THE

FOUNDATIONS OF LATIN

A BOOK FOR BEGINNERS

BY

CHARLES E. BENNETT
PROFESSOR OF LATIN IN CORNELL UNIVERSITY

Boston

ALLYN AND BACON

1899

COPYRIGHT, 1898, BY
CHARLES E. BENNETT.

Norwood Press
J. S. Cushing & Co. — Berwick & Smith
Norwood Mass. U.S.A.

PREFACE.

TWENTY years ago the beginner's Latin books published in this country followed the plan of an orderly development, first of the forms, and then of the syntax, of the language. Since that time a different practice has been inaugurated, and most books for beginners now present no connected and systematic development either of forms or of syntax. The conjugation of the verb, for example, is not given connectedly and continuously, but is variously dismembered and scattered throughout the book. So in the syntax the different constructions of a case or a mood are not presented in connection with each other, but are mutually detached and introduced one by one, here and there.

This plan has long seemed to me pedagogically unsound, and in practice I fear that it has not enabled us to realize the best results in our elementary Latin instruction. To me no principle of teaching seems more vital and fundamental than that of presenting together to the pupil those things that naturally belong together. This conviction is not merely founded in theory, but has been steadily forced upon me by actual experience. Hence it has appeared to me psychologically more natural in elementary Latin teaching to present in conjunction with each other the different declensions of nouns, the several conjugations of the verb, the various constructions of the accusative, the genitive, the ablative, *etc.* That these different categories which I have just enumerated do naturally belong together and have an organic connection seems to be recognized by the universal custom of so presenting them in our Latin grammars.

Again, it is of great importance that the pupil should, in his first introduction to Latin, learn in conjunction with each other those facts that he is ultimately to associate together. This is impossible with the method of arrangement which I am criticising. Pupils spend a part of the first year, or possibly the whole of it, on the beginner's book. They then, in connection with their reading of Latin authors, make a systematic study of the grammar for the next three years. Is there not an unreasonable waste of energy, if the order of presentation in the one book is made to deviate widely from that followed in the other? And is there not a corresponding economy of time and effort, if the pupil becomes familiar in the beginner's book with the arrangement which must ultimately be followed in the grammar?

As justification for the prevalent custom of dismembering the declensions and conjugations in our beginner's books, it is doubtless urged that the acquisition of the forms is difficult, and that the plan of gradual presentation is intended to facilitate the process of learning them. But is it not a fallacy to imagine that any such hesitating, timid policy is likely to be successful in guiding the pupil to a mastery of his inflections? Is not the plan of resolute, systematic, sustained attack upon the declensions and conjugations the more logical, and has any other ever yielded as good results in actual experience? Certainly to me Latin pupils to-day seem to know their forms less accurately than did the pupils of twenty years ago, and this impression I find entertained by teachers of prominence in our best institutions.

The foregoing considerations have impelled me in this book to present the forms before the syntax, and in both forms and syntax to follow the usual order of the Latin grammars. The only deviations from rigid conformity with this programme have been the following:

The inflection of the present indicative of *sum* and of a paradigm of the present indicative active of a verb of the first conjugation are given at the outset.

Adjectives of the first and second declensions are given immediately after the second declension of nouns.

Such syntactical principles as are necessary for the comprehension and construction of simple sentences are also given in the earliest lessons; for example, the rules for subject, object, predicate nouns, appositives, agreement of adjectives with noun, and of verb with subject. But a very little here is amply sufficient for all rational needs until the forms have been acquired. '*One thing at a time*' is a good motto; and until the inflections are learned, and well learned, the peculiarities of Latin syntax would better be kept in the background.

The English-Latin exercises for the first thirty-two chapters (III.–XXXIV.) are intentionally detached from the lessons and placed together after Chapter LX., where they are numbered to correspond with the lessons with which they may be used. My purpose was to discourage the use of English-Latin exercises during the acquisition of the forms. Experience shows that the writing of even the simplest Latin exercises at the outset of one's study takes no small amount of time. These simple sentences involve a multitude of little details, — vocabulary, syntax, word-order, *etc.*, — as well as a knowledge of the inflections themselves. Of the ultimate indispensableness of such exercises, there is no question, but, during the acquisition of the forms, a rather long personal experience as teacher of elementary Latin has taught me to believe that the teacher can by skilful oral exercises and blackboard work on the forms themselves accomplish vastly more toward their mastery by the pupil than by devoting any amount of time to the writing of Latin exercises. The writing of Latin is admirably adapted to giving drill in Latin syntax, but it is not the most effective way of teaching the forms. The amount of drill in the forms gained by a written exercise requiring half an hour in its preparation would hardly be as much as can be given in five minutes by the brisk oral questioning of an entire class or by simultaneous blackboard work ; nor would it be nearly so effective. I would therefore earnestly advise deferring the English-Latin exercises until the beginning of the syntax, where such exercises regularly accompany each lesson. Pupils who have mastered their forms will find no difficulty with the English-Latin exercises in Chapters XXXIV.–LX., even though they have not written the exercises of Chapters III.–XXXIV.

Special pains have been taken to make the English-Latin exercises throughout the book as simple as is consistent with the end they are intended to serve. Many elementary books appear to me to make this part of the work too difficult, and give for beginners sentences and passages which no freshman class that I have ever seen could render in Latin with credit.

The Vocabulary of the sixty chapters into which the body of the book is divided, consists of about 750 words, exclusive of proper names. These were selected on the following plan : I first made a list of the words common to Caesar and Nepos. There are some 1800 of these. This list was then reduced to its present size by eliminating all words used less than fifteen times in Caesar.[1] The Vocabulary, therefore, consists of the 750 words in most frequent use by Caesar and Nepos, and should consequently serve equally well as an introduction to either author. My first disposition had been to make the Vocabulary considerably larger, but in working out the details of the book I became fully persuaded of the wisdom of keeping the Vocabulary within

---

[1] As the sentences of the Latin exercises are based mainly on passages in Caesar, it was found convenient to add a small list of words of very frequent occurrence in that author but not found in Nepos. These are mainly military terms, such as *legio, cohors, turris, agger, fossa,* etc.

narrow limits. The pupil cannot surmount all difficulties at the outset. If he secures a solid foundation in the way of forms and syntax, a vocabulary will be quickly gained with the beginning of continuous reading.

The sentences, in the great majority of cases, are taken directly from Caesar's *Commentaries*. Often a word has been added or omitted, or a tense has been changed, but the Latin will be recognized as essentially Caesar's. The number of sentences given in each exercise is intentionally limited to ten or a dozen, which ought to be entirely adequate.

The Selections for Reading which follow the lessons are the traditional fables along with the Roman history originally prepared by Professor Jacobs, from whose *Latin Reader* I have taken them. They are sufficiently easy, are interesting, and the Latin is in the main correct. In a few cases, where Jacob's text shows inconsistency with classical usage, I have ventured to make the necessary changes.

In arranging the work by Chapters rather than by Lessons, it has been my purpose to preserve unity of subject-matter as far as possible. A 'chapter' does not necessarily mean that its contents are to be taken at a single lesson. With many pupils it will probably be found possible to take most of the chapters in one exercise, but where that is not feasible, the matter can easily be divided according to the necessities of the case.

I have received generous help from friends in the preparation of this book, and desire here to recognize my obligations to Mr. C. L. Durham, Professor H. C. Elmer, and Mr. F. O. Bates of this University for their counsel and assistance.

CHARLES EDWIN BENNETT.

CORNELL UNIVERSITY, ITHACA, N. Y.,
April 17, 1898.

TABLE OF CONTENTS.

PART I.

SOUNDS, ACCENT, QUANTITY.

PART II.

INFLECTIONS.

PART III.

SYNTAX.

ABBREVIATIONS.

abl.	= *ablative.*	interrog.	= *interrogative.*
acc.	= *accusative.*	intr.	= *intransitive.*
adj.	= *adjective.*	lit.	= *literally.*
adv.	= *adverb, adverbial.*	masc.	= *masculine.*
c.	= *common (gender).*	n., neut.	= *neuter.*
comp.	= *comparative.*	nom.	= *nominative.*
conj.	= *conjunction.*	p., pp.	= *page, pages.*
dat.	= *dative.*	pass.	= *passive.*
decl.	= *declension.*	pl., plu.	= *plural.*
dep.	= *deponent.*	prep.	= *preposition.*
e.g.	= *exempli gratia = for example.*	pres.	= *present.*
		pron.	= *pronoun.*
etc.	= *et cetera = and so forth.*	rel.	= *relative.*
f.	= *feminine.*	sc.	= *supply.*
gen.	= *genitive.*	sing.	= *singular.*
i.e.	= *id est = that is.*	sup., super.	= *superlative.*
impers.	= *impersonal, impersonally.*	tr., trans.	= *transitive.*
indecl.	= *indeclinable.*	w.	= *with.*
indic.	= *indicative.*	1, with verbs	= 1st conjugation.
inf.	= *infinitive.*		

PART I.

SOUNDS, QUANTITY, ACCENT.

———◆———

CHAPTER I.[1]

1.   ALPHABET.

The Latin Alphabet is the same as the English except that the Latin has no *w*.

2.   SOUNDS CLASSIFIED.

The vowels are **a, e, i, o, u, y**. The other letters are Consonants. The Diphthongs are **ae, oe, au, eu, ui**.

3.   PRONUNCIATION.[2]

a) **Vowels**.

ā[3] as in *father* ;	ă as in the first syllable of *ahd* ;
ē as in *they* ;	ĕ as in *met* ;
ī as in *machine* ;	ĭ as in *pin* ;
ō as in *note* ;	ŏ as in *obey*, *melody* ;
ū as in *rude* ;	ŭ as in *put* ;
	y like French *u*, German *ü*.

---

[1] On the arrangement of this book by chapters, see Preface.

[2] The system of pronunciation here given is that employed by the ancient Romans themselves. It is often called the ' Roman Method.'

[3] Vowels which are long in quantity are indicated by a horizontal line above them, as ā, ī, ō, *etc*. Short vowels either have the curved mark (ă, ŏ), or are left unmarked.

b) **Diphthongs.**

ae like *ai* in *aisle;*
oe like *oi* in *oil;*
au like *ow* in *how;*

eu with its two elements, **e** and **u**, pronounced in rapid succession;
ui occurs mainly in *cui* and *huic*. These are pronounced as though spelled *kwee* and *wheek*.

c) **Consonants.**

b, d, f, h, k, l, m, n, p, qu are pronounced as in English except that *bs, bt* are pronounced *ps, pt*.

c is always pronounced as *k*.

t is always pronounced as plain *t*, never with the sound of *sh*, as in Eng. *oration*.

g always as in *get;* when *ngu* precedes a vowel, **gu** has the sound of *gw*, as in **anguis, languidus.**

j[1] has the sound of *y* as in *yet*.

r was probably slightly trilled with the tip of the tongue.

s always as in *sin, gas;* in **suādeō, suāvis, suēscō,** and in compounds and derivatives of these words, **su** has the sound of *sw*.

v like *w*.

x always as *ks;* never like Eng. *gz* or *z*.

z is best pronounced as Eng. *z*.

ph, ch, th, are to be pronounced practically like our simple *p, k, t*. Doubled letters like **ll, mm, tt,** *etc.*, should be pronounced with an endeavor to articulate both members of the combination distinctly.

4.   QUANTITY.

A. **Quantity of Vowels.**

A vowel is long or short according to *the length of time* consumed in its pronunciation. As will be seen by comparing the sounds given in § 3, the long sounds take considerably more time to pronounce than the short ones. For example, the ı of *machine* takes more time than the ı of *pin*. No absolute rule can be given for determining the quantity of Latin vowels. The pupil can become familiar with them only by observing the quantity as marked in

---

[1] Some books print i instead of j.

the paradigms, the vocabularies, and the exercises. Yet the following principles are of aid : —

1. *A vowel is long,* —

    a) before **nf, ns,** and before **gn** in nouns and adjectives ending in -gnus, -gna, -gnum ; as **īnfāns, dīgnus, sīgnum** ; also in derivatives of words in -gnus, -gna, -gnum ; as **sīgnificō**.

    b) when the result of contraction ; as **nīlum,** for **nihilum**.

    c) before **j** ; as **hūjus**.

2. *A vowel is short,* —

    a) before **nt, nd** ; as **amant, amandus**. A few rare exceptions occur in cases of compounds whose first member has a long vowel ; as **nōndum** (for **nōn dum**).

    b) before another vowel or **h**[1] ; as **meus, trahō**. Some exceptions occur, chiefly in proper names derived from the Greek ; as **Aenēās**.

N.B.—Long vowels should always be *pronounced* long (that is the only thing that '*long*' means) ; short vowels should be pronounced short.

B. Quantity of Syllables.

A syllable is long or short according to *the length of time* it takes to pronounce such syllable.

1. *A syllable is long* (that is, it takes a long time to pronounce it), —

    a) if it contains a long vowel ; as **māter, māgnus, dīus**.[2]

    b) if it contains a diphthong ; as **causae, foedus**.[2]

    c) if it contains a short vowel followed by **x, z,** or any two consonants (except a mute followed by **l** or **r**)[3] ; as **axis, restat, gaza, amantis**.[4]

2. *A syllable is regularly short* if it contains a short vowel followed by a vowel, by a single consonant, or by a mute with **l** or **r** ; as **mea, amat, patris, volucris**.[5]

---

[1] **h** was pronounced so lightly as to be entirely disregarded, whether singly or in combination.

[2] Such syllables are sometimes said to be long by nature.

[3] The mutes are **p, c, t; b, d, g.**

[4] Such syllables are sometimes said to be long by position.

[5] Such syllables are sometimes said to be short by position.

5. ACCENT.

1. There are as many syllables in a Latin word as there are separate vowels and diphthongs.

2. Words of two syllables are accented upon the first; as **tégit, môrem.**

3. Words of more than two syllables are accented upon the penult (next to the last) if that is a long syllable, otherwise upon the antepenult (second from the last); as **amāvī, miníster, míserum.**

6. EXERCISE.

Pronounce the following words, observing carefully the proper sound of each letter, and placing the accent upon the proper syllable. Remember to pronounce all long vowels long, all short vowels short. Take care of the vowels, and the syllables will take care of themselves.

1. Mājōrum, amīcus, Athēnae. 2. Queō, pāscō, poscō. 3. Juvenis, porrēctūra, abiimus. 4. Amīcitia, obtineō, antīquus. 5. Eurōpa, Charmidēs, exemplum. 6. Ingerō, exiguitās, sanguis. 7. Olympus, mittō, nātiōnēs. 8. Foedus, dīgnātiō, cōnsēnsus. 9. Pervolat, efferre, īnstituerat. 10. Arguō, cui, Philippī. 11. Percussus, rēxī, pereō. 12. Jam, suāvitās, suēscō. 13. Concēdō, sīgnātor, referō. 14. Īnserō, obserō, persuādet.

PART II.

INFLECTIONS.

———◆———

CHAPTER II.

7. THE PARTS OF SPEECH.

The Parts of Speech in Latin are the same as in English; *viz.*, Nouns, Adjectives, Pronouns, Verbs, Adverbs, Prepositions, Conjunctions, and Interjections; but the Latin has no article.

8. INFLECTION.

Of these eight parts of speech, the first four are capable of **Inflection**, that is, of undergoing change of form to express modifications of meaning. In the case of Nouns, Adjectives, and Pronouns, this process is called **Declension**; in the case of Verbs, **Conjugation**.

9. NOUNS.

1. A Noun is the name of a *person, place, thing*, or *quality*; as **Caesar**, *Caesar*; **Rōma**, *Rome*; **penna**, *feather*; **virtūs**, *courage*.

2. Nouns have Gender, Number, and Case.

10. GENDER.

1. There are in Latin, as in English, three Genders: the Masculine, Feminine, and Neuter.

2. Gender in Latin may be either natural (that is, based on sex, as gender always is in English) or grammatical (not based on sex).

3. *Natural Gender.* In Latin only nouns denoting *persons* have natural gender, and these are Masculine, if they denote males, as **nauta,** *sailor;* Feminine, if they denote females, as **māter,** *mother.*

4. *Grammatical Gender.* When nouns have grammatical gender, the gender is determined : —

A. **By signification.** Thus : —

  a) Names of *Rivers, Winds,* and *Months* are Masculine; as, **Sēquana,** *Seine;* **Eurus,** *East Wind;* **Aprīlis,** *April.*

  b) Names of *Trees, Countries, Towns,* and *Islands* are Feminine; as, **quercus,** *oak;* **Pontus,** *Pontus;* **Corinthus,** *Corinth;* **Rhodus,** *Rhodes.*

  c) Indeclinable nouns are Neuter; as, **nefās,** *wrong.*

B. **By ending.**

  The principles for gender by ending are given later, under the five declensions.

11.   NUMBER.

Latin has two Numbers, the Singular and the Plural. The Singular denotes one object; the Plural more than one.

12.   CASES.

1. There are six Cases in Latin : —

Nominative,	Case of Subject;
Genitive,	Objective with *of;*
Dative,	Objective with *to* or *for;*
Accusative,	Case of Direct Object;
Vocative,	Case of Address;
Ablative,	Objective with *by, from, in, with.*

2. LOCATIVE. Vestiges of another case, the **Locative** (denoting place where), occur in names of towns and in a few other words.

3. OBLIQUE CASES. The Genitive, Dative, Accusative, and Ablative are called **Oblique Cases**.

4. FORMATION OF THE CASES. The different cases were originally formed by joining certain **case-endings** to a fundamental part called the **stem**. Thus **portam** (Accusative Singular) was formed by joining the case-ending **m**, to the stem **porta-**. But in most cases the final vowel of the stem has united so closely with the original case-ending, that the latter has become more or less obscured. The apparent case-ending thus resulting is called a **termination**.

13. THE FIVE DECLENSIONS.

There are five Declensions in Latin, distinguished from each other by the final letter of the Stem, and also by the Termination of the Genitive Singular, as follows: —

DECLENSION.	FINAL LETTER OF STEM.	GEN. TERMINATION.
First	ā	-ae
Second	ŏ	-ī
Third	{ ĭ Some consonant }	-ĭs
Fourth	ŭ	-ūs
Fifth	ē	-ĕī

Cases alike in Form.

1. The Vocative is regularly like the Nominative, except in the Singular of nouns in -us of the Second Declension.

2. The Dative and Ablative Plural are always alike.

3. In Neuters the Accusative and Nominative are always alike, and in the Plural end in -ă.

4. In the Third, Fourth, and Fifth Declensions, the Accusative Plural is regularly like the Nominative.

CHAPTER III.

FIRST DECLENSION. — *ā*-STEMS.

Pure Latin nouns of the First Declension regularly end, in the Nominative Singular, in -ă, weakened from -ā, and are of the Feminine Gender. They are declined as follows: —

Porta, *gate;* stem, portă-.

SINGULAR.

CASES.		MEANINGS.	TERMINATIONS.
Nom.	porta	*a gate* (as subject)	-ă
Gen.	portae	*of a gate*	-ae
Dat.	portae	*to* or *for a gate*	-ae
Acc.	portam	*a gate* (as object)	-am
Voc.	porta	*O gate!*	-ă
Abl.	portā	*with, by, from, in a gate*	-ā

PLURAL.

Nom.	portae	*gates* (as subject)	-ae
Gen.	portārum	*of gates*	-ārum
Dat.	portīs	*to* or *for gates*	-īs
Acc.	portās	*gates* (as object)	-ās
Voc.	portae	*O gates!*	-ae
Abl.	portīs	*with, by, from, in gates*	-īs

1. The Latin has no article, and **porta** may mean either *a gate* or *the gate;* and in the Plural, *gates* or *the gates.*

15. Peculiarities of Nouns of the First Declension.

1. EXCEPTIONS IN GENDER. Nouns denoting males are Masculine; as, **nauta,** *sailor;* **agricola,** *farmer.*

2. Special Case-Endings, —

    a) The Locative Singular ends in -ae; as, **Rōmae,** *at Rome.*

    b) **Dea,** *goddess,* and **fīlia,** *daughter,* commonly form the Dative and Ablative Plural with the termination -ābus; as **deābus, fīliābus.** This is in order to distinguish these words from the corresponding cases of **deus,** *god,* and **fīlius,** *son.*

16. Paradigm of the Present Indicative Active of a Verb of the First Conjugation.

SINGULAR.	PLURAL.

1. amō,[1] *I love.*   amāmus, *we love.*
amās, *thou lovest, you love.*   amātis, *you love.*
amat, *he, she, it loves.*   amant, *they love.*

2. In Latin the Subject of the verb, if a personal pronoun (*I, thou, he, we,* etc.), is not expressed unless emphatic, but is implied in the verb.

17. Principles of Syntax.

1. The Subject of the Verb stands in the Nominative.

2. The Object of the Verb stands in the Accusative.

3. The Verb agrees with its Subject in Number and Person.

18. VOCABULARY.

accūsō, *I accuse.*
agricola, ae, m., *farmer.*
cōpia, ae, f., *plenty*; in plural,
     cōpiae, ārum, *troops.*
et, conj., *and.*
fīlia, ae, f., *daughter.*
Galba, ae, m., *Galba* (a man's name).

incitō, *I urge on, encourage.*
incola, ae, m., *inhabitant.*
īnsula, ae, f., *island.*
Italia, ae, f., *Italy.*
laudō, *I praise.*
vāstō, *I lay waste.*
vocō, *I call, summon.*

EXERCISES.[2]

19. 1. Agricolae, agricolā, agricolārum.   2. Īnsulae, īnsulīs. 3. Italiae, Galbae.   4. Fīlia, fīliārum, fīliābus.   5. Incolae, incolīs.   6. Cōpiārum, cōpiīs.

20. 1. Fīliās agricolae laudāmus.[3]   2. Galba cōpiās incitat. 3. Cōpiae Galbae Italiam vāstant.   4. Galbam laudāmus. 5. Cōpiās Galbae laudō.   6. Incolās īnsulārum accūsātis. 7. Galba agricolam vocat.   8. Īnsulās vāstāmus.   9. Galbam et agricolās vocāmus.   10. Fīliās agricolae vocō.

---

[1] All verbs of the First Conjugation are inflected like amō. Such verbs are given in the General Vocabulary with the numeral 1.

[2] For exercises on the translation of English into Latin, see p. 155 and Preface.

[3] The verb in Latin ordinarily stands at the end of the sentence.

CHAPTER IV.

21.   SECOND DECLENSION. — ŏ–STEMS.

Pure Latin nouns of the Second Declension end in **-us,
-er, -ir**, Masculine; **-um**, Neuter; and are declined as follows : —

		Hortus, *garden;* stem, **hortŏ-.**	TERMINATION.	**Bellum,** *war;* stem, **bellŏ-.**	TERMINATION.
SINGULAR.	*Nom.*	hortus	-us	bellum	-um
	Gen.	hortī	-ī	bellī	-ī
	Dat.	hortŏ	-ŏ	bellŏ	-ŏ
	Acc.	hortum	-um	bellum	-um
	Voc.	horte	-e	bellum	-um
	Abl.	hortŏ	-ŏ	bellŏ	-ŏ
PLURAL.	*Nom.*	hortī	-ī	bella	-a
	Gen.	hortōrum	-ōrum	bellōrum	-ōrum
	Dat.	hortīs	-īs	bellīs	-īs
	Acc.	hortŏs	-ŏs	bella	-a
	Voc.	hortī	-ī	bella	-a
	Abl.	hortīs	-īs	bellīs	-īs

		Puer, *boy;* stem, **puerŏ-.**	**Ager,** *field;* stem, **agrŏ-.**	**Vir,** *man;* stem, **virŏ-.**	TERMINATION.
SINGULAR.	*Nom.*	puer	ager	vir	Wanting
	Gen.	puerī	agrī	virī	-ī
	Dat.	puerŏ	agrŏ	virŏ	-ŏ
	Acc.	puerum	agrum	virum	-um
	Voc.	puer	ager	vir	Wanting
	Abl.	puerŏ	agrŏ	virŏ	-ŏ
PLURAL.	*Nom.*	puerī	agrī	virī	-ī
	Gen.	puerōrum	agrōrum	virōrum	-ōrum
	Dat.	puerīs	agrīs	virīs	-īs
	Acc.	puerŏs	agrŏs	virŏs	-ŏs
	Voc.	puerī	agrī	virī	-ī
	Abl.	puerīs	agrīs	virīs	-īs

22. Peculiarities of Inflection in the Second Declension.

1. Most nouns in -er in common use are declined like **ager**, not like **puer**.

2. Nouns in -ius and -ium throughout the best period of the language formed the Genitive Singular in -ī (instead of -iī) ; as, —

Nom. ingenium	fīlius
Gen. ingénī	fīlī

These Genitives accent the penult, even when it is short.

3. The Locative Singular ends in -ī ; as, **Corinthī**, *at Corinth.*

23. Inflection of the Present Indicative of the Verb *sum.*

sum, *I am.*	**sumus,** *we are.*
ĕs,[1] *thou art, you are.*	**ĕstis,**[1] *you are.*
ĕst,[1] *he, she, it is.*	**sunt,** *they are.*

24. **Principles of Syntax.**

1. A Predicate Noun (that is, a noun limiting its subject through the medium of the verb *to be,* or some similar word, as *seem, become*) agrees with its subject in case ; as, —

    Mercurius est deus, *Mercury is a god.*

2. An Appositive agrees in case with the word which it explains ; as, —

    Mercurius, deus, *Mercury, the god.*

25. **VOCABULARY.**

amīcus, I, m., *friend.*
auxilium, I (iī), n., *aid, help.*
Belgae, ārum, m. plu., *Belgians,* a Gallic tribe.
castra, ōrum, n. pl., *a camp.*
Gallī, ōrum, m. pl., *Gauls.*
Germānī, ōrum, m. pl., *Germans.*
implōrō, *I entreat.*
oppidum, I, n., *town, walled town.*

oppūgnō, *I attack, assault.*
perīculum, I, n., *danger.*
proelium, I (iī), n., *battle.*
Sēquanī, ōrum, m. pl., *Séquani,* a Gallic tribe.
vexō, *I harass, annoy ; ravage.*
vīcus, I, m., *village.*
vītō, *I avoid.*

---

[1] Pronounce these words severally, **ĕs, ĕst, ĕstis,** not **ēs, ēst, ēstis.**

EXERCISES.

26. 1. Oppidī, oppidōrum.   2. Estis, es.   3. Vīcō, vīcīs.
4. Perīcula, perīculōrum.   5. Amīcī, amīcōrum, amīcīs.   6. Auxilium, auxiliō.   7. Agrī, agrīs.

27. 1. Sumus amīcī[1] Gallōrum.   2. Belgae et Sēquanī
auxilium implōrant.   3. Sēquanī agricolās, incolās vīcōrum,
vexant.   4. Germānī oppida Belgārum oppūgnant.   5. Germānī sunt agricolae.   6. Galba, amīcus Gallōrum, castra Germānōrum oppūgnat.   7. Amīcōs Gallōrum laudāmus.   8. Cōpiae
Galbae Sēquanōs proeliō vexant.   9. Perīcula et bella vītāmus.

---

[1] A predicate noun may (and often does) follow the verb.

CHAPTER V.

28.   ADJECTIVES.

Adjectives denote *quality*.   They are declined like nouns,
and fall into two classes, —
1. Adjectives of the First and Second Declensions.
2. Adjectives of the Third Declension.

Adjectives of the First and Second Declensions.

In these the Masculine is declined like **hortus, puer,**
or **ager,** the Feminine like **porta,** and the Neuter like
bellum.

29. Thus, Masculine like **hortus** : —

Bonus, *good.*

SINGULAR.

	MASCULINE.	FEMININE.	NEUTER.
Nom.	bonus	bona	bonum
Gen.	bonī	bonae	bonī
Dat.	bonŏ	bonae	bonŏ
Acc.	bonum	bonam	bonum
Voc.	bone	bona	bonum
Abl.	bonŏ	bonā	bonŏ

PLURAL.

Nom.	bonī	bonae	bona
Gen.	bonŏrum	bonārum	bonŏrum
Dat.	bonīs	bonīs	bonīs
Acc.	bonŏs	bonās	bona
Voc.	bonī	bonae	bona
Abl.	bonīs	bonīs	bonīs

30. Masculine like **puer** : —

Tener, *tender.*

SINGULAR.

	MASCULINE.	FEMININE.	NEUTER.
Nom.	tener	tenera	tenerum
Gen.	tenerī	tenerae	tenerī
Dat.	tenerŏ	tenerae	tenerŏ
Acc.	tenerum	teneram	tenerum
Voc.	tener	tenera	tenerum
Abl.	tenerŏ	tenerā	tenerŏ

PLURAL.

	MASCULINE.	FEMININE.	NEUTER.
Nom.	tenerī	tenerae	tenera
Gen.	tenerŏrum	tenerārum	tenerŏrum
Dat.	tenerīs	tenerīs	tenerīs
Acc.	tenerŏs	tenerās	tenera
Voc.	tenerī	tenerae	tenera
Abl.	tenerīs	tenerīs	tenerīs

31. Masculine like **ager** : —

Sacer, *sacred.*

SINGULAR.

	MASCULINE.	FEMININE.	NEUTER.
Nom.	sacer	sacra	sacrum
Gen.	sacrī	sacrae	sacrī
Dat.	sacrŏ	sacrae	sacrŏ
Acc.	sacrum	sacram	sacrum
Voc.	sacer	sacra	sacrum
Abl.	sacrŏ	sacrā	sacrŏ

PLURAL.

	MASCULINE.	FEMININE.	NEUTER.
Nom.	sacrī	sacrae	sacra
Gen.	sacrŏrum	sacrārum	sacrŏrum
Dat.	sacrīs	sacrīs	sacrīs
Acc.	sacrŏs	sacrās	sacra
Voc.	sacrī	sacrae	sacra
Abl.	sacrīs	sacrīs	sacrīs

1. Most adjectives in -er are declined like **sacer.** Of adjectives in common use only the following are declined like **tener** : **asper,** *rough ;* **līber,** *free ;* **miser,** *wretched.*

32. **Principles of Syntax.**

1. An Adjective agrees with the noun which it limits in Gender, Number, and Case.

2. An Adjective limiting its noun directly is called an *attributive* adjective, as **via longa**, *a long journey;* an Adjective limiting its noun through the medium of the verb **esse,** *to be,* or some similar verb, is a *predicate* adjective, as **via est longa,** *the journey is long;* **via vidētur longa,** *the journey seems long.*

33. VOCABULARY.

Britannia, ae, f., *Britain.*	parō, *I prepare, get ready.*
dīmicō, *I contend.*	parvus, a, um, *small.*
Helvētiī, ōrum, m. pl., *Helvetii,*	populus, ī, m., *people.*
a Gallic tribe.	pulcher, chra, chrum, *beautiful.*
jūmentum, ī, n., *beast of burden.*	Rōmānus, a, um, *Roman;* — as
lēgātus, ī, m., *lieutenant.*	noun, m., *a Roman.*
māgnus, a, um, *large, great.*	superō, *I overcome.*
multus, a, um, *much;* pl., *many.*	victōria, ae, f., *victory.*
numerus, ī, m., *number.*	

EXERCISES.

34. 1. Populī Rōmānī, populō Rōmānō. 2. Māgnae[1] victōriae, māgnārum victōriārum. 3. Multa jūmenta, multīs jūmentīs. 4. Multae īnsulae, multās īnsulās. 5. Fīliae pulchrae, fīliābus pulchrīs. 6. Parvī vīcī, parvōrum vīcōrum.

35. 1. Fīliae agricolae sunt pulchrae et bonae. 2. Populus Rōmānus Gallōs superat. 3. Galba, lēgātus Rōmānus, māgnum oppidum Sēquanōrum oppūgnat. 4. Sēquanī multīs proeliīs dīmicant. 5. Britannia est māgna īnsula. 6. Victōria populī Rōmānī est māgna. 7. Īnsula est parva. 8. Helvētiī māgnum numerum jūmentōrum parant. 9. Māgnae cōpiae dīmicant.

---

[1] The attributive adjective (see § 32, 2) in Latin, as in English, more commonly precedes the word which it limits. This is especially true of adjectives of *number, amount,* etc. Yet other adjectives when used attributively often follow the noun; see, for example, § 34, 5; 35, 2.

CHAPTER VI.

36. NOUNS OF THE THIRD DECLENSION.

Nouns of the Third Declension end in -a, -e, -ĭ, -ŏ, -y, -c, -l, -n, -r, -s, -t, -x. The Third Declension includes several distinct classes of Stems, —

    I. Pure Consonant-Stems.

    II. ɪ-Stems.

    III. Mixed Stems. (Consonant Stems which have partially adapted themselves to the inflection of ɪ-Stems.)

Consonant-Stems.

37. 1. In these the stem appears in its unaltered form in all the oblique cases; so that the actual case-endings may be clearly recognized.

2. Consonant-Stems fall into several natural subdivisions, according as the stem ends in a **Mute, Liquid, Nasal,** or **Spirant.**

Mute-Stems.

38. Mute-Stems may end, —

1. In a Labial (b or p); as, **trab-s; prīncep-s.**
2. In a Guttural (g or c); as, **rēmex (rēmeg-s); dux (duc-s).**
3. In a Dental (d or t); as, **lapis (lapid-s); mīles (mīlet-s).**

ɪ. STEMS IN A LABIAL MUTE (b, p).

39. **Trabs,** f., *beam.*   **Prīnceps,** m., *chief.*

	SINGULAR.		CASE-ENDING.
Nom.	trabs	prīnceps	-s
Gen.	trabis [1]	prīncipis [1]	-is
Dat.	trabī	prīncipī	-ī
Acc.	trabem	prīncipem	-em
Voc.	trabs	prīnceps	-s
Abl.	trabe [2]	prīncipe [2]	-e

---

[1] Pronounce ĭs, not īs.   [2] Pronounce ĕ, not ē.

	PLURAL.		CASE-ENDING.
Nom.	trabēs [1]	prīncipēs [1]	-ēs
Gen.	trabum	prīncipum	-um
Dat.	trabĭbus	prīncipĭbus	-ĭbus
Acc.	trabēs [1]	prīncipēs [1]	-ēs
Voc.	trabēs [1]	prīncipēs [1]	-ēs
Abl.	trabĭbus	prīncipĭbus	-ĭbus

2. STEMS IN A GUTTURAL MUTE (g, c).

40. In these the termination -s of the Nominative Singular unites with the guttural, thus producing -x.

Rēmex, m., *rower*.   **Dux, c., *leader*.**

	SINGULAR.	PLURAL.	SINGULAR.	PLURAL.
Nom.	rēmex	rēmigēs	dux	ducēs
Gen.	rēmigis	rēmigum	ducis	ducum
Dat.	rēmigī	rēmigĭbus	ducī	ducĭbus
Acc.	rēmigem	rēmigēs	ducem	ducēs
Voc.	rēmex	rēmigēs	dux	ducēs
Abl.	rēmige	rēmigĭbus	duce	ducĭbus

3. STEMS IN A DENTAL MUTE (d, t).

41. In these the final d or t of the Stem disappears in the Nominative Singular before the ending -s.

Lapis, m., *stone*.   **Mīles, m., *soldier*.**

	SINGULAR.	PLURAL.	SINGULAR.	PLURAL.
Nom.	lapis	lapidēs	mīles	mīlitēs
Gen.	lapidis	lapidum	mīlitis	mīlitum
Dat.	lapidī	lapidĭbus	mīlitī	mīlitĭbus
Acc.	lapidem	lapidēs	mīlitem	mīlitēs
Voc.	lapis	lapidēs	mīles	mīlitēs
Abl.	lapide	lapidĭbus	mīlite	mīlitĭbus

---

[1] Pronounce ēs, not ēz.

Liquid Stems.

42. These end usually in -r; a few end in -l.

	Victor, m., *conqueror.*		**Aequor, n., sea.**	
	SINGULAR.	PLURAL.	SINGULAR.	PLURAL.
Nom.	victor	victōrēs	aequor	aequora
Gen.	victōris	victōrum	aequoris	aequorum
Dat.	victōrī	victōribus	aequorī	aequoribus
Acc.	victōrem	victōrēs	aequor	aequora
Voc.	victor	victōrēs	aequor	aequora
Abl.	victōre	victōribus	aequore	aequoribus

1. Masculine and Feminine Stems ending in a liquid form the Nominative and Vocative Singular without case-ending.

2. The case-ending is also lacking in the Nominative, Accusative, and Vocative Singular of *all neuters* of the Third Declension.

43.   **VOCABULARY.**

agger, eris, m., *embankment, rampart.*
altus, a, um, *high, deep.*
Caesar, aris, m., *Caesar.*
cōnfīrmō, *I establish.*
cōnsul, ulis, m., *consul.*
cum, *with,* prep. with abl.
eques, itis, m., *horseman;* plu., *cavalry.*

Gallia, ae, f., *Gaul.*
imperō, *I demand.*
Mārcellus, I, m., *Marcellus.*
obses, idis, c.,[1] *hostage.*
pater, tris, m., *father.*
pāx, pācis, f., *peace.*
virtūs, tūtis, f., *valor, virtue.*

EXERCISES.

44. 1. Pater cōnsulis.   2. Aggerēs altī, aggeribus altīs. 3. Pāx bona.   4. Cōnsulēs bonī, cōnsulum bonōrum.   5. Multī obsidēs, multīs obsidibus.

45. 1. Equitēs cum māgnō perīculō proeliō dīmicant.   2. Multī mīlitēs castra Gallōrum oppūgnant.   3. Galba māgnum numerum obsidum imperat.   4. Prīncipēs Galliae pācem cōnfīrmant. 5. Virtūtem ducum et mīlitum Rōmānōrum laudāmus.   6. Agger castrōrum est altus.   7. Galba et Mārcellus sunt cōnsulēs. 8. Dux rēmigēs laudat.   9. Caesar māgnās cōpiās parat. 10. Mīlitēs cum equitibus dīmicant.

---

[1] Common gender; *i.e.,* either m. or f.   But such nouns are ordinarily treated as masculine.

CHAPTER VII.

THIRD DECLENSION (CONTINUED).

Nasal Stems.

46. These end in -n, which often disappears in the Nom. Sing.

Leō, m., *lion.* **Nōmen**, n., *name.*

	SINGULAR.	PLURAL.	SINGULAR.	PLURAL.
Nom.	leō	leōnēs	nōmen	nōmina
Gen.	leōnis	leōnum	nōminis	nōminum
Dat.	leōnī	leōnibus	nōminī	nōminibus
Acc.	leōnem	leōnēs	nōmen	nōmina
Voc.	leō	leōnēs	nōmen	nōmina
Abl.	leōne	leōnibus	nōmine	nōminibus

Spirant or s-Stems.

47. Mōs., m., *custom.* **Genus**, n., *race.* **Honor**, m., *honor.*

SINGULAR.

Nom.	mōs	genus	honor
Gen.	mōris	generis	honōris
Dat.	mōrī	generī	honōrī
Acc.	mōrem	genus	honōrem
Voc.	mōs	genus	honor
Abl.	mōre	genere	honōre

PLURAL.

Nom.	mōrēs	genera	honōrēs
Gen.	mōrum	generum	honōrum
Dat.	mōribus	generibus	honōribus
Acc.	mōrēs	genera	honōrēs
Voc.	mōrēs	genera	honōrēs
Abl.	mōribus	generibus	honōribus

1. Note that the final **s** of the stem becomes r (between vowels) in the oblique cases. In some words, as **honor**, the r of the oblique cases has, by analogy, crept into the Nominative, displacing the earlier **s**.

19

Ĭ-Stems.

A. *Masculine and Feminine* I-*Stems.*

48. These regularly end in -is in the Nominative Singular, and always have -ium in the Genitive Plural. Originally the Accusative Singular ended in -im, the Ablative Singular in -ī, and the Accusative Plural in -īs; but these endings have been largely displaced by -em, -e, and -ēs, the endings of Consonant-Stems.

49. Turris, f., *tower;*   Hostis, c., *enemy;*
      stem, turri-.   stem, hosti-.

	SINGULAR.		TERMINATION.
Nom.	turris	hostis	-is
Gen.	turris	hostis	-is
Dat.	turrī	hostī	-ī
Acc.	turrim	hostem	-im, -em
Voc.	turris	hostis	-is
Abl.	turrī	hoste	-ī, -e

	PLURAL.		
Nom.	turrēs	hostēs	-ēs
Gen.	turrium	hostium	-ium
Dat.	turribus	hostibus	-ibus
Acc.	turrīs or -ēs	hostīs or -ēs	-īs, -ēs,
Voc.	turrēs	hostēs	-ēs
Abl.	turribus	hostibus	-ibus

B. *Neuter* I-*Stems.*

50. These end in the Nominative Singular in -e, -al, and -ar. They always have -ī in the Ablative Singular, -ia in the Nominative, Accusative, and Vocative Plural, and -ium in the Genitive Plural, thus holding more steadfastly to the ı-character than do Masculine and Feminine I-Stems.

	Sedīle, *seat*; stem, sedīli-.	Animal, *animal*; stem, animāli-.	Calcar, *spur*; stem, calcāri-.	
		SINGULAR.		TERMINATION.
Nom.	sedīle	animal	calcar	Wanting
Gen.	sedīlis	animālis	calcāris	-is
Dat.	sedīlī	animālī	calcārī	-ī
Acc.	sedīle	animal	calcar	Wanting
Voc.	sedīle	animal	calcar	Wanting
Abl.	sedīlī	animālī	calcārī	-ī
		PLURAL.		
Nom.	sedīlia	animālia	calcāria	-ia
Gen.	sedīlium	animālium	calcārium	-ium
Dat.	sedīlibus	animālibus	calcāribus	-ibus
Acc.	sedīlia	animālia	calcāria	-ia
Voc.	sedīlia	animālia	calcāria	-ia
Abl.	sedīlibus	animālibus	calcāribus	-ibus

1. In most words of this class the final -i of the stem is lost in the Nominative Singular; in others it appears as -e.

Mixed Stems.

(Consonant-Stems that have partially adapted themselves to the inflection of I-stems.)

51. Many Consonant-Stems have so far adapted themselves to the inflection of I-stems as to take -ium in the Genitive Plural, and -īs in the Accusative Plural. Their true character as Consonant-Stems, however, is shown by the fact that they never take -im in the Accusative Singular, or -ī in the Ablative Singular. The following words are examples of this class: —

	SINGULAR.		PLURAL.	
	Caedēs, f., *slaughter*; stem, caed-.	Arx, f., *citadel*; stem, arc-.	Caedēs, f., *slaughter*; stem, caed-.	Arx, f., *citadel*; stem, arc-.
Nom.	caedēs	arx	caedēs	arcēs
Gen.	caedis	arcis	caedium	arcium
Dat.	caedī	arcī	caedibus	arcibus
Acc.	caedem	arcem	caedēs, -īs	arcēs, -īs
Voc.	caedēs	arx	caedēs	arcēs
Abl.	caede	arce	caedibus	arcibus

1. The following classes of nouns belong to Mixed Stems: —

a) Nouns in -ĕs, with Genitive in -is; as, nūbĕs, aedĕs, *etc.*

b) Many monosyllables in -s or -x preceded by one or more consonants; as, urbs, mōns.

c) Most nouns in -ns and -rs; as, oliĕns, oohors.

52.   **VOCABULARY.**

arbor, oris, f., *tree.*

cīvitās, tātis, f., *state.*

flūmen, inis, n., *river.*

hostis, is, c., *enemy.*

in, *in, on,* prep. with the abl. denoting rest in a place.

mare, is, n., *sea.*

mēns, mentis, f., *mind.*

mōns, montis, m., *mountain.*

nōmen, inis, n., *name.*

oocupō, *I take possession of, seize.*

paucī, ae, a, *few, a few;* used only in plu.

Rhēnus, Ī, m., *the Rhine.*

silva, ae, f., *forest.*

timor, ōris, m., *fear.*

turris, is, f., *tower.*

EXERCISES.

53. 1. Arborēs silvae.   2. Cīvitātum, cīvitātibus.   3. Hostēs, hostīs.   4. Māgna animālia, māgnīs animālibus.   5. Montēs altī, montibus altīs.   6. Timōrēs mīlitum.

54. 1. Mīlitēs Rōmānī turrīs hostium oppūgnant.   2. In māgnō marī sunt multae īnsulae.   3. Nōmen flūminis est Rhēnus.   4. Multa animālia sunt in silvā.   5. Arborēs sunt altae.   6. Timor mentēs mīlitum occupat.   7. Caesar hostēs proeliō superat.   8. Equitēs Rōmānī cum hostibus dīmicant.   9. Caesar montem occupat.   10. Paucae cīvitātēs pācem cōnfīrmant.

CHAPTER VIII.

GENDER IN THIRD DECLENSION.—THE FOURTH AND FIFTH DECLENSIONS.

55. General Principles of Gender in the Third Declension.

1. Nouns in -ŏ, -or, -ŏs, -er, -ĕs are Masculine.

2. Nouns in -ās, -ēs, -is, -ys, -x, -s (preceded by a consonant); -dŏ, -gŏ (Genitive -inis); -iŏ (abstract and collective), -ūs (Genitive -ūtis or -ūdis) are Feminine.

3. Nouns ending in -a, -e, -ī, -y, -c, -l, -n, -t, -ar, -ur, -ŭs are Neuter.

4. There are many exceptions to the foregoing principles. These are noted in the Vocabularies.

FOURTH DECLENSION.— *ŭ*-STEMS.

56. Nouns of the Fourth Declension end in -us Masculine, and -ū Neuter. They are declined as follows:—

| | Frūctus, *fruit.* | | Cornū, *horn.* | |
	SINGULAR.	PLURAL.	SINGULAR.	PLURAL.
Nom.	frūctus	frūctūs	cornū	cornua
Gen.	frūctūs	frūctuum	cornūs	cornuum
Dat.	frūctuī	frūctibus	cornū	cornibus
Acc.	frūctum	frūctūs	cornū	cornua
Voc.	frūctus	frūctūs	cornū	cornua
Abl.	frūctū	frūctibus	cornū	cornibus

1. A few nouns in -us of the Fourth Declension are feminine, particularly **manus**, *hand,* and **domus**, *house.*

FIFTH DECLENSION.— *ē*-STEMS.

57. Nouns of the Fifth Declension end in -ēs, and are declined as follows:—

Diēs, m., *day.*   **Rēs**, f., *thing.*

SINGULAR.	PLURAL.		SINGULAR.	PLURAL.
Nom.	diēs	diēs	rēs	rēs
Gen.	diēī	diērum	rĕī	rērum
Dat.	diēī	diēbus	rĕī	rēbus
Acc.	diem	diēs	rem	rēs
Voc.	diēs	diēs	rēs	rēs
Abl.	diē	diēbus	rē	rēbus

1. The ending of the Genitive and Dative Singular is -ĕī, instead of -ēī, when a consonant precedes; as spĕī, rĕī.

2. With the exception of **diēs** and **rēs**, most nouns of the Fifth Declension are not declined in the Plural.

3. Nouns of the Fifth Declension are regularly Feminine, except **diēs**, *day*, and **merīdiēs**, *mid-day*, and even **diēs** is sometimes Feminine in the Singular.

58.   VOCABULARY.

aciēs, ēī, f., *line of battle.*
collocō, *I place, arrange, station.*
cornū, ūs, n., *horn;* in military sense, *wing* of an army.
dē, *concerning*, prep. w. abl.
dexter, tra, trum, *right.*
dubitō, *I doubt, am in doubt.*
fidēs, eī, f., *fidelity, loyalty.*

legiō, ōnis, f., *legion.*
manus, ūs, f., *hand;* in military sense, *band, force.*
nūntiō, *I announce, report.*
portus, ūs, m., *harbor.*
reliquus, a, um, *remaining.*
senātus, ūs, m., *senate.*
spēs, speī, f., *hope.*

EXERCISES.

59. 1. Fideī, dē fidē.   2. Manūs, manibus.   3. In aciē. 4. Cornua, cornuum.   5. Portūs, portibus.   6. Senātūs, senātuī.

60. 1. Gallī cum māgnā manū legiōnem Rōmānam oppūgnant. 2. Reliquae legiōnēs sunt in dextrō cornū.   3. In portū est parva īnsula.   4. Galba dē fidē Gallōrum dubitat.   5. Caesar multās rēs senātuī nūntiat.   6. Mīlitēs in aciē collocat.   7. Sumus in māgnā spē victōriae.   8. Portūs īnsulae sunt bonī.   9. Senātum Rōmānum accūsāmus.   10. Dē multīs rēbus dubitant.

CHAPTER IX.

ADJECTIVES (Continued).

Nine Irregular Adjectives.

61. Here belong —

alius, *another;*   alter, *the other;*
üllus, *any;*   nüllus, *none, no;*
uter, *which?* (of two);   neuter, *neither;*
sölus, *alone;*   tötus, *whole;*

ünus, *one, alone.*

They are declined as follows : —

SINGULAR.

	Masculine.	Feminine.	Neuter.	Masculine.	Feminine.	Neuter.
Nom.	alius	alia	aliud	alter	altera	alterum
Gen.	alterĭus	alterĭus	alterĭus [1]	alterĭus	alterĭus	alterĭus
Dat.	aliī	aliī	aliī	alterī	alterī	alterī
Acc.	·alium	aliam	aliud	alterum	alteram	alterum
Voc.	——	——	——	——	——	——
Abl.	aliŏ	aliă	aliŏ	alterŏ	alterā	alterŏ
Nom.	uter	utra	utrum	tötus	töta	tötum
Gen.	utrĭus	utrĭus	utrĭus	tötĭus	tötĭus	tötĭus
Dat.	utrī	utrī	utrī	tötī	tötī	tötī
Acc.	utrum	utram	utrum	tötum	tötam	tötum
Voc.	——	——	——	——	——	——
Abl.	utrŏ	utră	utrŏ	tötŏ	tötă	tötŏ

1. All these words lack the Vocative.
2. The Plural is regular, and is declined like *bonus.*

ADJECTIVES OF THE THIRD DECLENSION.

62. These fall into three classes, —

1. Adjectives of three terminations in the Nominative Singular, — one for each gender.

---

1 This is regularly used, instead of alīus.

2. Adjectives of two terminations.
3. Adjectives of one termination.

a. With the exception of Comparatives, and a few other words mentioned below (see § 68. 1), all Adjectives of the Third Declension follow the inflection of Ĭ-stems; *i.e.* they have the Ablative Singular in -Ĭ, the Genitive Plural in -ium, the Accusative Plural in -Ĭs (as well as -ēs) in the Masculine and Feminine, and the Nominative and Accusative Plural in -ia in the Neuter.

Adjectives of Three Terminations.

63. These are declined as follows : —

Ācer, *sharp.*

SINGULAR.

	MASCULINE.	FEMININE.	NEUTER.
Nom.	ācer	ācris	ācre
Gen.	ācris	ācris	ācris
Dat.	ācrī	ācrī	ācrī
Acc.	ācrem	ācrem	ācre
Voc.	ācer	ācris	ācre
Abl.	ācrī	ācrī	ācrī

PLURAL.

Nom.	ācrēs	ācrēs	ācria
Gen.	ācrium	ācrium	ācrium
Dat.	ācribus	ācribus	ācribus
Acc.	ācrēs, -Ĭs	ācrēs, -Ĭs	ācria
Voc.	ācrēs	ācrēs	ācria
Abl.	ācribus	ācribus	ācribus

1. **Celer, celeris, celere,** *swift,* retains the e before r, but lacks the Genitive Plural.

64. VOCABULARY.

ager, agrĭ, m., *field.*
celer, eris, ere, *swift.*
cohors, rtis, f., *cohort.*
collis, is, m., *hill.*
conjūrō, *I conspire.*
dēlectō, *I delight.*

dōnō, *I present.*
equester, tris, tre, *equestrian.*
prīnceps, cipis, m., *chief.*
sine, *without,* prep. w. abl.
terra, ae, f., *land.*

EXERCISES.

65. 1. Alia terra, alterius terrae. 2. Aliud perīculum, aliōrum perīculōrum. 3. Tōtī cohortī, tōtīus collis. 4. Nūllī agrī, nūllīus agrī. 5. Aliī legiōnī, aliae legiōnēs.

66. 1. Prīncipēs tōtīus Galliae conjūrant. 2. Dē aliīs rēbus dubitāmus. 3. Sine ūllō timōre alterum oppidum oppūgnant. 4. Aliō proeliō dīmicat. 5. Nūllōs mīlitēs alterius cohortis laudāmus. 6. Ūnam legiōnem in dextrō cornū collocat. 7. Collem aliīs cohortibus occupat. 8. Germānīs sōlīs agrōs dōnat. 9. Equestrī proeliō dīmicat. 10. Spēs celeris victōriae legiōnēs dēlectat.

CHAPTER X.

ADJECTIVES (Continued).

Adjectives of Two Terminations.

67.   **Fortis,** *strong.*   **Fortior,** *stronger.*

SINGULAR.

	M. AND F.	NEUT.	M. AND F.	NEUT.
Nom.	fortis	forte	fortior	fortius
Gen.	fortis	fortis	fortiōris	fortiōris
Dat.	fortī	fortī	fortiōrī	fortiōrī
Acc.	fortem	forte	fortiōrem	fortius
Voc.	fortis	forte	fortior	fortius
Abl.	fortī	fortī	fortiōre, -I	fortiōre, -I

PLURAL.

	M. AND F.	NEUT.	M. AND F.	NEUT.
Nom.	fortēs	fortia	fortiōrēs	fortiōra
Gen.	fortium	fortium	fortiōrum	fortiōrum
Dat.	fortibus	fortibus	fortiōribus	fortiōribus
Acc.	fortēs, -Is	fortia	fortiōrēs, -Is	fortiōra
Voc.	fortēs	fortia	fortiōrēs	fortiōra
Abl.	fortibus	fortibus	fortiōribus	fortiōribus

1. **Fortior** is the Comparative of **fortis.** All Comparatives are regularly declined in the same way.

Adjectives of One Termination.

68.   **Fēlīx,** *happy.*   **Prūdēns,** *prudent.*

SINGULAR.

	M. AND F.	NEUT.	M. AND F.	NEUT.
Nom.	fēlīx	fēlīx	prūdēns	prūdēns
Gen.	fēlīcis	fēlīcis	prūdentis	prūdentis
Dat.	fēlīcī	fēlīcī	prūdentī	prūdentī
Acc.	fēlīcem	fēlīx	prūdentem	prūdēns
Voc.	fēlīx	fēlīx	prūdēns	prūdēns
Abl.	fēlīcī	fēlīcī	prūdentī	prūdentī

PLURAL.

	M. AND F.	NEUT.	M. AND F.	NEUT.
Nom.	fēlīcēs	fēlīcia	prūdentēs	prūdentia
Gen.	fēlīcium	fēlīcium	prūdentium	prūdentium
Dat.	fēlīcibus	fēlīcibus	prūdentibus	prūdentibus
Acc.	fēlīcēs, -Is	fēlīcia	prūdentēs, -Is	prūdentia
Voc.	fēlīcēs	fēlīcia	prūdentēs	prūdentia
Abl.	fēlīcibus	fēlīcibus	prūdentibus	prūdentibus

Vetus, *old.*   ### Plūs, *more.*

SINGULAR.

	M. AND F.	NEUT.	M. AND F.	NEUT.
Nom.	vetus	vetus	——	plūs
Gen.	veteris	veteris	——	plūris
Dat.	veterī	veterī	——	———
Acc.	veterem	vetus	——	plūs
Voc.	vetus	vetus	——	———
Abl.	vetere	vetere	——	plūre

PLURAL.

	M. AND F.	NEUT.	M. AND F.	NEUT.
Nom.	veterēs	vetera	plūrēs	plūra
Gen.	veterum	veterum	plūrium	plūrium
Dat.	veteribus	veteribus	plūribus	plūribus
Acc.	veterēs	vetera	plūrēs, -īs	plūra
Voc.	veterēs	vetera	——	———
Abl.	veteribus	veteribus	plūribus	plūribus

1. It will be observed that **vetus** is declined as a pure Consonant-Stem; *i.e.*, Ablative Singular in -e, Genitive Plural in -**um**, Nominative Plural Neuter in -a, and Accusative Plural Masculine and Feminine in -**ēs** only. In the same way are declined **dīves**, *rich;* **pauper,** *poor*.

2. **Plūs**, in the Singular, is used only as a substantive.

69.   VOCABULARY.

aditus, ūs, m., *approach.*

adulēscēns, entis, m., *young man.*

commūnis, e, *common.*

complūrēs, ra, gen. -**ium,** *very many.*

concilium, ī (iī), n., *council.*

dēlīberō, *I deliberate, consult.*

difficilis, e, *difficult.*

ferāx, gen., **ferācis,** *fertile.*

fidēs, eī, f., *protection.*

Haeduī, ōrum, m. plu., *Haedui,* a Gallic tribe.

incolumis, e, *unharmed, uninjured.*

lēgātus, ī, m., *envoy.*

nāvālis, e, *naval.*

nōbilis, e, *noble.*

omnis, e, *all, every.*

tribūnus, ī, m., *tribune.*

Venetī, ōrum, m. pl., *Veneti,* a Gallic tribe.

EXERCISES.

70. 1. Agrōrum ferācium, in agrīs ferācibus.   2. Omnibus aditibus, omnīs aditūs.   3. Nōbilis adulēscentis, nōbilium adulēscentium.   4. Proelia nāvālia, proeliīs nāvālibus.   5. Concilia commūnia, conciliīs commūnibus.

71. 1. Mīlitēs Rōmānī sunt incolumēs.   2. Cum omnibus cōpiīs oppidum oppūgnat.   3. Helvētiī agrōs ferācēs Haeduōrum vexant.   4. Tribūnōs omnium legiōnum vocat.   5. Complūrēs lēgātī fidem Caesaris implōrant.   6. Belgae in conciliō commūnī dē bellō dēlīberant.   7. Nōbilēs adulēscentēs accūsat. 8. Rōmānī Venetōs proeliō nāvālī superant.   9. Omnēs aditūs sunt difficilēs.

CHAPTER XI.

COMPARISON OF ADJECTIVES.

72. 1. There are three degrees of Comparison, — the Positive, the Comparative, and the Superlative.

2. The Comparative is regularly formed by adding -ior (Neut. -ius), and the Superlative by adding -issimus (-a, -um), to the Stem of the Positive deprived of its final vowel; as, —

altus, *high*,	altior, *higher*,	altissimus,	{ *highest, very high.*
fortis, *brave*,	fortior,	fortissimus.	
fēlīx, *fortunate*,	fēlīcior,	fēlīcissimus.	

3. Adjectives in -er form the Superlative by appending -rimus to the Nominative of the Positive. The Comparative is regular. Thus : —

pulcher, *beautiful*,	pulchrior,	pulcherrimus.
celer, *swift*,	celerior,	celerrimus.

4. Five Adjectives in -ilis form the Superlative by adding -limus to the Stem of the Positive deprived of its final vowel. The Comparative is regular. Thus : —

facilis, *easy*,	facilior,	facillimus.
difficilis, *difficult*,	difficilior	difficillimus.
similis, *like*,	similior,	simillimus.
dissimilis, *unlike*,	dissimilior,	dissimillimus.
humilis, *low*,	humilior,	humillimus.

73.   **Irregular Comparison.**

Several Adjectives vary the Stem in Comparison; *viz.* : —

bonus, *good*,	melior,	optimus.
malus, *bad*,	pējor,	pessimus.
parvus, *small*,	minor,	minimus.
māgnus, *large*,	mājor,	māximus.
multus, *much*,	plūs,	plūrimus.

74.   **Defective Comparison.**

1. Positive lacking entirely, —

———	prior, *former,*	prīmus, *first.*
———	citerior, *on this side,*	citimus, *near.*
———	ulterior, *farther,*	ultimus, *farthest.*
———	propior, *nearer,*	proximus, *nearest.*

2. Positive occurring only in special cases, —

posterus, *following,* posterior, *later,* { postrēmus, *last.* / postumus, *posthumous.* }

exterus, *foreign,* exterior, *outer,* { extrēmus, / extimus, } *outermost.*

īnferus, *low,* īnferior, *lower,* { īnfimus, / īmus, } *lowest.*

superus, *high,* superior, *higher,* { suprēmus, *last.* / summus, *highest.* }

75.   **VOCABULARY.**

Allobrogēs, um, m. pl., *Allobroges,* a Gallic tribe.
altitūdō, inis, f., *depth, height.*
Avāricum, ī, n., *Avaricum,* a Gallic town.
fortis, e, *brave.*

Genēva, ae, f., *Geneva,* a town of the Allobroges.
quattuor, indecl., *four.*
quīnque, indecl., *five.*
urbs, urbis, f., *city.*
vallis, is, f., *valley.*

EXERCISES.

76. 1. Mājōra perīcula, māximīs perīculīs. 2. Minōribus castrīs, minōrum castrōrum. 3. Māximī oppidī, māxima oppida. 4. Urbēs pulchriōrēs, urbium pulcherrimārum. 5. Vallēs mājōrēs, in vallibus mājōribus.

77. 1. Belgae sunt fortissimī omnium Gallōrum. 2. Reliquae cohortēs minōra castra oppūgnant. 3. Altitūdō flūminis est minima. 4. In castrīs mājōribus sunt quīnque legiōnēs. 5. Māximās cōpiās parāmus. 6. Quattuor cohortēs in prīmā aciē sunt. 7. Genēva est extrēmum oppidum Allobrogum. 8. Mīlitēs cum minōre perīculō dīmicant. 9. Avāricum est pulcherrima urbs tōtīus Galliae. 10. Aditūs sunt difficillimī.

CHAPTER XII.

78. Adverbs are for the most part derived from adjectives, and depend upon them for their comparison.

1. Adverbs derived from adjectives of the First and Second Declensions form the Positive by changing -ī of the Genitive Singular to -ĕ; those derived from adjectives of the Third Declension, by changing -is of the Genitive Singular to -iter; as, —

cārus,	cārĕ, *dearly;*
pulcher,	pulchrĕ, *beautifully;*
ācer,	ācriter, *fiercely.*

a) But Adjectives in -ns, and a few others, add -ter (instead of -iter), to form the Adverb; as, —

sapiēns,	sapienter, *wisely;*
audāx,	audācter, *boldly.*

2. The Comparative of all Adverbs regularly consists of the Accusative Singular Neuter of the Comparative of the Adjective; while the Superlative of the Adverb is found by changing the -ī of the Genitive Singular of the Superlative of the Adjective to -ĕ. Thus —

(cārus)	cārĕ, *dearly,*	cārius,	cārissimĕ.
(pulcher)	pulchrĕ, *beautifully,*	pulchrius,	pulcherrimĕ.
(ācer)	ācriter, *fiercely,*	ācrius,	ācerrimĕ.
(audāx)	audācter, *boldly,*	audācius,	audācissimĕ.

79. Adverbs Peculiar in Comparison and Formation.

benĕ, *well,*	melius,	optimĕ.
malĕ, *ill,*	pējus,	pessimĕ.
māgnopere, *greatly,*	magis,	māximĕ.
multum, *much,*	plūs,	plūrimum.
nōn multum, } *little,* parum,	minus,	minimĕ.
saepe, *often,*	saepius,	saepissimĕ.
prope, *near,*	propius,	proximĕ.

33

80 **Numerals.**

1. For the declension of **ūnus**, *one*, see p. 25.
2. Duo, *two*, and **trēs**, *three*, are declined as follows:

Nom.	duo	duae	duo
Gen.	duōrum	duārum	duōrum
Dat.	duōbus	duābus	duōbus
Acc.	duōs, duo	duās	duo
Abl.	duōbus	duābus	duōbus

Nom.	trēs	tria
Gen.	trium	trium
Dat.	tribus	tribus
Acc.	trēs (trīs)	tria
Abl.	tribus	tribus

3. The units from four to ten, and all the tens from ten to one hundred are indeclinable. Hundreds are declined like the plural of *bonus.*

4. **Mīlle**, *thousand*, is regularly an adjective in the Singular, and indeclinable. In the Plural it is a substantive (followed by the Genitive of the objects enumerated), and is declined, —

Nom.	mīlia	*Acc.*	mīlia
Gen.	mīlium	*Voc.*	mīlia
Dat.	mīlibus	*Abl.*	mīlibus

81. **VOCABULARY.**

ācriter, *sharply, fiercely* (from ācer).
audācter, *courageously* (from audāx).
cōgitō, *I think.*
dēfēnsiō, ōnis, f., *defence.*
diū, adv., *a long time.*
facile, *easily* (from facilis).
fortiter, *bravely* (from fortis).
fuga, ae, f., *flight.*
impetus, ūs, m., *onset, attack.*

Instō, *I press on.*
magis, *more, rather*; comp. of māgnopere.
māximē, *especially*; sup. of māgnopere.
perturbō, *I agitate.*
pūgnō, *I fight.*
quam, *than.*
tardō, *I retard, check.*
trecentī, ae, a, *three hundred.*

EXERCISES.

82. 1. Trecentōrum equitum.　　2. Cum tribus fīliābus.
3. Tria oppida, in tribus oppidīs.　　4. Duo mīlia equitum, mīlle
equitēs.　　5. In duābus terrīs.

83. 1. Hostēs diū[1] et ācriter pūgnant.　　2. Mīlitēs magis dē
fugā quam dē dēfēnsiōne castrōrum cōgitant.　　3. Jūmenta
Gallōs māximē dēlectant.　　4. Timor mentēs mīlitum māgnopere
perturbat.　　5. Duae legiōnēs audācius īnstant.　　6. Trecentī
Germānī sunt in castrīs.　　7. Mīlitēs ācerrimē et fortissimē pūgnant.　　8. Caesar impetum hostium facile tardat.　　9. Tria
mīlia equitum in proeliō pūgnant.　　10. Equitēs minus audācter
īnstant.

---

[1] The adverb usually stands immediately before the word which it modifies.

CHAPTER XIII.

PRONOUNS.

84. A Pronoun is a word that indicates something without naming it.

I. Personal Pronouns.

85. These correspond to the English *I, you, he, she, it,*
etc., and are declined as follows : —

	First Person.	*Second Person.*	*Third Person.*
		SINGULAR.	
Nom.	ego, *I*	tū, *thou*	is, *he* ; ea, *she* ; id, *it*
Gen.	meī	tuī	(For Declension, see § 94.)
Dat.	mihi	tibi	
Acc.	mē	tē	
Voc.	——	tū	
Abl.	mē	tē	
		PLURAL.	
Nom.	nōs, *we*	vōs, *you*	
Gen.	{ nostrum { nostrī	{ vestrum { vestrī	
Dat.	nōbīs	vōbīs	
Acc.	nōs	vōs	
Voc.	——	vōs	
Abl.	nōbīs	vōbīs	

II. Reflexive Pronouns.

86. These refer to the subject of the sentence or clause
in which they stand ; like *myself, yourself,* in '*I see myself,*'
etc. They are declined as follows : —

36

First Person.	Second Person.	Third Person.
Supplied by oblique cases of **ego.**	Supplied by oblique cases of **tū.**	
Gen. meī, *of myself*	tuī, *of thyself*	suī
Dat. mihi, *to myself*	tibi, *to thyself*	sibi
Acc. mē, *myself*	tē, *thyself*	sē *or* sēsē
Voc. ——	——	——
Abl. mē, *with myself, etc.*	tē, *with thyself, etc.*	sē *or* sēsē

1. The Reflexive of the Third Person serves for *all genders* and for *both numbers.* Thus **suī** may mean, *of himself, herself, itself,* or *of themselves;* and so with the other cases of **suī.**

III. **Possessive Pronouns.**

87. These are strictly adjectives of the First and Second Declensions, and are inflected as such. They are —

First Person.	Second Person.
meus, -a, -um, *my;*	tuus, -a, -um, *thy;*
noster, nostra, nostrum, *our;*	vester, vestra, vestrum, *your;*

Third Person.

suus, -a, -um, *his, her, its, their.*

1. **Suus** is exclusively Reflexive; as, —

pater suōs līberōs amat, *the father loves his children.*

Otherwise, *his, her, its,* are regularly expressed by the Genitive Singular of **is,** *viz.* **ējus;** and *their,* by the Genitive Plural, **eōrum, eārum.**

IV. **Demonstrative Pronouns.**

88. These point out an object as **here** or **there,** or as **previously mentioned.** They are —

hīc, *this;* **iste, ille, is,** *that;* **īdem,** *the same.*

Hīc, *this.*

	SINGULAR.			PLURAL.		
	MASCULINE.	FEMININE.	NEUTER.	MASCULINE.	FEMININE.	NEUTER.
Nom.	hīc	haec	hōc	hī	hae	haec
Gen.	hūjus	hūjus	hūjus	hōrum	hārum	hōrum
Dat.	huic	huic	huic	hīs	hīs	hīs
Acc.	hunc	hanc	hōc	hōs	hās	haec
Abl.	hōc	hāc	hōc	hīs	hīs	hīs

89. VOCABULARY.

ad, *to,*[1] *towards,* prep. w. acc.
amīcē, *in a friendly manner.*
cārus, a, um, *dear.*
culpō, *I blame.*
Dumnorīx, īgis, m., *Dumnorix,*
  a chief of the Haedui.
gladius, ī (iī), m., *sword.*
grātus, a, um, *pleasing, welcome.*
imperātor, ōris, m., *commander.*
jūdicō, *I judge, adjudge.*

memoria, ae, f., *memory, recollec-*
  tion.
officium, ī (iī), n., *duty.*
praestō, *I perform.*
probō, *I approve.*
quoque, *also,* always placed after
  the word it modifies.
salūs, ūtis, f., *safety.*
verbum, ī, n., *word.*

EXERCISES.

90. 1. Mihi, nōbīs, nōs. 2. Suī, sibi. 3. Tē, vōbīs, vestrī.
4. Pater meus,[2] pater noster, patrum nostrōrum. 5. Patris tuī,
patrēs vestrī. 6. Hūjus patris, hōrum patrum.

91. 1. Ego officium meum[3] imperātōrī praestō. 2. Caesar
nōs ācriter accūsat. 3. Tua nostrī memoria mihi est grāta.
4. Ad sē Dumnorīgem vocat. 5. Caesar dē vōbīs amīcissimē
jūdicat. 6. Tū quoque verba mea probās. 7. Ego mē accūsō.
8. Sē culpant. 9. Hīc[3] pater fīliās suās vocat. 10. Vestra
salūs, mīlitēs, huic imperātōrī cāra est. 11. Equitēs nostrī
gladiīs suīs pūgnant.

---

[1] English *to* is rendered by *ad* in Latin, if there is an idea of *motion;* otherwise
the Dative is used.

[2] The Possessive Pronouns, unless emphatic, are ordinarily placed after the
noun which they limit.

[3] The Demonstrative Pronoun, like an adjective, agrees in Gender, Number,
and Case with the noun it limits.

CHAPTER XIV.

DEMONSTRATIVE PRONOUNS (CONTINUED).—THE INTENSIVE PRONOUN.

92. **Iste,** *that, that of yours.*

| | SINGULAR. | | | PLURAL. | | |
	MASCULINE.	FEMININE.	NEUTER.	MASCULINE.	FEMININE.	NEUTER.
Nom.	iste	ista	istud	istī	istae	ista
Gen.	istīus	istīus	istīus	istōrum	istārum	istōrum
Dat.	istī	istī	istī	istīs	istīs	istīs
Acc.	istum	istam	istud	istōs	istās	ista
Abl.	istō	istā	istō	istīs	istīs	istīs

93. **Ille,** *that, that one, he,* is declined like iste.

94. **Is,** *he, this, that.*

| | SINGULAR. | | | PLURAL. | | |
	MASCULINE.	FEMININE.	NEUTER.	MASCULINE.	FEMININE.	NEUTER.
Nom.	is	ea	id	eī, iī, (ī)	eae	ea
Gen.	ējus	ējus	ējus	eōrum	eārum	eōrum
Dat.	eī	eī	eī	eīs, iīs	eīs, iīs	eīs, iīs
Acc.	eum	eam	id	eōs	eās	ea
Abl.	eō	eā	eō	eīs, iīs	eīs, iīs	eīs, iīs

95. **Īdem,** *the same.*

| | SINGULAR. | | | PLURAL. | | |
	MASCULINE.	FEMININE.	NEUTER.	MASCULINE.	FEMININE.	NEUTER.
Nom.	īdem	eadem	idem	{ eīdem / iīdem }	eaedem	eadem
Gen.	ējusdem	ējusdem	ējusdem	eōrundem	eārundem	eōrundem
Dat.	eīdem	eīdem	eīdem	eīsdem	eīsdem	eīsdem
Acc.	eundem	eandem	idem	eōsdem	eāsdem	eadem
Abl.	eōdem	eādem	eōdem	eīsdem	eīsdem	eīsdem

The Nom. Plu. Masc. also has **īdem,** and the Dat. Abl. Plu. **īsdem** or **iīsdem.**

39

V. **The Intensive Pronoun.**

96. The Intensive Pronoun in Latin is **ipse.** It corresponds to the English *myself, etc.*, in '*I myself, he himself.*'

	SINGULAR.			PLURAL.		
	MASCULINE.	FEMININE.	NEUTER.	MASCULINE.	FEMININE.	NEUTER.
Nom.	ipse	ipsa	ipsum	ipsī	ipsae	ipsa
Gen.	ipsīus	ipsīus	ipsīus	ipsōrum	ipsārum	ipsōrum
Dat.	ipsī	ipsī	ipsī	ipsīs	ipsīs	ipsīs
Acc.	ipsum	ipsam	ipsum	ipsōs	ipsās	ipsa
Abl.	ipsō	ipsā	ipsō	ipsīs	ipsīs	ipsīs

97.   VOCABULARY.

bene, *well.*
causa, ae, f., *cause, condition.*
exercitus, ūs, m., *army.*
facultās, ātis, f., *supply.*
ignāvus, a, um, *cowardly.*
labor, ōris, m., *labor.*

opīniō, ōnis, f., *opinion, expectation.*
porta, ae, f., *gate.*
servus, ī, m., *slave.*
sex, indecl., *six.*
summus, *highest, greatest*; sup. of
superus (§ 74, 2).

EXERCISES.

98. 1. Illīus[1] opīniōnis, illae opīniōnēs.   2. Ejusdem exercitūs, in eōdem exercitū.   3. Eae causae, dē eīs causīs. 4. Eōrundem labōrum, eīsdem labōribus.   5. Servī ipsīus,[2] ipsōs servōs.

99. 1. Istī mīlitēs sunt ignāvī.   2. Officia illī praestāmus. 3. In illō exercitū sunt multī servī.   4. Ējus nōmen est Galba. 5. Dē eā causā bene jūdicat.   6. Sex cohortēs ējus legiōnis portās ipsās oppidī oppūgnant.   7. Dē eīsdem rēbus jūdicāmus. 8. In eādem causā sunt aliī Gallī.   9. Eīdem equitēs illum laudant.   10. In eō oppidō est summa facultās omnium rērum.

---

[1] The Demonstrative Pronouns regularly precede the noun which they limit.
[2] The Intensive Pronoun stands sometimes before, sometimes after, the noun which it limits.

CHAPTER XV.

RELATIVE, INTERROGATIVE, AND INDEFINITE PRONOUNS.

VI. The Relative Pronoun.

100. The Relative Pronoun is **quī**, *who*. It is declined : —

	SINGULAR.			PLURAL.		
	MASCULINE.	FEMININE.	NEUTER.	MASCULINE.	FEMININE.	NEUTER.
Nom.	quī	quae	quod	quī	quae	quae
Gen.	cūjus	cūjus	cūjus	quōrum	quārum	quōrum
Dat.	cui	cui	cui	quibus	quibus	quibus
Acc.	quem	quam	quod	quōs	quās	quae
Abl.	quō	quā	quō	quibus	quibus	quibus

VII. Interrogative Pronouns.

101. The Interrogative Pronouns are **quis**, *who ?* (substantive) and **quī**, *what ? what kind of ?* (adjective).

1. **Quis,** *who ?*

	SINGULAR.		PLURAL.
	MASC. AND FEM.	NEUTER.	
Nom.	quis	quid	Plural forms are rare.
Gen.	cūjus	cūjus	When they occur they
Dat.	cui	cui	follow the declension
Acc.	quem	quid	of the Relative Pro-
Abl.	quō	quō	noun.

2. **quī,** *what ? what kind of ?* is declined precisely like the Relative Pronoun ; *viz.* **quī, quae, quod,** *etc.*

VIII. Indefinite Pronouns.

102. These have the general force of *some one, any one,* as shown in the following list : —

41

SUBSTANTIVES.			ADJECTIVES.		
M. AND F.	NEUT.		MASC.	FEM.	NEUT.
quis,	quid,	{ *any one, anything.*	quī,	quae *or* qua, quod, *any.*	
aliquis,	aliquid,	{ *some one, something.*	aliquī,	aliqua,	aliquod, *some.*
quisquam,	quidquam,	{ *any one, anything.*	No corresponding adjective.		
quispiam,	quidpiam,	{ *any one, anything.*	quispiam,	quaepiam,	quodpiam, *any.*
quisque,	quidque, *each.*		quisque,	quaeque,	quodque, *each.*
quivīs, quaevīs, quidvīs, quīlibet, quaelibet, quidlibet,		{ *any one, anything you wish.*	quivīs, quīlibet,	quaevīs, quaelibet,	quodvīs, quodlibet, { *any you wish.*
quīdam, quaedam, quiddam,		{ *a certain person* or *thing.*	quīdam,	quaedam,	quoddam, { *a certain.*

1. In the Indefinite Pronouns, only the pronominal part is declined. Thus: Genitive Singular **alicūjus, cūjuslibet,** *etc.*

2. Note that **aliquī** has **aliqua** in the Nominative Singular Feminine, also in the Nominative and Accusative Plural Neuter. **Quī** has both **qua** and **quae** in these same cases.

3. **Quīdam** forms Accusative Singular **quendam, quandam**; Genitive Plural **quōrundam, quārundam**; the **m** being assimilated to **n** before **d**.

4. There are two Indefinite Relatives, — **quīcumque** and **quisquis,** *whoever*. **Quīcumque** declines only the first part; **quisquis** declines both, but has only **quisquis, quidquid, quōquō** in common use.

103.   Principle of Syntax.

Agreement of Relative Pronouns. The Relative Pronoun agrees with its Antecedent in Gender and Number, but its Case is determined by its construction in the clause in which it stands; as, —

mulier quam vidēbāmus, *the woman whom we saw;*
bona quae dēsīderāmus, *the blessings which we miss.*

104. VOCABULARY.

armō, *I arm.*
dubitō, *I hesitate, waver.*
dux, ducis, m., *leader.*
errō, *I err, am mistaken.*
fugō, *I put to flight.*
hīberna, ōrum, n. plu., *winter-quarters.*

homō, minis, c., *man, human being.*
praeda, ae, f., *booty.*
sī, *if.*
spērō, *I hope, hope for*; governs the acc.

EXERCISES.

105. 1. Mīles quīdam, mīlitibus quibusdam. 2. Quis[1] homō? Quid[1] oppidum? 3. Cuique cīvitātī, cūjusque servī. 4. Praeda aliqua, in proeliō aliquō. 5. Homō quīlibet, hominis cūjuslibet.

106. 1. Cohortēs quāsdam in hībernīs collocat. 2. Sī quisquam salūtem spērat, errat. 3. Dux mīlitibus, quī oppidum oppūgnant, praedam dōnat. 4. Legiōnēs laudat quae hostīs fugant. 5. Servōs armat quī in castrīs sunt. 6. Collem quendam occupat. 7. Quis hunc hominem accūsat? 8. Caesar prīncipēs cūjusque cīvitātis ad sē vocat. 9. Quid oppidum oppūgnātis?

---

[1] **Quis** and **quid** are sometimes used as interrogative adjectives. They have the force of *what?* whereas **quī, quod** mean rather *what kind of?*

CHAPTER XVI.

CONJUGATION.

107. The Inflection of Verbs is called Conjugation.

108. Verbs have Voice, Mood, Tense, Number, Person:

1. Two Voices, — Active and Passive.
2. Three Moods, — Indicative, Subjunctive, Imperative.
3. Six Tenses, — Present, Imperfect, Future, Perfect, Pluperfect, Future Perfect.

But the Subjunctive lacks the Future and Future Perfect; while the Imperative employs only the Present and Future.

4. Two Numbers, — Singular and Plural.
5. Three Persons, — First, Second, and Third.

109. These make up the so-called *Finite Verb.* Besides this, we have the following Noun and Adjective Forms: —

1. Noun Forms, — Infinitive, Gerund, and Supine.
2. Adjective Forms, — Participles (including the Gerundive).

THE FOUR CONJUGATIONS.

110. There are in Latin four regular Conjugations, distinguished from each other by the vowel of the termination of the Present Infinitive Active, as follows: —

CONJUGATION.	INFINITIVE TERMINATION.	DISTINGUISHING VOWEL.
I.	-āre	ā
II.	-ēre	ē
III.	-ĕre	ĕ
IV.	-īre	ī

111. PRINCIPAL PARTS. The Present Indicative, Present Infinitive, Perfect Indicative, and the Perfect Participle [1] constitute the **Principal Parts** of a Latin verb, — so called because they contain the different stems, from which the full conjugation of the verb may be derived.

---

[1] Where the Perfect Participle is not in use, the Future Active Participle, if it occurs, is given as one of the Principal Parts.

Indicative of *sum*.

112. The irregular verb **sum** is so important for the conjugation of all other verbs that its inflection is given at the outset.

PRINCIPAL PARTS.

PRES. IND.	PRES. INF.	PERF. IND.	FUT. PARTIC.[1]
sum	esse	fuī	futūrus

PRESENT TENSE.

SINGULAR.	PLURAL.
sum, *I am,*	sumus, *we are,*
es, *thou art,*	estis, *you are,*
est, *he is ;*	sunt, *they are.*

IMPERFECT.

eram, *I was,*	erāmus, *we were,*
erās, *thou wast,*	erātis, *you were,*
erat, *he was ;*	erant, *they were.*

FUTURE.

erŏ, *I shall be,*	erimus, *we shall be,*
eris, *thou wilt be,*	eritis, *you will be,*
erit, *he will be ;*	erunt, *they will be.*

PERFECT.

fuī, *I have been, I was,*[2]	fuimus, *we have been, we were,*
fuistī, *thou hast been, thou wast,*	fuistis, *you have been, you were,*
fuit, *he has been, he was ;*	fuĕrunt, ⎫ *they have been, they were.* fuēre, ⎭

PLUPERFECT.

fueram, *I had been,*	fuerāmus, *we had been,*
fuerās, *thou hadst been,*	fuerātis, *you had been,*
fuerat, *he had been ;*	fuerant, *they had been.*

FUTURE PERFECT.

fuerŏ, *I shall have been,*	fuerimus, *we shall have been,*
fueris, *thou wilt have been,*	fueritis, *you will have been,*
fuerit, *he will have been ;*	fuerint, *they will have been.*

---

[1] The Perfect Participle is wanting in **sum**.

[2] These two meanings are designated respectively as the Present Perfect (*I have been*) and the Historical Perfect (*I was*).

113.   **VOCABULARY.**

ante, *before, in front of,* prep. w.
acc.
Bibulus, I, m., *Bibulus,* a man's
name.
firmus, a, um, *firm, strong.*
fossa, ae, f., *ditch, trench.*

ibi, *adv., there, in that place.*
inopia, ae, f., *lack, need.*
nondum, *not yet.*
quondam, *formerly.*
septem, indecl., *seven.*
ubi, *where,* rel. and interr. adv.

EXERCISES.

114. 1. Erātis, fuerat, fuistis.   2. Estis, fuerimus, fuerant.
3. Eritis, erant, fuēre.   4. Fuistī, erimus, erās.   5. Fuerās,
fueris, fueritis.

115. 1. Fossa erat ante oppidum.   2. Hī lēgātī in castrīs
Caesaris fuerant.   3. Haec cīvitās quondam fuerat fīrmissima.
4. Hae septem legiōnēs in Italiā erant.   5. Quis fuit dux hōrum
mīlitum?   6. Caesar et Bibulus cōnsulēs fuērunt.   7. Māgna
erit inopia omnium rērum.   8. Ubi fuistis?   9. In oppidō
Haeduōrum fuimus.   10. Nōndum ibi fuerāmus.

CHAPTER XVII.

116.   SUBJUNCTIVE OF *sum*.[1]

PRESENT.

SINGULAR.	PLURAL.
sim, *may I be,*	sīmus, *let us be,*
sīs, *mayest thou be,*	sītis, *be ye, may you be,*
sit, *let him be, may he be ;*	sint, *let them be.*

IMPERFECT.

essem, *I should be,*	essēmus, *we should be,*
essēs, *thou wouldst be,*	essētis, *you would be,*
esset, *he would be ;*	essent, *they would be.*

PERFECT.

fuerim, *I may have been,*	fuerimus, *we may have been,*
fueris, *thou mayst have been,*	fueritis, *you may have been,*
fuerit, *he may have been ;*	fuerint, *they may have been.*

PLUPERFECT.

fuissem, *I should have been,*	fuissēmus, *we should have been,*
fuissēs, *thou wouldst have been,*	fuissētis, *you would have been,*
fuisset, *he would have been ;*	fuissent, *they would have been.*

Imperative.

Pres. es, *be thou,*	este, *be ye.*
Fut. estō, *thou shalt be,*	estōte, *ye shall be,*
estō, *he shall be ;*	suntō, *they shall be.*

Infinitive.   Participle.

Pres. esse, *to be,*
Perf. fuisse, *to have been.*
Fut. futūrus esse,[2] *to be about to be.*   *Fut.* futūrus,[3] *about to be.*

---

[1] The meanings of the different tenses of the Subjunctive are so many and so varied, particularly in subordinate clauses, that no attempt can be made to give them here. For fuller information the pupil is referred to the Syntax.

[2] For **futūrus esse** the form **fore** is often used.

[3] Declined like **bonus, -a, -um.**

117. VOCABULARY.

amīcitia, ae, f., *friendship.*

beātus, a, um, *happy.*

brevis, e, *short, brief.*

cīvis, cīvis, c., *citizen, fellow citizen.*

clēmēns, gen., entis, *merciful.*

contentus, a, um, *contented.*

fēlīx, gen., fēlīcis, *fortunate, happy.*

inter, *among, between,* prep. with acc.

lēx, lēgis, f., *law.*

perpetuus, a, um, *perpetual.*

puer, puerī, m., *boy.*

sub, *under,* prep. with abl.

EXERCISES.

118. 1. Fuisse, futūrus esse. 2. Sit, sītis. 3. Fuisset, fuissēmus. 4. Es, estō, suntō. 5. Essēs, essētis, essēmus.

119. 1. Sint meī cīvēs incolumēs, sint beātī. 2. Fēlīcēs sīmus. 3. Sub hōc imperātōre contentī fuissēmus. 4. Lēgēs brevēs suntō. 5. Es bonus imperātor. 6. Estō clēmēns. 7. Este fortēs mīlitēs. 8. Hī puerī futūrī sunt adulēscentēs. 9. Inter nōs sit amīcitia perpetua.

CHAPTER XVIII.

FIRST (OR *ā*-) CONJUGATION.

120. **Active Voice.** — Amō, *I love.*

PRINCIPAL PARTS.

Pres. Ind.	Pres. Inf.	Perf. Ind.	Perf. Pass. Partic.
amō	amāre	amāvī	amātus

Indicative Mood.

PRESENT TENSE.

SINGULAR.	PLURAL.
amō, *I love,*	amāmus, *we love,*
amās, *you love,*	amātis, *you love,*
amat, *he loves ;*	amant, *they love.*

IMPERFECT.

amābam, *I was loving, I loved,*	amābāmus, *we were loving, etc.,*
amābās, *you were loving, etc.,*	amābātis, *you were loving, etc.,*
amābat, *he was loving, etc. ;*	amābant, *they were loving, etc.*

FUTURE.

amābō, *I shall love,*	amābimus, *we shall love,*
amābis, *you will love,*	amābitis, *you will love,*
amābit, *he will love ;*	amābunt, *they will love.*

PERFECT.

amāvī, *I have loved, I loved,*	amāvimus, *we have loved, we loved,*
amāvistī, *you have loved, you loved,*	amāvistis, *you have loved, you loved,* [*they loved.*
amāvit, *he has loved, he loved ;*	amāvērunt, -ēre, *they have loved,*

PLUPERFECT.

amāveram, *I had loved,*	amāverāmus, *we had loved,*
amāverās, *you had loved,*	amāverātis, *you had loved,*
amāverat, *he had loved ;*	amāverant, *they had loved.*

FUTURE PERFECT.

amāverō, *I shall have loved,*	amāverimus, *we shall have loved,*
amāveris, *you will have loved,*	amāveritis, *you will have loved,*
amāverit, *he will have loved ;*	amāverint, *they will have loved.*

1. VERB STEMS. Observe that the Present, Imperfect, and Future are formed by adding the proper endings to one and the same stem, **am-**. This is called the **Present Stem**. Similarly the Perfect, Pluperfect, and Future Perfect are formed from the stem **amāv-**. This is called the **Perfect Stem**.

121. VOCABULARY.

animus, ī, m., *mind.*

Ariovistus, ī, m., *Ariovistus,* king of the Germans.

classis, is, f., *fleet.*

cōnsilium, ī (iī) n., *plan.*

ē, ex, *from, out of,* prep. w. abl., **ex** must be used before vowels or **h.**

gēns, gentis, f., *tribe.*

jam, adv., *already.*

jugum, ī, n., *yoke; ridge* (of mountains).

lītus, oris, n., *shore.*

locus, ī, m., *place,* plu. **loca, ōrum, n.**

nāvis, is, f., *ship, boat.*

pars, partis, f., *part, side.*

saepe, adv., *often.*

EXERCISES.

122. 1. Laudābimus, laudāvistis. 2. Laudāverant, laudābat, laudābit. 3. Jūdicāvimus, jūdicāverimus, jūdicāverās. 4. Superābit, superābās. 5. Occupant, occupāvērunt.

123. 1. Ariovistus castra minōra oppūgnābat. 2. Hunc locum ex duābus partibus oppūgnāvērunt. 3. Nāvēs et rēmigēs parābimus. 4. Omnia lītora classibus occupāvit. 5. Timor animōs omnium occupāverat. 6. In summō jugō montis duās legiōnēs collocāvimus. 7. Dē bellō vōs ipsī jūdicābitis. 8. Hās gentēs, mīlitēs, jam saepe superāvistis. 9. Legiōnēs in proeliō dīmicābant. 10. Quis hōc cōnsilium probābit?

CHAPTER XIX.

124. ACTIVE OF *amō* (CONTINUED).

Subjunctive.

PRESENT.

SINGULAR.	PLURAL.
amem, *may I love,*	amēmus, *let us love,*
amēs, *may you love,*	amētis, *may you love,*
amet, *let him love;*	ament, *let them love.*

IMPERFECT.

amārem, *I should love,*	amārēmus, *we should love,*
amārēs, *you would love,*	amārētis, *you would love,*
amāret, *he would love;*	amārent, *they would love.*

PERFECT.

amāverim, *I may have loved,*	amāverimus, *we may have loved,*
amāveris, *you may have loved,*	amāveritis, *you may have loved,*
amāverit, *he may have loved;*	amāverint, *they may have loved.*

PLUPERFECT.

amāvissem, *I should have loved,*	amāvissēmus, *we should have loved,*
amāvissēs, *you would have loved,*	amāvissētis, *you would have loved,*
amāvisset, *he would have loved;*	amāvissent, *they would have loved.*

Imperative.

Pres. amā, *love thou;*	amāte, *love ye.*
Fut. amātō, *thou shalt love;*	amātōte, *ye shall love,*
amātō, *he shall love;*	amantō, *they shall love.*

Infinitive.

Pres. amāre, *to love.*
Perf. amāvisse, *to have loved.*
Fut. amātūrus esse, *to be about to love.*

Participle.

Pres. amāns,[1] *loving.*
(Gen. amantis)
Fut. amātūrus, *about to love.*

Gerund.

Gen. amandī, *of loving,*
Dat. amandō, *for loving,*
Acc. amandum, *loving,*
Abl. amandō, *by loving.*

Supine.

Acc. amātum, *to love.*
Abl. amātū, *to love, be loved.*

---

[1] For declension of amāns, see § 68, prūdēns.

1. **VERB STEMS.** Observe that the Present and Imperfect Subjunctive, the entire Imperative, the Present Infinitive, Present Participle, and the Gerund are formed from the Present Stem. The Perfect and Pluperfect Subjunctive, along with the Perfect Infinitive, are formed from the Perfect Stem. The Future Participle, Future Infinitive, and the Supine are formed from a third stem **amāt-**, known as the **Participial Stem.**

125.   **VOCABULARY.**

arma, ōrum, n. plu., *arms.*

bellō,[1] *I make war, carry on war.*

cupidus, a, um, *fond, eager.*

hōra, ae, f., *hour.*

intrā, *within*, prep. w. acc.

medius, a, um, *middle, middle of.*

multitūdō, dinis, f., *multitude.*

nunc, *now*, temporal adv.

patria, ae, f., *country, fatherland.*

pedes, itis, m., *foot-soldier ;* in plu., *infantry.*

plānitiēs, ēī, f., *plain.*

temptō, 1, *I attempt, make trial of.*

vadum, ī, n., *ford.*

EXERCISES.

126. 1. Parā, parantō.   2. Parāvisse, parandī, parandō. 3. Bellāre, bellātūrus esse.   4. Temptēmus, temptāvissēmus. 5. Laudātō, laudāvisse, laudāvisset.

127. 1. Patriam amēmus !   2. Hōc oppidum sine ūllō perīculō oppūgnāvissēmus.   3. Arma, mīlitēs, parāte ! 4. Caesar vadum hūjus flūminis temptāre parat.   5. In mediā plānitiē nunc dīmicātūrī sumus.   6. Helvētiī erant cupidī bellandī. 7. Intrā ūnam hōram classēs hostium superāvissēmus.   8. Cum māgnā multitūdine peditum oppidum oppūgnāre parābat.

---

[1] Verbs of the First Conjugation are so regular that their Principal Parts are not given in full. They are indicated in the Vocabularies by the figure 1, and unless otherwise stated, their Principal Parts are regularly formed in **-ō, -āre, -āvī, -ātus,** precisely like **amō.**

CHAPTER XX.

FIRST (OR *ā-*) CONJUGATION.

128. **Passive Voice.** — Amor, *I am loved.*

	PRES. IND.	PRES. INF.	PERF. IND.
PRINCIPAL PARTS. —	amor	amārī	amātus sum

Indicative Mood.

PRESENT TENSE.

SINGULAR.	*I am loved.*	PLURAL.
amor		amāmur
amāris		amāminī
amātur		amantur

IMPERFECT.
I was loved.

amābar	amābāmur
amābāris, *or* -re	amābāminī
amābātur	amābantur

FUTURE.
I shall be loved.

amābor	amābimur
amāberis, *or* -re	amābiminī
amābitur	amābuntur

PERFECT.
I have been loved or *I was loved.*

amātus (-a, -um) sum	amātī (-ae, -a) sumus
amātus es	amātī estis
amātus est	amātī sunt

PLUPERFECT.
I had been loved.

amātus eram	amātī erāmus
amātus erās	amātī erātis
amātus erat	amātī erant

FUTURE PERFECT.
I shall have been loved.

amātus erō	amātī erimus
amātus eris	amātī eritis
amātus erit	amātī erunt

53

1. VERB STEMS. Observe that the Present, Imperfect, and Future belong to the Present Stem, the remaining tenses to the Participial Stem.

129. VOCABULARY.

adventus, ūs, m., *arrival.*
centum, indecl., *hundred.*
exspectō, 1, *I expect, await.*
fīnitimus, a, um, *neighboring.*
frūmentum, ī, n., *grain.*

frūstrā, adv., *in vain.*
funditor, tōris, m., *slinger.*
postrīdiē, adv., *on the next day.*
postulō, 1, *I demand.*
vulnerō, 1, *I wound.*

EXERCISES.

130. 1. Laudābor, laudāminī, laudābuntur. 2. Vocātus sum, vocātī erant. 3. Vulnerantur, vulnerābāmur. 4. Exspectāmur, exspectābantur. 5. Culpātī erāmus, culpātī erunt.

131. 1. Reliqua pars exercitūs frūstrā exspectābātur. 2. Hī fortēs mīlitēs superātī sunt. 3. Amīcitia cum fīnitimīs cīvitātibus cōnfīrmāta[1] erat. 4. Centum funditōrēs vulnerātī sunt. 5. Frūmentum postulātur. 6. Adventus ējus postrīdiē nūntiātus est. 7. Nāvēs et rēmigēs parābuntur. 8. Hae cōpiae armātae[1] sunt. 9. Haec oppida oppūgnāta[1] erant. 10. Haec victōria equitum nostrōrum jam nūntiāta erat.

---

[1] Observe that in the compound tenses of the Passive the Participle agrees in Gender and Number with its subject, precisely like an adjective.

CHAPTER XXI.

132.   PASSIVE OF *amō* (CONTINUED).

Subjunctive.

PRESENT.
May I be loved, let him be loved.

SINGULAR.	PLURAL.
amer	amēmur
amēris, *or* -re	amēminī
amētur	amentur

IMPERFECT.
I should be loved, he would be loved.

amārer	amārēmur
amārēris, *or* -re	amārēminī
amārētur	amārentur

PERFECT.
I may have been loved.

amātus sim	amātī sīmus
amātus sīs	amātī sītis
amātus sit	amātī sint

PLUPERFECT.
I should have been loved, he would have been loved.

amātus essem	amātī essēmus
amātus essēs	amātī essētis
amātus esset	amātī essent

Imperative.

Pres. amāre, *be thou loved;*	amāminī, *be ye loved.*
Fut. amātor, *thou shalt be loved,*	
amātor, *he shall be loved;*	amantor, *they shall be loved.*

Infinitive.

Pres. amārī, *to be loved.*
Perf. amātus esse, *to have been loved.*
Fut. amātum īrī, *to be about to be loved.*

Participle.

Perf.   amātus, *having been loved.*
Gerund. amandus, *to be loved, deserving to be loved.*

55

1. **VERB STEMS.** Observe that the Present and Imperfect Subjunctive, the entire Imperative, the Present Infinitive, and the Gerundive belong to the Present Stem, the remaining forms to the Participial Stem. The Perfect Stem is not represented in the Passive.

133. VOCABULARY.

castellum, I, n., *fort.*
convocō, 1, *I call together.*
dīligentia, ae, f., *diligence.*
equus, I, m., *horse.*
excitō, 1, *I stir up, rouse.*

expūgnō, 1, *I take by storm.*
nōn, *not.*
statim, *at once, immediately.*
templum, I, n., *temple.*
vix, *scarcely, with difficulty.*

EXERCISES.

134. 1. Laudētur, laudēmur, culpentur.   2. Laudātus esset, laudātī essēmus.   3. Excitārī, excitātus esse, superandus.   4. Convocātus, culpātus.   5. Superātī essēmus, culpātī essent.   6. Parārī, parandus.

135. 1. Arma et equī statim parentur.   2. Māgnae classēs summā dīligentiā parandae sunt.   3. Hī hostēs nōn ūnā legiōne superātī essent.   4. Sine nōbīs hōc castellum vix expūgnātum esset.   5. Senātus in hōc templum convocētur.   6. Sine tē hae māgnae cōpiae nōn parātae essent.   7. Dīligentia mīlitum nostrōrum laudētur.   8. Hī mīlitēs vix laudātī essent.

CHAPTER XXII.

SECOND (OR ē-) CONJUGATION. — ACTIVE VOICE.

PRINCIPAL PARTS.

	PRES. IND.	PRES. INF.	PERF. IND.	PERF. PASS. PARTIC
136.	moneŏ	monēre	monuī	monĭtus

Indicative Mood.

PRESENT TENSE. *I advise.*

SINGULAR.	PLURAL.
moneŏ	monēmus
monēs	monētis
monet	monent

IMPERFECT. *I was advising,* or *I advised.*

monēbam	monēbāmus
monēbās	monēbātis
monēbat	monēbant

FUTURE. *I shall advise.*

monēbŏ	monēbimus
monēbis	monēbitis
monēbit	monēbunt

PERFECT. *I have advised,* or *I advised.*

monuī	monuimus
monuistī	monuistis
monuit	monuērunt, *or* -ēre

PLUPERFECT. *I had advised.*

monueram	monuerāmus
monuerās	monuerātis
monuerat	monuerant

FUTURE PERFECT. *I shall have advised.*

monuerŏ	monuerimus
monueris	monueritis
monuerit	monuerint

137. **Subjunctive.**

PRESENT. *May I advise, let him advise.*

SINGULAR.	PLURAL.
moneam	moneāmus
moneās	moneātis
moneat	moneant

IMPERFECT. *I should advise, he would advise.*

monĕrem	monĕrēmus
monĕrēs	monĕrētis
monĕret	monĕrent

PERFECT. *I may have advised.*

monuerim	monuerimus
monueris	monueritis
monuerit	monuerint

PLUPERFECT. *I should have advised, he would have advised.*

monuissem	monuissēmus
monuissēs	monuissētis
monuisset	monuissent

Imperative.

Pres. monē, *advise thou ;*	monēte, *advise ye.*
Fut. monētō, *thou shalt advise,*	monētōte, *ye shall advise.*
monētō, *he shall advise ;*	monentō, *they shall advise.*

Infinitive.

Pres. monēre, *to advise.*
Perf. monuisse, *to have advised.*
Fut. monitūrus esse, *to be about to advise.*

Participle.

Pres. monēns, *advising.*
(Gen. monentis.)
Fut. monitūrus, *about to advise.*

Gerund.

Gen. monendī, *of advising,*
Dat. monendō, *for advising,*
Acc. monendum, *advising,*
Abl. monendō, *by advising.*

Supine.

Acc. monitum, *to advise,*
Abl. monitū, *to advise, be advised.*

1. VERB STEMS. The Present, Perfect, and Participial Stems include the same moods and tenses in the Second, Third, and Fourth Conjugations as in the First.

138. VOCABULARY.

angustus, a, um, *narrow.*

dēbeō, ēre, uī, itus, *I owe;* with another verb, *I ought.*

deus, ī, m., *god.*

equitātus, ūs, m., *cavalry.*

fīnis, is, m., *end, boundary ;* in plu., *territory.*

fortiter, *bravely.*

habeō, ēre, uī, itus, *I have, possess.*

maneō, ēre, mānsī, mānsūrus, *I remain.*

mīlitāris, e, *military.*

moveō, ēre, mōvī, mōtus, *I move.*

prohibeō, ēre, uī, itus, *I keep off, keep away* (tr.).

sīgnum, ī, n., *sign, standard.*

sustineō, ēre, sustinuī, *I withstand.*

timeō, ēre, uī, *I fear.*

videō, ēre, vīdī, vīsus, *I see.*

EXERCISES.

139. 1. Habēbimus, habuimus, habeāmus. 2. Sustinuistis, sustinuerat. 3. Timēbat, timēbit, timeant. 4. Vīdit, vīderat, 5. Mānsistī, mānserās, mānseris.

140. 1. Hae cīvitātēs in amīcitiā Haeduōrum mānserant. 2. Helvētiī fīnēs angustōs habēbant. 3. Hostēs sīgna mīlitāria jam vīderant. 4. Impetum equitātūs nostrī fortiter sustinuērunt. 5. Helvētiī ex eō locō castra movent. 6. Quis eōs timēbit? 7. Hostēs prohibēre dēbēmus. 8. Deī hostēs prohibeant ! 9. Hostēs prohibēte ! 10. Māgnum numerum equitum et peditum habēbimus.

CHAPTER XXIII.

SECOND CONJUGATION. — PASSIVE VOICE.

	Pres. Ind.	Pres. Inf.	Perf. Ind.
141. Principal Parts. —	moneor	monērī	monitus sum

Indicative Mood.

PRESENT TENSE.

SINGULAR.	*I am advised.*	PLURAL.
moneor		monēmur
monēris		monēminī
monētur		monentur

IMPERFECT.
I was advised.

monēbar	monēbāmur
monēbāris, or -re	monēbāminī
monēbātur	monēbantur

FUTURE.
I shall be advised.

monēbor	monēbimur
monēberis, *or* -re	monēbiminī
monēbitur	monēbuntur

PERFECT.
I have been advised, I was advised.

monitus sum	monitī sumus
monitus es	monitī estis
monitus est	monitī sunt

PLUPERFECT.
I had been advised.

monitus eram	monitī erāmus
monitus erās	monitī erātis
monitus erat	monitī erant

FUTURE PERFECT.
I shall have been advised.

monitus erō	monitī erimus
monitus eris	monitī eritis
monitus erit	monitī erunt

142. **Subjunctive.**

PRESENT.

May I be advised, let him be advised.

SINGULAR.	PLURAL.
monear	moneāmur
moneāris, *or* -re	moneāminī
moneātur	moneantur

IMPERFECT.

I should be advised, he would be advised.

monĕrer	monĕrēmur
monĕrēris, *or* -re	monĕrēminī
monĕrētur	monĕrentur

PERFECT.

I may have been advised.

monitus sim	monitī sīmus
monitus sīs	monitī sītis
monitus sit	monitī sint

PLUPERFECT.

I should have been advised, he would have been advised.

monitus essem	monitī essēmus
monitus essēs	monitī essētis
monitus esset	monitī essent

Imperative.

Pres. monĕre, *be thou advised;*   monēminī, *be ye advised.*
Fut. monētor, *thou shalt be advised,*
monētor, *he shall be advised.*   monentor, *they shall be advised.*

Infinitive.	**Participle.**
Pres. monĕrī, *to be advised.*	
Perf. monitus esse, *to have been advised.*	*Perf.* monitus, *advised.*
Fut. monitum īrī, *to be about to be advised.*	*Gerund.* monendus, *to be advised, deserving to be advised.*

143. VOCABULARY.

admodum, *quite, very much.*
aequus, a, um, *level.*
apertus, a, um, *open.*
augeŏ, ēre, auxī, auctus, *I increase.*
barbarus, a, um, *barbarian;* as noun, m., *a barbarian.*
celeriter, *quickly.*
compleŏ, ēre, ēvī, ētus, *I fill up.*
contineŏ, ēre, uī, *I confine, hold in check.*

imber, imbris, m., *rainstorm.*
moveŏ, ēre, mōvī, mōtus, *I move; touch, affect.*
perterreŏ, ēre, uī, itus, *I terrify.*
suspīciŏ, ōnis, f., *suspicion.*
teneŏ, ēre, uī, *I hold.*
vāstŏ, 1, *I lay waste.*
vetus, gen. veteris, *old.*
videor, ērī, vīsus sum (passive of videŏ), *be seen; seem, appear.*

EXERCISES.

144. 1. Movētur, movēbantur. 2. Perterrentur, perterrēbantur, perterritī erant. 3. Contineātur, continēbuntur
4. Vidērī, vīsus esse, videndus. 5. Augērī, auctus esse.

145. 1. Mīlitēs in castrīs imbribus continēbantur. 2. Barbarī admodum perterritī sunt. 3. Equitēs hostium in aequō
locō vīsī sunt. 4. Memoriā nostrae veteris amīcitiae movēbar.
5. Suspīciōnēs Gallōrum augēbantur. 6. Agrī nostrī vāstārī nōn
dēbent. 7. Equitēs nostrī illud oppidum expūgnāvisse videntur.
8. Fossae celeriter complēbuntur. 9. Loca aperta tenēbantur.
10. Timōrēs nostrī auctī sunt.

CHAPTER XXIV.

THIRD (OR CONSONANT) CONJUGATION. — ACTIVE VOICE.

PRINCIPAL PARTS.

	PRES. IND.	PRES. INF.	PERF. IND.	PERF. PASS. PARTIC.
146.	regō	regere	rēxī	rēctus

Indicative Mood.

PRESENT TENSE.

SINGULAR.	*I rule.*	PLURAL.
regō		regimus
regis		regitis
regit		regunt

IMPERFECT.
I was ruling, or *I ruled.*

regēbam		regēbāmus
regēbās		regēbātis
regēbat		regēbant

FUTURE.
I shall rule.

regam		regēmus
regēs		regētis
reget		regent

PERFECT.
I have ruled, or *I ruled.*

rēxī		rēximus
rēxistī		rēxistis
rēxit		rēxērunt, *or* -ēre

PLUPERFECT.
I had ruled.

rēxeram		rēxerāmus
rēxerās		rēxerātis
rēxerat		rēxerant

FUTURE PERFECT.
I shall have ruled.

rēxerō		rēxerimus
rēxeris		rēxeritis
rēxerit		rēxerint

147. **Subjunctive.**

PRESENT.

May I rule, let him rule.

SINGULAR.	PLURAL.
regam	regāmus
regās	regātis
regat	regant

IMPERFECT.

I should rule, he would rule.

regerem	regerēmus
regerēs	regerētis
regeret	regerent

PERFECT.

I may have ruled.

rēxerim	rēxerimus
rēxeris	rēxeritis
rēxerit	rēxerint

PLUPERFECT.

I should have ruled, he would have ruled.

rēxissem	rēxissēmus
rēxissēs	rēxissētis
rēxisset	rēxissent

Imperative.

Pres. rege, *rule thou;*	regite, *rule ye.*
Fut. regitō, *thou shalt rule,*	regitōte, *ye shall rule.*
regitō, *he shall rule;*	reguntō, *they shall rule.*

Infinitive.	**Participle.**
Pres. regere, *to rule.*	*Pres.* regēns, *ruling.*
Pref. rēxisse, *to have ruled.*	(Gen. regentis.)
Fut. rēctūrus esse, *to be about to rule.*	*Fut.* rēctūrus, *about to rule.*

Gerund.	**Supine.**
Gen. regendī, *of ruling,*	
Dat. regendō, *for ruling.*	
Acc. regendum, *ruling,*	*Acc.* rēctum, *to rule,*
Abl. regendō, *by ruling.*	*Abl.* rēctū, *to rule, be ruled.*

1. VERB STEMS. See § 137, 1.

148. VOCABULARY.

auxilia, ōrum, n. plu., *auxiliary troops, auxiliaries.*

citerior, ius, adj., *nearer, hither.*

committō, ere, mīsī, missus, *I bring together* ; with proelium, *to join battle.*

cōnstituō, ere, uī, ūtus, *I decide, determine.*

contendō, ere, tendī, tentum,[1] *I hurry, hasten.*

dēfendō, ere, fendī, fēnsus, *I defend.*

gerō, ere, gessī, gestus, *I carry on, perform* ; with bellum, *to wage.*

hīc, *here, at this place.*

Hispānia, ae, f., *Spain.*

in, *into* ; prep. with acc.

in, *on, in,* prep. w. abl. of place where.

īnstruō, ere, ūxī, ūctus, *I draw up, arrange.*

iter, itineris, n., *journey, march.*

litterae, ārum, f., *a letter.*

mittō, ere, mīsī, missus, *I send.*

pōnō, ere, posuī, positus, *I put, place, establish.*

praesidium, ī (iī), n., *garrison.*

prōvincia, ae, f., *province.*

redūcō, ere, dūxī, ductus, *I lead back.*

relinquō, ere, līquī, līctus, *I leave, leave behind.*

EXERCISES.

149. 1. Mittēbat, mittent.   2. Mīsit, mīserātis, mīsērunt. 3. Relīquisset, relīquisse, relinquēns.   4. Īnstrūxerat, īnstrūxerimus.   5. Posuimus, posuerat, pōnant.

150. 1. Litterās in Hispāniam citeriōrem[2] mīsit.   2. In hanc prōvinciam māgnīs itineribus contendēbat.   3. Illās prōvinciās audācter dēfendite.   4. Galba legiōnēs in castra redūxerat.   5. Caesar aciem in mediō colle īnstrūxit.   6. Bellum gerere cōnstituimus.   7. Proelium committāmus.   8. Partem auxiliōrum ibi relīquerat.   9. Hīc praesidium posuērunt.   10. Hās prōvinciās fortiter dēfendēmus.

---

[1] In the case of intransitive verbs, the Perfect Passive Participle is given in the neuter form.

[2] That is, Spain north of the Ebro.

CHAPTER XXV.

THIRD CONJUGATION.—PASSIVE VOICE.

	Pres. Ind.	Pres. Inf.	Perf. Ind.
151. Principal Parts.—	regor	regī	rēctus sum

Indicative Mood.

PRESENT TENSE.

SINGULAR.	*I am ruled.*	PLURAL.
regor		regimur
regeris		regiminī
regitur		reguntur

IMPERFECT.
I was ruled.

regēbar		regēbāmur
regēbāris, *or* -re		regēbāminī
regēbātur		regēbantur

FUTURE.
I shall be ruled.

regar		regēmur
regēris, *or* -re		regēminī
regētur		regentur

PERFECT.
I have been ruled, or *I was ruled.*

rēctus sum		rēctī sumus
rēctus es		rēctī estis
rēctus est		rēctī sunt

PLUPERFECT.
I had been ruled.

rēctus eram		rēctī erāmus
rēctus erās		rēctī erātis
rēctus erat		rēctī erant

FUTURE PERFECT.
I shall have been ruled.

rēctus erō		rēctī erimus
rēctus eris		rēctī eritis
rēctus erit		rēctī erunt

152. **Subjunctive.**

PRESENT.

May I be ruled, let him be ruled.

SINGULAR.	PLURAL.
regar	regāmur
regāris, *or* -re	regāminī
regātur	regantur

IMPERFECT.

I should be ruled, he would be ruled.

regerer	regerēmur
regerēris, *or* -re	regerēminī
regerētur	regerentur

PERFECT.

I may have been ruled.

rēctus sim	rēctī sīmus
rēctus sīs	rēctī sītis
rēctus sit	rēctī sint

PLUPERFECT.

I should have been ruled, he would have been ruled.

rēctus essem	rēctī essēmus
rēctus essēs	rēctī essētis
rēctus esset	rēctī essent

Imperative.

Pres. regere, *be thou ruled;*   regiminī, *be ye ruled.*
Fut. regitor, *thou shalt be ruled,*
    regitor, *he shall be ruled;*   reguntor, *they shall be ruled.*

Infinitive.

Pres. regī, *to be ruled.*
Perf. rēctus esse, *to have been ruled.*
Fut. rēctum īrī, *to be about to be ruled.*

Participle.

Perf. rēctus, *ruled.*
Gerund. regendus, *to be ruled, deserving to be ruled.*

153.   VOCABULARY.

cōgō, ere, coēgī, coāctus, *I force,*
  compel.
contrā, *against,* prep. w. acc.
dēdūcō, ere, dūxī, ductus, *I lead*
  away.
ducentī, ae, a, *two hundred.*
dūcō, ere, dūxī, ductus, *I lead.*
expedītus, a, um, *unencumbered,*
  light-armed.
intereā, adv., *in the meanwhile.*

īnstruō, ere, strūxī, strūctus,
  I fit out.
longus, a, um, *long;* nāvis longa,
  war-ship.
mūnītiō, ōnis, f., *fortification.*
quā, *where.*
superior, ius, *higher.*
trādō, ere, didī, ditus, *I hand over.*
tum, *then, at that time.*
ulterior, ius, *farther.*

EXERCISES.

154. 1. Dēdūcitur, dēductī erant.   2. Cōgimur, coāctī
sumus.   3. Dūcantur, ductī essent, ductus esse.   4. Mittēmur,
mittentur, missī sumus.   5. Relinquēbāmur, relinquēbātur, relin-
quētur.

155. 1. Intereā castella quoque posita sunt.   2. Duae
cohortēs ad aliam partem mūnītiōnum dēdūcuntur.   3. Venetī
hās nāvēs relinquere cōguntur.   4. Trēs legiōnēs in Galliam
ulteriōrem[1] missae sunt, quā bellum tum gerēbātur.   5. Duae
legiōnēs expedītae contrā hostēs dūcentur.   6. Nāvēs longae
omnibus rēbus īnstrūctae erant.   7. In locīs superiōribus proelium commissum est.   8. Ducentī obsidēs Caesarī trāditī sunt.

---

[1] That is, Gaul beyond the Alps.

CHAPTER XXVI.

FOURTH (OR *ĭ*-) CONJUGATION. — ACTIVE VOICE.

PRINCIPAL PARTS.

PRES. IND.	PRES. INF.	PERF. IND.	PERF. PASS. PARTIC.
156. audiŏ	audīre	audīvī	audītus

Indicative Mood.

PRESENT TENSE.

SINGULAR.	*I hear.*	PLURAL.
audiŏ		audīmus
audīs		audītis
audit		audiunt

IMPERFECT.

I was hearing, or *I heard.*

audiĕbam		audiĕbāmus
audiĕbās		audiĕbātis
audiĕbat		audiĕbant

FUTURE.

I shall hear.

audiam		audiēmus
audiēs		audiētis
audiet		audient

PERFECT.

I have heard, or *I heard.*

audīvī		audīvimus
audīvistī		audīvistis
audīvit		audīvērunt, *or* -ēre

PLUPERFCT.

I had heard.

audīveram		audīverāmus
audīverās		audīverātis
audīverat		audīverant

FUTURE PERFECT.

I shall have heard.

audīverŏ		audīverimus
audīveris		audīveritis
audīverit		audīverint

157.　　　　　　　　**Subjunctive.**

PRESENT.

May I hear, let him hear.

SINGULAR.	PLURAL.
audiam	audiāmus
audiās	audiātis
audiat	audiant

IMPERFECT.

I should hear, he would hear.

audīrem	audīrēmus
audīrēs	audīrētis
audīret	audīrent

PERFECT.

I may have heard.

audīverim	audīverimus
audīveris	audīveritis
audīverit	audīverint

PLUPERFECT.

I should have heard, he would have heard.

audīvissem	audīvissēmus
audīvissēs	audīvissētis
audīvisset	audīvissent

Imperative.

Pres.	audī, *hear thou;*	audīte, *hear ye.*
Fut.	audītō, *thou shalt hear,*	audītōte, *ye shall hear,*
	audītō, *he shall hear;*	audiuntō, *they shall hear.*

Infinitive.

Pres.	audīre, *to hear.*
Perf.	audīvisse, *to have heard.*
Fut.	audītūrus esse, *to be about to hear.*

Participle.

Pres.	audiēns, *hearing.*
	(Gen. audientis.)
Fut.	audītūrus, *about to hear.*

Gerund.

Gen.	audiendī, *of hearing,*
Dat.	audiendō, *for hearing,*
Acc.	audiendum, *hearing,*
Abl.	audiendō, *by hearing.*

Supine.

Acc.	audītum, *to hear,*
Abl.	audītū, *to hear, be heard.*

1. VERB STEMS. See § 137, 1.

158. VOCABULARY.

agmen, minis, n., *army* (on the march); *column.*
antèā, *previously, before.*
conveniō, īre, vēnī, ventum, *come together.*
eōdem, adv., *to the same place.*
fāma, ae, f., *report.*
ferè, *almost, about, practically.*
impediō, īre, īvī (iī), ītus, *I impede, hinder.*
mora, ae, f., *delay.*

mūniō, īre, īvī, ītus, *I fortify.*
nūntius, ī (iī), m., *messenger.*
occāsiō, ōnis, f., *occasion, opportunity.*
posteā, *afterwards.*
reperiō, īre, repperī, repertus, *I discover.*
undique, adv., *from all parts or sides.*
veniō, īre, vēnī, ventum, *I come.*

EXERCISES.

159. 1. Vēnerat, veniet, veniat. 2. Repperimus, reppererāmus. 3. Mūnīvērunt, mūnient, mūnīvimus. 4. Convēnisse, impedītūrus esse. 5. Mūniendō, mūnīvissent.

160. 1. Caesar reliquās cōpiās quae nōndum convēnerant exspectābat. 2. Lēgātī ferē tōtīus Galliae undique conveniunt. 3. Eōdem convēnimus. 4. Hōs nūntiōs audiāmus. 5. Haec castra, mīlitēs, sine morā mūnīte. 6. Hanc fāmam anteā audīverāmus. 7. Equitātus noster agmen hostium impediet. 8. Nōn facile occāsiōnem posteā reperiēmus. 9. Complūrēs nūntiī vēnērunt.

CHAPTER XXVII.

FOURTH CONJUGATION. — PASSIVE VOICE.

	PRES. IND.	PRES. INF.	PERF. IND.
161. PRINCIPAL PARTS. —	audior	audīrī	audītus sum

Indicative Mood.

PRESENT TENSE.

SINGULAR.	*I am heard.*	PLURAL.
audior		audīmur
audīris		audīminī
audītur		audiuntur

IMPERFECT.
I was heard.

audiēbar		audiēbāmur
audiēbāris, *or* -re		audiēbāminī
audiēbātur		audiēbantur

FUTURE.
I shall be heard.

audiar		audiēmur
audiēris, *or* -re		audiēminī
audiētur		audientur

PERFECT.
I have been heard, or *I was heard.*

audītus sum		audītī sumus
audītus es		audītī estis
audītus est		audītī sunt

PLUPERFECT.
I had been heard.

audītus eram		audītī erāmus
audītus erās		audītī erātis
audītus erat		audītī erant

FUTURE PERFECT.
I shall have been heard.

audītus erō		audītī erimus
audītus eris		audītī eritis
audītus erit		audītī erunt

72

162.   Subjunctive.

PRESENT.

May I be heard, let him be heard.

SINGULAR.	PLURAL.
audiar	audiāmur
audiāris, *or* -re	audiāminī
audiātur	audiantur

IMPERFECT.

I should be heard, he would be heard.

audīrer	audīrēmur
audīrēris, *or* -re	audīrēminī
audīrētur	audīrentur

PERFECT.

I may have been heard.

audītus sim	audītī sīmus
audītus sīs	audītī sītis
audītus sit	audītī sint

PLUPERFECT.

I should have been heard, he would have been heard.

audītus essem	audītī essēmus
audītus essēs	audītī essētis
audītus esset	audītī essent

Imperative.

Pres. audīre, *be thou heard;*   audīminī, *be ye heard.*
Fut. audītor, *thou shalt be heard,*
     audītor, *he shall be heard;*   audiuntor, *they shall be heard.*

Infinitive.

Pres. audīrī, *to be heard.*
Perf. audītus esse, *to have been heard.*
Fut. audītum īrī, *to be about to be heard.*

Participle.

Perf.   audītus, *heard.*
Gerund. audiendus, *to be heard, deserving to be heard.*

163.   VOCABULARY.

angustiae, ārum, f. pl., *a narrow pass.*
aqua, ae, f., *water.*
captīvus, ī, m., *captive.*
circumveniō, īre, vēnī, ventus, *I surround.*
extrā, *outside, beyond,* prep. w. acc.
idōneus, a, um, *suitable.*
inveniō, īre, vēnī, ventus, *I find, come upon.*
nātūra, ae, f., *nature.*

nihil, indecl., n., *nothing.*
opus, operis, n., *work, fortification.*
paene, *almost, nearly.*
poena, ae, f., *punishment.*
prōcurrō, ere, cucurrī, cursum, *I run forward.*
regio, ōnis, f., *region.*
simul, *together, at the same time.*
temere, *rashly.*
vōx, vōcis, f., *voice, word.*

EXERCISES.

164. 1. Invenītur, inventus erat. 2. Impedīmur, impediēbātur, impedīrī. 3. Impedītus, impedītī erāmus. 4. Inventus esse, inveniendus. 5. Inveniētur, inventī erunt, inventus esset.

165. 1. Locus idōneus, nātūrā mūnītus, repertus est. 2. Nihil dē poenā captīvōrum audītum erat. 3. Peditēs nostrī altitūdine aquae impediēbantur. 4. Angustiīs impediēmur. 5. Castra māgnis operibus mūnīta sunt. 6. Vōcēs mīlitum simul audiēbantur. 7. Māgna cōpia frūmentī in hīs regiōnibus inventa est. 8. Ūna cohors, quae temere extrā aciem prōcucurrerat, paene circumventa est. 9. Nihil reperiētur.

CHAPTER XXVIII.

VERBS IN -iŏ OF THE THIRD CONJUGATION.

166. 1. Verbs in -iŏ of the Third Conjugation take the endings of the Fourth Conjugation, wherever the latter endings have two successive vowels. This occurs only in the Present System (§ 120, 1 ; 124, 1).

167.   **Active Voice.** — Capiŏ, *I take.*

PRINCIPAL PARTS.

Pres. Ind.	Pres. Inf.	Perf. Ind.	Perf. Pass. Partic.
capiŏ,	capere,	cēpī,	captus.

Indicative Mood.

PRESENT TENSE.

SINGULAR.	PLURAL.
capiŏ, capis, capit ;	capimus, capitis, capiunt.

IMPERFECT.

capiēbam, -iēbās, -iēbat ;	capiēbāmus, -iēbātis, -iēbant.

FUTURE.

capiam, -iēs, -iet ;	capiēmus, -iētis, -ient.

PERFECT.

cēpī, -istī, -it ;	cēpimus, -istis, -ērunt, *or* -ēre.

PLUPERFECT.

cēperam, -erās, -erat ;	cēperāmus, -erātis, -erant.

FUTURE PERFECT.

cēperŏ, -eris, -erit ;	cēperimus, -eritis, -erint.

Subjunctive.

SINGULAR.	PRESENT.	PLURAL.

PRESENT.

capiam, -iās, -iat ;   capiāmus, -iātis, -iant.

IMPERFECT.

caperem, -erēs, -eret ;   caperēmus, -erētis, -erent.

PERFECT.

cēperim, -eris, -erit ;   cēperimus, -eritis, -erint.

PLUPERFECT.

cēpissem, -issēs, -isset ;   cēpissēmus, -issētis, -issent.

Imperative.

Pres. cape ;   capite.
Fut. capitō,   capitōte,
         capitō ;   capiuntō.

Infinitive.	Participle.

Pres. capere.   *Pres.* capiēns.
Perf. cēpisse.
Fut. captūrus esse.   *Fut.* captūrus.

Gerund.	Supine.

Gen. capiendī,
Dat. capiendō,
Acc. capiendum,   *Acc.* captum,
Abl. capiendō.   *Abl.* captū.

168.   **Passive Voice.** — Capior, *I am taken.*

	PRES. IND.	PRES. INF.	PERF. IND.
PRINCIPAL PARTS. —	capior,	capī,	captus sum.

Indicative Mood.

PRESENT TENSE.

capior, caperis, capitur ;   capimur, capiminī, capiuntur.

IMPERFECT.

capiēbar, -iēbāris, -iēbātur ;   capiēbāmur, -iēbāminī, iēbantur.

FUTURE.

capiar, -iēris, -iētur ;   capiēmur, -iēminī, -ientur.

SINGULAR. PERFECT. PLURAL.

captus sum, es, est; captī sumus, estis, sunt.

PLUPERFECT.

captus eram, erās, erat; captī erāmus, erātis, erant.

FUTURE PERFECT.

captus erō, eris, erit; captī erimus, eritis, erunt.

Subjunctive.

PRESENT.

capiar, -iāris, -iātur; capiāmur, -iāminī, -iantur.

IMPERFECT.

caperer, -erēris, -erētur; caperēmur, -erēminī, -erentur.

PERFECT.

captus sim, sīs, sit; captī sīmus, sītis, sint.

PLUPERFECT.

captus essem, essēs, esset; captī essēmus, essētis, essent.

Imperative.

Pres. capere; capiminī.
Fut. capitor,
capitor; capiuntor.

Infinitive.	**Participle.**
Pres. capī.	
Perf. captus esse.	*Perf.* captus.
Fut. captum īrī.	*Gerund.* capiendus.

169. VOCABULARY.

accipiō, ere, cēpī, ceptus, *I receive.*

capiō, ere, cēpī, captus, *I take, adopt; capture.*

dīripiō, ere, ripuī, reptus, *I plunder.*

faciō, ere, fēcī, factus, *I make, do;* passive irregular; cf. § 193.

fīlius, ī (iī), m., *son.*

fugiō, ere, fūgī, fugitūrus, *I flee.*

interficiō, ere, fēcī, fectus, *I kill.*

lībertās, tātis, f., *liberty.*

mājōrēs, um, m. plu., *ancestors.*

mandātum, ī, n., *command, order.*

nātiō, ōnis, f., *nation, tribe.*

palūs, lūdis, f., *marsh.*

pōns, pontis, m., *bridge.*

rēx, rēgis, m., *king.*

rūrsus, *again.*

subitō, *suddenly.*

supplicium, ī (iī), n., *torture, punishment.*

EXERCISES.

170. 1. Accipiunt, accipiēbāmus, accipiāmus.   2. Fugit, fūgerant, fūgisse.   3. Faciēbat, facient.   4. Accipitur, accipiētur, acceptus erat.   5. Accipī, accipiendus, acceptus esset.

171. 1. In¹ eō flūmine pontem fēcerat.   2. Prīncipēs hārum nātiōnum bellum facient.   3. Hostēs rūrsus subitō impetum fēcērunt.   4. Lībertātem ā mājōribus accēpimus.   5. Haec mandāta accepta erant.   6. Duo fīliī hūjus rēgis captī sunt.   7. Aliud cōnsilium capiāmus.   8. Hostēs in palūdēs fūgērunt.   9. Obsidēs māgnīs suppliciīs interfectī sunt.   10. Hōc oppidum dīripiēbātur.

CHAPTER XXIX.

DEPONENT VERBS.

172. Deponent Verbs have, in the main, Passive *forms* with Active or Neuter *meaning*. But —

> *a*) They have the following Active forms: Future Infinitive, Present and Future Participles, Gerund, and Supine.
> *b*) They have the following Passive meanings: always in the Gerundive, and sometimes in the Perfect Passive Participle; as, —

> **sequendus,** *to be followed*; **adeptus,** *having been attained.*

173. Paradigms of Deponent Verbs are —

I. Conj.	**mīror, mīrārī, mīrātus sum,** *admire.*
II. Conj.	**vereor, verērī, veritus sum,** *fear.*
III. Conj.	**sequor, sequī, secūtus sum,** *follow.*
IV. Conj.	**largior, largīrī, largītus sum,** *give.*
III. (in -ior)	**patior, patī, passus sum,** *suffer.*

---

¹ The Romans said 'make a bridge on a river,' where we say 'across a river.'

Indicative Mood.

	I.	II.	III.	IV.	III. (in -ior).
Pres.	mīror	vereor	sequor	largior	patior
	mīrāris	verēris	sequeris	largīris	pateris
	mīrātur	verētur	sequitur	largītur	patitur
	mīrāmur	verēmur	sequimur	largīmur	patimur
	mīrāminī	verēminī	sequiminī	largīminī	patiminī
	mīrantur	verentur	sequuntur	largiuntur	patiuntur
Impf.	mīrābar	verēbar	sequēbar	largiēbar	patiēbar
Fut.	mīrābor	verēbor	sequar	largiar	patiar
Perf.	mīrātus sum	veritus sum	secūtus sum	largītus sum	passus sum
Plup.	mīrātus eram	veritus eram	secūtus eram	largītus eram	passus eram
F. P.	mīrātus erō	veritus erō	secūtus erō	largītus erō	passus erō

Subjunctive.

Pres.	mīrer	verear	sequar	largiar	patiar
Impf.	mīrārer	verērer	sequerer	largīrer	paterer
Perf.	mīrātus sim	veritus sim	secūtus sim	largītus sim	passus sim
Plup.	mīrātus essem	veritus essem	secūtus essem	largītus essem	passus essem

Imperative.

Pres.	mīrāre	verēre	sequere	largīre	patere
Fut.	mīrātor	verētor	sequitor	largītor	patitor

Infinitive.

Pres.	mīrārī	verērī	sequī	largīrī	patī
Perf.	mīrātus esse	veritus esse	secūtus esse	largītus esse	passus esse
Fut.	mīrātūrus esse	veritūrus esse	secūtūrus esse	largītūrus esse	passūrus esse

Participles.

Pres.	mīrāns	verēns	sequēns	largiēns	patiēns
Fut.	mīrātūrus	veritūrus	secūtūrus	largītūrus	passūrus
Perf.	mīrātus	veritus	secūtus	largītus	passus
Ger.	mīrandus	verendus	sequendus	largiendus	patiendus

Gerund.

	mīrandī	verendī	sequendī	largiendī	patiendī
	mīrandō, *etc.*	verendō, *etc.*	sequendō, *etc.*	largiendō, *etc.*	patiendō, *etc.*

Supine.

	mīrātum, -tū	veritum, -tū	secūtum, -tū	largītum, -tū	passum, -sū

174.　　　　VOCABULARY.

adorior, orīrī, ortus sum, *I attack.*
audeō, ēre, ausus sum, semi-
　dep.,[1] *I dare.*
colloquor, ī, locūtus sum, *I con-*
　verse, confer.
cōnor, ārī, ātus sum, *I endeavor,*
　attempt.
ēgredior, ī, gressus sum, *I march*
　out.
Īnsidiae, ārum, f. plu., *ambush.*
Jūra, ae, f., *the Jura,* chain of
　mountains on west of Switzer-
　land.
moror, ārī, ātus sum, *I tarry,*
　delay.

nēmō, c., *no one,* dat. nēminī,
　acc. nēminem; gen. and abl.
　not used.
paulum, adv., *a little.*
Pompējus, ī, m., *Pompey.*
proficīscor, ī, fectus sum, *I set*
　out.
prōgredior, ī, gressus sum, *I ad-*
　vance, go forward.
propter, *on account of,* prep. w.
　acc.
resistō, ere, restitī, *I resist.*
revertor, tī, *I return.*
Rhodanus, ī, m., *the Rhone.*

EXERCISES.

175. 1. Audēbimus, ausī erant, ausus.　　2. Adoriēbātur, adortus, adortus est.　　3. Prōgredimur, prōgressus, prōgredientur.　　4. Adoriendus, morāns, collocūtī erāmus.　　5. Cōnābar, cōnātus sum.

176. 1. Hostēs agmen nostrum ex īnsidiīs adortī sunt.　　2. Nēmō resistere ausus est.　　3. Caesar dē salūte commūnī cum Pompējō colloquēbātur.　　4. Helvētiī ex suīs fīnibus ēgressī sunt.　　5. Inter montem Jūram et flūmen Rhodanum iter facere cōnantur.　　6. Propter hās causās proficīscēmur.　　7. Hostēs nōn diū morātī sunt.　　8. Equitēs paulum prōgressī revertuntur.　　9. Īnsidiās verēbāmur.

---

[1] A few verbs have active forms in the Present system, but passive forms elsewhere. These are called semi-deponent.

CHAPTER XXX.

PERIPHRASTIC CONJUGATION.

177. There are two Periphrastic Conjugations, — the Active and the Passive. The Active is formed by combining the Future Active Participle with the auxiliary **sum**, the Passive by combining the Gerundive with the same auxiliary.

Active Periphrastic Conjugation. — Indicative Mood.

Pres.	amātūrus (-a, -um) sum,	*I am about to love.*
Imp.	amātūrus eram,	*I was about to love.*
Fut.	amātūrus erō,	*I shall be about to love.*
Perf.	amātūrus fuī,	*I have been (was) about to love.*
Plup.	amātūrus fueram,	*I had been about to love.*
Fut. P.	amātūrus fuerō,	*I shall have been about to love.*

Subjunctive.

Pres.	amātūrus sim,	*may I be about to love.*
Imp.	amātūrus essem,	*I should be about to love.*
Perf.	amātūrus fuerim,	*I may have been about to love.*
Plup.	amātūrus fuissem,	*I should have been about to love.*

Infinitive.

Pres.	amātūrus esse,	*to be about to love.*
Perf.	amātūrus fuisse,	*to have been about to love.*

Passive Periphrastic Conjugation. — Indicative Mood.

Pres.	amandus (-a, -um) sum,	*I am to be loved, must be loved.*
Imp.	amandus eram,	*I was to be loved.*
Fut.	amandus erō,	*I shall deserve to be loved.*
Perf.	amandus fuī,	*I was to be loved.*
Plup.	amandus fueram,	*I had deserved to be loved.*
Fut. P.	amandus fuerō,	*I shall have deserved to be loved.*

Subjunctive.

Pres.	amandus sim,	*may I deserve to be loved.*
Imp.	amandus essem,	*I should deserve to be loved.*
Perf.	amandus fuerim,	*I may have deserved to be loved.*
Plup.	amandus fuissem,	*I should have deserved to be loved.*

Infinitive.

Pres.	amandus esse,	*to deserve to be loved.*
Perf.	amandus fuisse,	*to have deserved to be loved.*

178.   **VOCABULARY.**

caedēs, is, f., *slaughter*.
cōnservō, 1, *I preserve*.
dēdō, ere, dēdidī, itus, *I give up, surrender*.
fortūna, ae, f., *fortune*.
incommodum, ī, n., *disaster*.

līberō, 1, *I set free*.
loquor, I, locūtus sum, *I speak*.
post, *after*, prep. w. acc.
recūsō, 1, *I refuse*.
tot, *so many*, indecl.
vīta, ae, f., *life*.

EXERCISES.

179. 1. Līberātūrus eram, līberātūrī erāmus.   2. Cōnservandus est, cōnservandī fuērunt.   3. Līberandī sunt, līberandī erunt.   4. Locūtūrus fuit, locūtūrī fuerant.

180. 1. Equitēs ex castrīs ēgressūrī sunt.   2. Post hōc proelium sē dēditūrī erant.   3. Nunc cum māgnā caede dīmicātūrī sunt.   4. Dē hīs tot incommodīs locūtūrus fuit.   5. Vītae nostrae et fortūnae cōnservandae sunt.   6. Hae urbēs sunt līberandae.   7. Auxilium nōn est recūsandum.[1]   8. Hostēs hōc oppidum dīreptūrī erant.   9. Haec oppida nōn dīripienda sunt.   10. Hae nāvēs longae omnibus rēbus īnstruendae sunt.

---

[1] est recūsandum = *recūsandum est;* such inversions are common.

CHAPTER XXXI.

IRREGULAR VERBS.

181. A number of Verbs are called Irregular. The most important are **sum, dŏ, ferŏ, volŏ, nŏlŏ, mălŏ, eŏ, fïŏ.** The peculiarity of these Verbs is that they append the personal endings in many forms directly to the stem, instead of employing a connecting vowel, as **fer-s** (2d Sing. of **fer-ŏ**) instead of **fer-ia.** They are but the relics of what was once in Latin a large class of Verbs.

182. The Inflection of **sum** has already been given. Its various compounds are inflected in the same way. Examples are —

| absum | abesse | āfuī | *am absent* |

Pres. Partic. absēns (absentis), *absent.*

| adsum | adesse | adfuī | *am present* |
| praesum | praeesse | praefuī | *am in charge of* |

Pres. Partic. praesēns (praesentis), *present.*

183. Possum. In its Present System **possum** is a compound of **pot-** (for **pote,** *able*) and **sum**; **potuī** is from an obsolete **potěre.**

PRINCIPAL PARTS.

| **possum,** | **posse,** | **potuī,** | *to be able* |

Indicative Mood.

	SINGULAR.	PLURAL.
Pres.	possum, potes, potest ;	possumus, potestis, possunt.
Imp.	poteram ;	poterāmus.
Fut.	poterō ;	poterimus.
Perf.	potuī ;	potuimus.
Plup.	potueram ;	potuerāmus.
Fut. P.	potuerō ;	potuerimus.

Subjunctive.

	SINGULAR.	PLURAL.
Pres.	possim, possīs, possit ;	possīmus, possītis, possint.
Imp.	possem ;	possēmus.
Perf.	potuerim ;	potuerimus.
Plup.	potuissem ;	potuissēmus.

Infinitive.   **Participle.**

Pres.	posse.	*Pres.* potēns (*as an adjective*).
Perf.	potuisse.	

184.   Dŏ, *I give.*

PRINCIPAL PARTS. — **dŏ,   dăre,   dedī,   dătus.**

Active Voice. —Indicative Mood.

Pres.	dō, dās, dat ;	dămus, dătis, dant.
Imp.	dăbam, *etc.* ;	dăbāmus.
Fut.	dăbō, *etc.* ;	dăbimus.
Perf.	dedī ;	dedimus.
Plup.	dederam ;	dederāmus.
Fut. P.	dederō ;	dederimus.

Subjunctive.

Pres.	dem ;	dēmus.
Imp.	dărem ;	dărēmus.
Perf.	dederim ;	dederimus.
Plup.	dedissem ;	dedissēmus.

Imperative.

Pres.	dă ;	dăte.
Fut.	dătō ;	dătōte.
	dătō ;	dantō

Infinitive.   **Participle.**

Pres.	dăre.	dāns.
Perf.	dedisse.	
Fut.	dătūrus esse.	dătūrus.

Gerund.   **Supine.**

dandī, *etc.*   dătum, dătū.

1. The Passive is inflected regularly with the short vowel. Thus: dărī, dătur, dăbătur, dărētur, *etc.*

185. **VOCABULARY.**

dēsum, dĕesse, dēfuī, *I am want-*
ing, fail.
excēdō, ere, cessī, cessūrus, *I*
depart from.
jūs jūrandum; gen. jūris jūrandī, n., *oath* (jūs and jūrandum are declined separately).
longē, adv., *far.*
negōtium, ī (iī), n., *business.*

omnīnō, adv., *altogether.*
pecūnia, ae, f., *money.*
potestās, tātis, f., *power, oppor-*
tunity.
pūblicus, a, um, *public.*
sententia, ae, f., *sentiment, opin-*
ion.
tālis, e, *such.*
vulnus, eris, n., *wound.*

EXERCISES.

186. 1. Potuerant, potuisse, potuissem.   2. Dedisse, dede-
rant, dent.   3. Adfuērunt, adfuisse, adsit.   4. Āfuisse, āfuissent,
aberunt.   5. Dabātur, darī, datī erant.

187. 1. Equitēs et nāvēs et frūmentum Rōmānīs dĕerant.
2. Potestās pūgnandī nōn dĕerit.   3. Pecūnia pūblica Pompējō
datur.   4. Mīlitibus sīgnum dedit.   5. Ducēs nostrī adfuērunt.
6. Omnēs lēgātī quī aderant jūs jūrandum dedērunt.   7. Hostēs
nōn longē aberant.   8. Tālēs sententiae probārī nōn possunt.
9. Hōc negōtium nōbīs dat.   10. Mīlitēs quī vulnera accēpĕ-
runt ex aciē excēdere nōn poterant.

CHAPTER XXXII.

IRREGULAR VERBS (CONTINUED).

188.   **Ferō,** *I bear.*

Active Voice.

PRINCIPAL PARTS. — **ferō,**   **ferre,**   **tulī,**   **lātus.**

Indicative Mood.

SINGULAR.	PLURAL.
Pres. ferō, fers, fert ;	ferimus, fertis, ferunt.[1]
Imp. ferēbam ;	ferēbāmus.
Fut. feram ;	ferēmus.
Perf. tulī ;	tulimus.
Plup. tuleram ;	tulerāmus.
Fut. P. tulerō ;	tulerimus.

Subjunctive.

Pres. feram ;	ferāmus.
Imp. ferrem ;	ferrēmus.
Perf. tulerim ;	tulerimus.
Plup. tulissem ;	tulissēmus.

Imperative.

Pres. fer ;	ferte.
Fut. fertō ;	fertōte.
fertō ;	feruntō.

Infinitive.   Participle.

Pres. ferre.	*Pres.* ferēns.
Perf. tulisse.	
Fut. lātūrus esse.	*Fut.* lātūrus.

Gerund.   Supine.

Gen. ferendī.	
Dat. ferendō.	
Acc. ferendum.	*Acc.* lātum.
Abl. ferendō.	*Abl.* lātū.

---

[1] It will be observed that not all the forms of **ferō** lack the connecting vowel. Some of them, as **ferimus, ferunt,** follow the regular inflection of verbs of the Third Conjugation.

Passive Voice.

feror,	ferrī,	lātus sum,	*to be borne.*

Indicative Mood.

	SINGULAR.	PLURAL.
Pres.	feror, ferris, fertur ;	ferimur, feriminī, feruntur.
Imp.	ferēbar ;	ferēbāmur.
Fut.	ferar ;	ferēmur.
Perf.	lātus sum ;	lātī sumus.
Plup.	lātus eram ;	lātī erāmus.
Fut. P.	lātus erō ;	lātī erimus.

Subjunctive.

Pres.	ferar ;	ferāmur.
Imp.	ferrer ;	ferrēmur.
Perf.	lātus sim ;	lātī sīmus.
Plup.	lātus essem ;	lātī essēmus.

Imperative.

Pres.	ferre ;	feriminī.
Fut.	fertor ;	————
	fertor ;	feruntor.

Infinitive.   Participle.

Pres.	ferrī.		
Perf.	lātus esse.	*Perf.*	lātus.
Fut.	lātum īrī.	*Ger.*	ferendus.

So also the Compounds —

afferō	afferre	attulī	allātus	*bring*
auferō	auferre	abstulī	ablātus	*take away*
cōnferō	cōnferre	contulī	collātus	*compare*
īnferō	īnferre	intulī	illātus	*bring against*
referō	referre	rettulī	relātus	*bring back*

189.   VOCABULARY.

afferō, ferre, attulī, allātus, *I bring.*

calamitās, tātis, f., *calamity.*

condiciō, ōnis, f., *condition, terms.*

cōnferō, ferre, tulī, collātus, *I bring together;* **sē cōnferre,** *betake one's self.*

ignōminia, ae, f., *ignominy, disgrace.*

impedīmentum, I, n., *hindrance;* in plu., *baggage.*

nē . . . quidem, *not even;* emphatic negative, emphasizing the expression placed between **nē** and **quidem.**

perferō, ferre, tulī, lātus, *I carry through, convey; endure.*

prōtinus, *forthwith, straightway.*

referō, ferre, rettulī, relātus, *I bring back.*

subsidium, ī(iī), n., *assistance.*

tumultus, ūs, m., *uprising.*

EXERCISES.

190. 1. Afferet, attulimus, attulisse.   2. Lātus esse, lātī essent, ferendus.   3. Perfertur, perferēbantur, perlātī sunt.   4. Refert, rettulērunt, rettulissent.   5. Rettulisse, relātī sunt, referuntur.

191. 1. Hostēs nē prīmum quidem impetum tulērunt.   2. Nōbīs subsidium ferēbat.   3. Pompējus sē prōtinus in castra contulit.   4. Helvētiī impedīmenta in ūnum locum contulērunt. 5. Hīc nūntius condiciōnēs pācis affert.   6. Fāma dē hōc tumultū allāta est.   7. Multās calamitātēs pertulimus.   8. Ea fāma ad Caesarem perlāta est. '   9. Sīgna mīlitāria referuntur. 10. Ignōminiam ferre nōn possumus.

CHAPTER XXXIII.

IRREGULAR VERBS (Continued).

192. **Volō, nōlō, mālō.**

PRINCIPAL PARTS.

volō,	velle,	voluī,	*to wish, be willing.*
nōlō,	nōlle,	nōluī,	*to be unwilling.*
mālō,	mālle,	māluī,	*to prefer.*

Indicative Mood.

Pres.	volō,	nōlō,	mālō,
	vīs,	nōn vīs,	māvīs,
	vult ;	nōn vult ;	māvult ;
	volumus,	nōlumus,	mālumus,
	vultis,	nōn vultis,	māvultis,
	volunt.	nōlunt.	mālunt.
Imp.	volēbam.	nōlēbam.	mālēbam.
Fut.	volam.	nōlam.	mālam.
Perf.	voluī.	nōluī.	māluī.
Plup.	volueram.	nōlueram.	mālueram.
Fut. P.	voluerō.	nōluerō.	māluerō.

Subjunctive.

Pres.	velim, -īs, -it, *etc.*	nōlim.	mālim.
Imp.	vellem, -ēs, -et, *etc.*	nōllem.	māllem.
Perf.	voluerim.	nōluerim.	māluerim.
Plup.	voluissem.	nōluissem.	māluissem.

Imperative.

Pres. nōlī, nōlīte.
Fut. nōlītō, nōlītō ; nōlītōte, nōluntō.

Infinitive.

Pres.	velle.	nōlle.	mālle.
Perf.	voluisse.	nōluisse.	māluisse.

Participle.

Pres. volēns. nōlēns.

193. **FĪŎ** (Passive of faciŏ).

PRINCIPAL PARTS. — **fīŏ, fierī,**[1] **factus sum,** *to become, be made, occur.*

Indicative Mood.

	SINGULAR.	PLURAL.
Pres.	fīō, fīs, fit ;	fīmus, fītis, fīunt.
Imp.	fīēbam ;	fīēbāmus.
Fut.	fīam ;	fīēmus.
Perf.	factus sum ;	factī sumus.
Plup.	factus eram ;	factī erāmus.
Fut. P.	factus erō ;	factī erimus.

Subjunctive.

Pres.	fīam ;	fīāmus.
Imp.	fierem ;	fierēmus.
Perf.	factus sim ;	factī sīmus.
Plup.	factus essem ;	factī essēmus.

Imperative.

Pres.	fī ;	fīte.

Infinitive.

Pres.	fierī.
Perf.	factus esse.
Fut.	factum·īrī.

Participle.

Perf.	factus.
Ger.	faciendus.

194. VOCABULARY.

causa, ae, f., *cause, reason.*

certus, a, um, *sure;* compar. certior in phrase certior fierī, *be informed (made more certain).*

concursus, ūs, m., *a running together.*

crēber, bra, brum, *frequent.*

dēserō, ere, seruī, sertus, *I abandon, desert.*

discēdō, ere, cessī, cessūrus, *I depart.*

hūc, adv., *hither.*

maritimus, a, um, *of the sea, maritime.*

ob, *on account of,* prep. w. acc.

ōra, ae, f., *coast.*

per, *through, by means of,* prep. w. acc.

perfuga, ae, m., *deserter.*

prō, *in front of,* prep. w. abl.

quārē, adv., *wherefore, why?*

repentīnus, a, um, *sudden.*

semper, *always.*

socius, ī (iī), m., *ally, comrade.*

---

[1] Note that the i is regularly short before er in this verb.

EXERCISES.

195. 1. Mālumus, māluimus, mālēbat. 2. Māvultis, māluisset, nōluisse. 3. Fīēbat, factum est, fīat. 4. Voluerātis, voluistī, volueris. 5. Volētis, volēbas, voluisse.

196. 1. Ob eam causam crēbra proelia fīēbant. 2. Ab ōrā maritimā discēdere nōlēbat. 3. Quārē sociōs nostrōs semper vexāre vultis? 4. Ex castrīs Gallōrum fit fuga repentīna. 5. Dē hīs rēbus per perfugās certior factus est. 6. Prō castrīs māgnus concursus fīēbat. 7. Hūc venīre nōluimus. 8. Officium suum dēserere nōluerat. 9. Māluissēmus in hīs locīs manēre. 10. Ab hōc oppidō discēdere nōluissem.

CHAPTER XXXIV.

IRREGULAR VERBS (Continued).

197.   **Eŏ.**

Principal Parts. — **eŏ, Ire, Ivī (iī), itum (est),** *to go.*

Indicative Mood.

	SINGULAR.	PLURAL.
Pres.	eō, īs, it ;	īmus, ītis, eunt.
Imp.	ībam ;	ībāmus.
Fut.	ībō ;	ībimus.
Perf.	īvī (iī);	īvimus (iimus).
Plup.	īveram (ieram);	īverāmus (ierāmus).
Fut. P.	īverō (ierō);	īverimus (ierimus).

Subjunctive.

	SINGULAR.	PLURAL.
Pres.	eam ;	eāmus.
Imp.	īrem ;	īrēmus.
Perf.	īverim (ierim);	īverimus (ierimus).
Plup.	īvissem (iissem, īssem);	īvissēmus (iissēmus, īssēmus).

Imperative.

	SINGULAR	PLURAL
Pres.	ī ;	īte.
Fut.	ītō ;	ītōte,
	ītō ;	euntō.

Infinitive. / Participle.

	Infinitive.		Participle.
Pres.	īre.	*Pres.*	iēns.
Perf.	īvisse (iisse, īsse).	(*Gen.* euntis).	
Fut.	itūrus esse.	*Fut.*	itūrus.

Gerund. / Supine.

Gerund.	Supine.
eundī, *etc.*	itum, itū.

1. Transitive compounds of **eŏ** admit the full Passive inflection ; as, **adeor, adīris, adītur,** *etc.*

DEFECTIVE VERBS.

Defective Verbs lack certain forms. The following are the most important : —

198.   USED MAINLY IN THE PERFECT SYSTEM.

Coepī, *I have begun.*   **Meminī,** *I remember.*   **Ōdī,** *I hate.*

Indicative Mood.

Perf.	coepī.	meminī.	ōdī.
Plup.	coeperam.	memineram.	ōderam.
Fut. P.	coeperō.	meminerō.	ōderō.

Subjunctive.

Perf.	coeperim.	meminerim.	ōderim.
Plup.	coepissem.	meminissem.	ōdissem.

Imperative.

Sing. mementō ; *Plur.* mementōte.

Infinitive.

Perf.	coepisse	meminisse.	ōdisse
Fut.	coeptūrus esse.		ōsūrus esse.

Participle.

Perf.	coeptus, *begun.*		ōsus.
Fut.	coeptūrus.		ōsūrus.

1. Note that **meminī** and **ōdī,** though Perfect in form, are Present in sense. Similarly the Pluperfect and Future Perfect have the force respectively of the Imperfect and Future; as, **memineram,** *I remembered*; **ōderō,** *I shall hate.*

199.   VOCABULARY.

adeō, īre, iī, itus, *I go to, visit.*
circiter, adv., *about.*
circumeō, īre, iī, itus, *I go around, surround.*
clam, *secretly.*
duodecim, indecl., *twelve.*
eō, adv., *thither, to that place.*
incipiō, ere, cēpī, ceptus, *I begin.*
ineō, īre, iī, itus, *I enter upon*;
    inīre cōnsilium, *form a plan.*

initium, ī (iī), n., *beginning.*
injūria, ae, f., *wrong, injustice.*
intereō, īre, iī, itūrus, *I perish.*
Mosa, ae, f., the river *Meuse.*
redeō, īre, iī, itum, *I return.*
sinister, tra, trum, *left.*
trāns, *across,* prep. w. acc.
trānseō, īre, iī, itus, *I cross.*
turpis, e, *base.*
unde, *whence.*

EXERCISES.

200. 1. Meminerat, meminerō, meminisse.   2. Adiisse, adiisset, adeāmus.   3. Eundō, itūrus esse, ierat.   4. Redīmus, rediimus, redeāmus.   5. Interībit, interierant.

201. 1. Hostēs sinistrum cornū circumīre cōnantur.   2. Māgna pars exercitūs interiit.   3. Caesar eō, unde redierat, proficīscitur.   4. Circiter duodecim mīlia Germānōrum Rhēnum trānsībant.   5. Hostēs trānseundī initium faciunt.   6. Equitēs, quī trāns Mosam ierant, nōndum redierant.   7. Hās nātiōnēs adībimus.   8. Barbarī cōnsilia dē bellō clam inīre incipiunt. 9. Hōc flūmen trānsīre coepērunt.   10. Hās injūriās meminerāmus.   11. Turpēs cīvīs ōdimus.

CHAPTER XXXV.

IMPERSONAL VERBS. — QUESTIONS AND ANSWERS.

Impersonal Verbs.

202. Impersonal Verbs correspond to the English, *it snows, it seems, etc.* They have no personal subject, but may take an Infinitive, a Clause, or a Neuter Pronoun; as, **mē pudet hōc fēcisse,** lit. *it shames me to have done this ;* **hōc decet,** *this is fitting.* Examples are : —

paenitet	paenitēre	paenituit	*it repents*
pudet	pudēre	puduit	*it causes shame*
miseret	miserēre	miseruit	*it causes pity*
licet	licēre	licuit	*it is lawful*
oportet	oportēre	oportuit	*it is fitting*
cōnstat	cōnstāre	cōnstitit	*it is evident*
accidit	accidere	accidit	*it happens*

Specially to be noted is the impersonal use of such Passive forms as, —

curritur	lit. *it is run*	*i.e. some one runs*
ventum est	lit. *it has been come*	*i.e. some one has come*
veniendum est	lit. *it must be come*	*i.e. somebody must come*

Questions and Answers.

203. Questions may be either Word-Questions or Sentence-Questions.

1. WORD-QUESTIONS. These are introduced by the various interrogative pronouns and adverbs; such as — **quis, quī, quō, quā,** *etc.* Thus : —

quis venit, *who comes ?*

quam diū manēbit, *how long will he stay ?*

2. SENTENCE-QUESTIONS. These are introduced —

a) By **nōnne** implying the answer '*yes*'; as, —

nōnne vidēs, *do you not see ?*

b) By **num** implying the answer '*no*'; as, —

> **num expectās,** *do you expect? (i.e. you don't expect, do you?)*

c) By the enclitic **-ne,** appended to the emphatic word, and simply asking for information; as, —

> **vidēsne,** *do you see?*

3. ANSWERS.

a) The answer YES is expressed by **ita, etiam, vērō, sānē,** or by repetition of the verb; as, —

> '**vīsne locum mūtēmus?**' '**sānē.**' '*Shall we change the place?*' '*Certainly.*'
> '**estisne vōs lēgātī?**' '**sumus.**' '*Are you envoys?*' '*Yes.*'

b) The answer No is expressed by **nōn, minimē, minimē vērō,** or by repeating the verb with a negative; as, —

> '**eane praeteriit?**' '**nōn.**' '*Has it passed?*' '*No.*'
> '**estne frāter intus?**' '**nōn est.**' '*Is your brother within?*' '*No.*'

204. **VOCABULARY.**

concurrō, ere, currī, concursum, *run together*.

dīcō, ere, dīxī, dictus, *I say*.

līberī, ōrum, c., *children* (freeborn).

melior, ius, *better*, comp. to bonus.

-nĕ, enclitic interrog. particle, asking for information.

neglegō, ere, ēxī, ēctus, *I neglect*.

nōnne, interrog. particle, expecting answer "yes."

num, interrog. particle, expecting answer "no."

profugiō, ere, fūgī, fugitūrus, *I flee, escape*.

quandō, *when*, interrog.

quō, *whither*, interrog. and rel. adv.

scrībō, ere, scrīpsī, scrīptus, *I write*.

vir, virī, m., *man*.

EXERCISES.

205. 1. Audācter resistendum est. 2. Undique ad sīgna concurritur.[1] 3. Eō conventum est.[2] 4. Nōnne hās litterās

---

[1] Lit. *it is run together, i.e. the men rush.*

[2] Lit. *it was assembled thither, i.e. men assembled there.*

scrīpsistī? Scrīpsī.   5. Num virī bonī patriam dēfendere recūsant?   Nōn recūsant.   6. Num hōs līberōs neglēxistī?
7. Quandō meliōrem virum vidēbis?   8. Hāsne sententiās pro-
bāvistis? Nōn probāvimus.   9. Quō profūgērunt?   10. Quid
dīxistī?

206. 1. When will you come to us?[1]   2. Where have you
been?   3. Where (= whither) have they gone?   4. What
would you have said?   5. Did you not see us?   6. You will not
neglect your duty, will you? No.   7. Have they returned?
Yes.   8. Would you have written this letter? No.   9. Who
will remain here?

---

[1] See p. 38, § 89, footnote 1.

PART III.

SYNTAX.

———◆———

CHAPTER XXXVI.

THE ACCUSATIVE.

207. 1. The Accusative is the case of the Direct Object.

208. The Direct Object may express either of the two following relations : —

A. The PERSON OR THING AFFECTED by the action; as, —
        cōnsulem interfēcit, *he slew the consul.*

B. The RESULT PRODUCED by the Action; as, —
        lĭbrum scrīpsī, *I wrote a book (i.e.* produced one).

1. This Accusative occurs especially in the case of a Neuter Pronoun or Adjective used Substantively; as, —
        hōc moneō, *I advise this, i.e. I give this advice;*
        hōc rogō, *I request this, i.e. I make this request.*

Two Accusatives — Direct Object and Predicate Accusative.

209. 1. Many Verbs of *Making, Choosing, Calling, Showing,* and the like, take two Accusatives, one of the Person or Thing Affected, the other a Predicate Accusative; as, —
        mē hērēdem fēcit, *he made me heir.*

Here mē is Direct Object, hērēdem Predicate Accusative.

2. The Predicate Accusative may be an Adjective as well as a Noun ; as, —

hominēs caecōs reddit cupiditās, *covetousness renders men blind.*

3. In the Passive the Direct Object becomes the Subject, and the Predicate Accusative becomes Predicate Nominative ; as, —

urbs Rōma vocāta est, *the city was called Rome.*

210. VOCABULARY.

aedificium, ī (iī), n., *building.*
alacer, cris, cre, *eager.*
appellō, 1, *I name, call.*
Bacēnis, is, f., *Bacenis,* a forest in Germany.
dēligō, ere, lēgī, lēctus, *I choose.*
dolor, ōris, m., *grief,*
efficiō, ere, fēcī, fectus, *I make, render.*
frāter, tris, m., *brother.*
hiemō, 1, *I pass the winter.*
incendō, ere, cendī, cēnsus, *I set on fire.*

inimīcus, ī, m., *a (personal) enemy.*
Lentulus, ī, m., *Lentulus,* a man's name.
Octodūrus, ī, m., *Octodurus,* a city of the *Veragri.*
opportūnus, a, um, *fit, opportune.*
praetor, ōris, m., *praetor.*
prīvātus, a, um, *private.*
pūgna, ae, f., *fight, battle.*
-que, *and,* enclitic conj.
sentiō, īre, sēnsī, sēnsus, *I feel.*

EXERCISES.

211. 1. Haec rēs hostēs ad pūgnam alacriōrēs effēcerat. 2. Populus Rōmānus Lentulum praetōrem fēcit. 3. Galba in vīcō quī Octodūrus appellātur hiemat. 4. Helvētiī hunc locum opportūnissimum jūdicāvērunt. 5. Caesarem dē hīs rēbus certiōrem faciunt. 6. Hīc homō dux dēlēctus est. 7. Suum frātrem inimīcum jūdicāverat. 8. Haec silva appellātur Bacēnis. 9. Helvētiī vīcōs reliquaque prīvāta aedificia incendunt. 10. Dolōrem sentīmus. 11. Māgnum exercitum parāvimus.

212. 1. We have made Galba leader. 2. Galba had been made leader. 3. The Helvetii called this town Geneva. 4. The valor of the commander made[1] the soldiers braver. 5. The Belgians were adjudged the bravest of the Gauls. 6. Caesar adjudged the Belgians the bravest of the Gauls. 7. Whom, O soldiers,[2] will you choose as commander?

---

[1] Use **efficiō.** [2] The Vocative regularly stands in the second place in the sentence.

CHAPTER XXXVII.

THE ACCUSATIVE (Continued).

Two Accusatives. — Person and Thing.

213. 1. Some Verbs take two Accusatives, one of the Person Affected, the other of the Result Produced, especially verbs of *Asking, Demanding, Teaching, etc. ;* as, —

> tē haec rogō, *I ask you this ;*
> tē litterās doceō, *I teach you (your) letters.*

2. But many verbs of *asking* (especially petō), instead of the Accusative of the Person, take ā with the Ablative ; as, —

> auxilium ā tē petō, *I request help from you.*

3. In the Passive construction the Accusative of the Person becomes the Subject, and the Accusative of the Thing is retained ; as, —

> is omnēs artēs ēdoctus est, *he was taught all accomplishments.*

Two Accusatives with Compounds.

214. 1. Transitive compounds of trāns may take two Accusatives, one dependent upon the Verb, the other upon the Preposition ; as, —

> mīlitēs flūmen trādūcit, *he leads his soldiers across the river.*

2. In the Passive the Accusative dependent upon the preposition is retained ; as, —

> mīlitēs flūmen trādūcēbantur, *the soldiers were being led across the river.*

Accusative of Time and Space.

215. *Duration of Time* and *Extent of Space* are denoted by the Accusative ; as, —

> quadrāgintā annōs vīxit, *he lived forty years ;*
> arborēs quīnquāgintā pedēs altae, *trees fifty feet high.*

Accusative of Limit of Motion.

216. 1. The Accusative of Limit of Motion is used —

a) With names of *Towns, Small Islands,* and *Peninsulas* ; as, —

Rōmam vēnī, *I came to Rome;*

b) With **domum, domōs, rūs** ; as, —

domum revertitur, *he returns home.*

2. Other designations of place than those above mentioned require a Preposition to denote Limit of Motion ; as, —

ad Italiam vēnit, *he came to Italy.*

217. VOCABULARY.

ā, ab *from*, prep. w. abl. ; before a vowel or **h**, the form **ab** must be used.

ac (atque), *and, and also* ; **ac** is not used before *vowels.*

annus, ī, m., *year.*

Athēnae, ārum, f., *Athens.*

bīduum, ī, n., *two days.*

cottīdiē, adv., *every day, daily.*

domus, ūs, f., *house, home.*

flāgitō, 1, *I demand.*

Hibērus, ī, m., *Hiberus,* a river in Spain.

interim, *in the meanwhile.*

moneō, ēre, uī, itus, *I advise, warn.*

obtineō, ēre, uī, tentus, *I occupy, hold.*

ops, opis, f. (nom. sing. is not used), *power, help;* in plu., *resources.*

passus, ūs, m., *pace* (five feet).

petō, ere, īvī (iī), ītus, *I seek, request.*

polliceor, ērī, itus sum, *I promise.*

rēgnum, ī, n., *kingdom.*

rogō, 1, *I ask.*

sescentī, ae, a, *six hundred.*

trādūcō, ere, dūxī, ductus, *I lead across.*

EXERCISES.

218. 1. Caesar interim cottīdiē Haeduōs frūmentum, quod pollicitī erant, flāgitat. 2. Ā tē opem petō. 3. Sine perīculō ac timōre cōpiās Hibērum trādūxit. 4. Sententiam rogātus est. 5. Hōc mē monēs. 6. Decem annōs rēgnum obtinuit. 7. Bīduum in hīs locīs morātus est. 8. Hic locus ab hostibus sescentōs passūs aberat. 9. Cōpiās domum redūxit. 10. Athēnās redierat. 11. In Galliam contendimus.

219. 1. I shall teach you all these things. 2. We had been taught these things. 3. I have demanded the money of you. 4. These envoys requested help from Caesar. 5. Have you been asked your opinion? 6. Caesar will lead his troops across the Rhine. 7. We remained here ten years. 8. The camp of the enemy is a thousand paces distant. 9. We shall come to Rome. 10. Return home.

CHAPTER XXXVIII.

THE DATIVE.

Dative of Indirect Object.

220. The commonest use of the Dative is to denote the person *to whom* something is *given, said,* or *done.* Thus:—

I. With transitive verbs in connection with the Accusative; as, —

> hanc pecūniam mihi dat, *he gives me this money.*

II. With many intransitive verbs; as, —

> nūllī labōrī cēdit, *he yields to no labor ;*
> tibi suscēnseō, *I am angry with you.*

a) Here belong many verbs signifying *favor, help, injure, please, displease, trust, distrust, command, obey, serve, resist, indulge, spare, pardon, envy, threaten, believe, persuade,* and the like; as, —

> Caesar populāribus favet, *Caesar favors (i.e. is favorable to) the popular party ;*
> amīcīs cōnfīdō, *I trust (to) my friends.*

III. With many verbs compounded with the prepositions: **ad, ante, com- (con-), in, inter, ob, post, prae, prō, sub, super,** and sometimes **circum**; as, —

> afflīctīs succurrit, *he helps the afflicted ;*
> exercituī praefuit, *he was in command of the army ;*
> Labiēnum exercituī praefēcit, *he put Labienus in charge of the army.*

103

221. VOCABULARY.

●ōnfīdō, ere, fīsus sum, semi-dep., *I trust.*

īnferō, ferre, tulī, illātus, *I bring upon.*

intersum, esse, fuī, *I am present at.*

Labiēnus, ī, m., *Labienus,* a lieutenant of Caesar.

mulier, eris, f., *woman.*

noceō, ēre, uī, itūrus, *I injure, harm.*

parcō, ere, pepercī, parsūrus, *I spare.*

persuādeō, ēre, suāsī, suāsum, *I persuade.*

placeō, ēre, uī, placitūrus, *I please.*

praeficiō, ere, fēcī, fectus, *I put in charge.*

praemium, ī (iī), n., *reward.*

praesum, esse, fuī, *I am in charge of.*

recēns, gen., recentis, *recent.*

rēs pūblica, gen., reī pūblicae, f., *state, republic.*

Sabīnus, ī, m., *Sabinus,* a lieutenant of Caesar.

sermō, ōnis, m., *conversation.*

terror, ōris, m., *terror, fear.*

EXERCISES.

222. 1. Reī pūblicae nocētis.   2. Caesar mulieribus pepercit.   3. Sabīnus eī māgnīs praemiīs persuāsit.   4. Caesar eī mūnītiōnī quam fēcerat Labiēnum praefēcit.   5. Laudat eōs quī huic negōtiō praefuerant.   6. Mīlitēs nostrī māximum terrōrem hostibus īnferunt.   7. Caesar huic legiōnī propter virtūtem māximē cōnfīdēbat.   8. Hōc cōnsilium nōbīs placet.   9. Ego huic sermōnī interfuī.   10. Mīlitibus propter recentem victōriam māgna praemia dōnat.

223. 1. We shall present rewards to our soldiers.   2. I had already given you[1] the letter.   3. Let us spare these children!   4. We have not injured you.   5. Trust these soldiers!   6. I had persuaded all these envoys.   7. I should easily have persuaded your brother.   8. We shall put you in charge of the smaller camp.   9. Caesar was in charge of many legions.   10. Who will bring war upon us?

---

[1] Observe that the special sign of the indirect object (*to, for*) is often lacking in English. The pupil must have regard to the meaning.

CHAPTER XXXIX.

THE DATIVE (CONTINUED).

Dative of Reference.

224. 1. The Dative of Reference denotes the person *to whom a statement refers, of whom it is true,* or *to whom it is of interest;* as, —

mihi ante oculōs versāris, *you hover before my eyes* (lit. *hover before the eyes to me*).

NOTE. — The Dative of Reference, unlike the Dative of Indirect Object, does not modify the verb, but rather the sentence as a whole. It is often used where, according to the English idiom, we should expect a Genitive.

Dative of Agency.

225. With the Gerundive the Dative is used to denote *agency*; as, —

haec nōbīs agenda sunt, *these things must be done by us;*
mihi eundum est, *I must go* (lit. *it must be gone by me*).

Dative of Possession.

226. The Dative of Possession occurs with the verb **esse** in such expressions as : —

mihi est liber, *I have a book* (lit. *a book is to me*).

Dative of Purpose.

227. The Dative of Purpose designates *the end toward which an action is directed* or *for which something exists;* as, —

castrīs locum dēligere, *to choose a place for a camp;*
nōbīs sunt odiō, *they are an object of hatred to us* (lit. *are to us for hatred*).

Dative with Adjectives.

228. The use of the Dative with Adjectives corresponds very closely to its use with verbs. Thus : —

105

It occurs with adjectives signifying: *friendly, unfriendly, similar, dissimilar, equal, near, related to, suitable, etc.*; as, —

> mihi inimīcus, *hostile to me* ;
> proximus rīpae, *next to the bank* ;
> castrīs idōneus locus, *a place suitable for a camp.*

229.　　　　　　VOCABULARY.

adversus, a, um, *adverse.*
colloquium, ī (iī), n., *conference.*
cōnspectus, ūs, m., *view, sight.*
dīcō, ere, dīxī, dictus, *I appoint.*
facinus, facinoris, n., *crime.*
pār, gen. paris, *equal.*
pēs, pedis, m., *foot.*
prōiciō, ere, jēcī, jectus, *I throw, cast.*

proximus, a, um, *nearest, next,*
　cf. § 74, 1.
scūtum, ī, n., *shield.*
tēlum, ī, n., *javelin.*
Trēverī, ōrum, m. plu., *Treveri,*
　a tribe of Belgians.
ūsus, ūs, m., *use, service.*
ventus, ī, m., *wind.*

EXERCISES.

230.　1. Hostēs nōbīs in cōnspectum vēnerant.　2. Omnēs sē Caesarī ad pedēs projēcērunt.　3. Patria nōbīs dēfendenda est.　4. Ācriter nōbīs resistendum est.[1]　5. Mīlitibus sunt scūta tēlaque.　6. Quīnque cohortēs castrīs praesidiō relīquit.　7. Ūna rēs mīlitibus māgnō ūsuī erat.　8. Diēs colloquiō dictus est.　9. Hīc ventus nōbīs adversus est.　10. Nūlla poena huic facinorī pār est.　11. Trēverī proximī Rhēnō sunt.

231.　1. This camp must be bravely defended by us.　2. We must make resistance (= it must be resisted by us; § 202).　3. The Helvetii had many villages.　4. The Romans had large fleets.　5. Let us appoint a day for a conference.　6. Caesar chose a place for a camp.　7. This place was suitable for a cavalry battle.　8. These villages are next the sea.　9. This thing was of great assistance[2] to us.

---

[1] See § 225, 2d example.
[2] Compare the seventh sentence in the Latin Exercise.

CHAPTER XL.

THE GENITIVE.

Genitive with Nouns.

232. With Nouns the Genitive is *the case which defines the meaning of the limited noun more closely.* Here belong especially : —

233. Genitive of Possession or Ownership; as, —

domus Cicerōnis, *Cicero's house.*

1. The Possessive Genitive is often used predicatively, especially with **esse** and **fierī**; as, —

domus est rēgis, *the house is the king's.*

234. Subjective Genitive. This denotes *the person who makes or produces something* or *who has a feeling*; as, —

dicta Platōnis, *the utterances of Plato* ;
timōrēs līberōrum, *the fears of the children.*

235. Objective Genitive. This denotes *the object of an action or feeling*; as, —

metus deōrum, *fear of the gods.*

236. Genitive of the Whole (Partitive Genitive). This designates the *whole* of which a part is taken, as, —

māgna pars hominum, *a great part of mankind.*

1. The Genitive of the Whole occurs especially with the Nominative or Accusative Singular Neuter of Pronouns, or of Adjectives used substantively, as, —

quid cōnsilī, *what purpose ?*
plūs auctōritātis, *more authority.*

237. Genitive of Quality. The Genitive modified by an Adjective is used to denote quality; as, —

    vir māgnae virtūtis, *a man of great virtue;*
    fossa quīndecim pedum, *a trench fifteen feet wide (or deep).*

238.   **VOCABULARY.**

āmittō, ere, mīsī, missus, *I lose.*
ancora, ae, f., *anchor.*
arcessō, ere, īvī, ītus, *I summon.*
armātūra, ae, f., *equipment.*
cēterī, ae, a, *the rest, the other.*
cūstōdia, ae, f., *custody.*
dīcō, ere, dīxī, dictus, *I utter.*
imperium, ī (iī), n., *rule, command.*
jūstus, a, um, *just.*
levis, e, *light.*

modus, ī, m., *manner, kind.*
nōnnūllus, a, um, *some* (§ 61).
pābulum, ī, n., *forage.*
quantus, a, um, *how much, how great.*
satis, *enough,* indecl.
supersum, esse, fuī, *I remain, am left.*
tantus, a, um, *so much, so great.*
vāllum, ī, n., *intrenchment.*
via, ae, f., *road, way.*

EXERCISES.

239. 1. Ancorae nāvium āmissae sunt. 2. Imperium populī Rōmānī jūstissimum erat. 3. Cēterīs cohortibus cūstōdiam captīvōrum trādidit. 4. Quantum viae superest? 5. Tantum pābulī dēerat. 6. Castrīs erat satis praesidī. 7. Dux peditēs levis armātūrae arcessīvit. 8. Erat vāllum decem pedum in altitūdinem. 9. Nōnnūllae sententiae ējus modī dīcēbantur.

240. 1. Caesar's legions were brave. 2. The onset of the Gauls was withstood. 3. This victory of our troops was most welcome to the Romans. 4. Your recollection of my favors is most welcome to me. 5. How much forage was in the camp? 6. There was not enough money.[1] 7. These soldiers were of the greatest valor. 8. Our soldiers filled up a trench ten feet in[2] depth.

---

[1] Translate: ' Not enough of money was.'
[2] Use **in** with the acc.

CHAPTER XLI.

THE GENITIVE (Continued).

Genitive with Adjectives.

241. The Genitive is used with many Adjectives *to limit the extent of their application.* Thus : —

1. With Adjectives signifying *desire, knowledge, familiarity, memory, participation, power, fulness,* and their opposites ; as, —

> **studiōsus discendī,** *desirous of learning;*
> **perītus bellī,** *skilled in war.*

Genitive with Verbs.

242. The Genitive is used with the following classes of Verbs : —

Memini, Reminīscor (*remember*), *Oblīvīscor* (*forget*)[1]; as, —

> **animus praeteritōrum meminit,** *the mind remembers the past.*

Admoneō, Commoneō, Commonefaciō.

243. These Verbs, in addition to an Accusative of the person, occasionally take a Genitive of the thing ; as, —

> **tē admoneō amīcitiae nostrae,** *I remind you of our friendship.*

Verbs of Judicial Action.

244. Verbs of *Accusing, Condemning, Convicting, Acquitting* take the Genitive of the *charge ;* as, —

> **mē fūrtī accūsat,** *he accuses me of theft.*

Genitive with Impersonal Verbs.

245. The Impersonals **pudet, paenitet, miseret, taedet, piget** take the Accusative of *the person affected,* along with

---

[1] These also often govern the Accusative, especially of a neut. pron. or adj.

the Genitive *of the person or thing toward whom the feeling is directed;* as, —

>   **pudet mē tuī,** *I am ashamed of you* (lit. *it shames me of you*).

Interest, Rēfert.

246. With **interest** (rarely with **rēfert**), the *person concerned* is denoted by the Genitive; as, —

>   **patris interest,** *it concerns the father.*

a. But instead of the Genitive of the personal pronouns, **meī, tuī,** *etc.,* the Latin uses the Ablative Singular Feminine of the Possessive, *viz.;* **meā, tuā,** *etc.;* as, —

>   **meā rēfert,** *it concerns me.*

247.   VOCABULARY.

admoneō, ēre, uī, itus, *I remind.*

beneficium, I (iī), n., *kindness, favor.*

contumēlia, ae, f., *insult.*

dēfectiō, ōnis, f., *revolt.*

etiam, *also.*

fūrtum, I, n., *theft.*

genus, eris, n., *kind.*

imperītus, a, um, *inexperienced.*

interest, *it concerns.*

oblīvīscor, I, oblītus sum, *forget.*

paenitet, *it causes regret.*

plēnus, a, um, *full.*

prīstinus, a, um, *pristine.*

EXERCISES.

248. 1. Plēna est vīta perīculōrum. 2. Hūjus generis pūgnae imperītī sumus. 3. Hārum contumēliārum meminimus. 4. Helvētiī prīstinae suae virtūtis nōn oblīvīscùntur. 5. Tē meōrum beneficiōrum admoneō. 6. Hunc puerum fūrtī accūsāmus. 7. Hūjus dēfectiōnis eōs paenitet. 8. Hōc reī pūblicae salūtisque commūnis interest. 9. Vestrā etiam interest.

249. 1. The Helvetii were fond of war. 2. They remembered the valor of their ancestors. 3. We shall not forget your favors. 4. I remind him of our friendship. 5. Do you remember this? 6. We regret this war. 7. It greatly concerns you. 8. This will concern all the soldiers.

CHAPTER XLII.

THE ABLATIVE.

250. The Latin Ablative unites in itself three cases which were originally distinct both in form and in meaning; viz. —
    The Ablative or from-case.
    The Instrumental or with-case.
    The Locative or where-case.

The uses of the Latin Ablative accordingly fall into Genuine Ablative uses, Instrumental uses, and Locative uses.

GENUINE ABLATIVE USES.

Ablative of Separation.

251. The Ablative of Separation is construed sometimes with, sometimes without, a preposition. The preposition is omitted especially with verbs of *freeing, depriving, lacking,* and with adjectives of similar meaning; as, —

cūrīs līberātus, *freed from cares.*

Ablative of Source.

252. The Ablative of Source is used with the participles nātus and ortus, to designate *parentage* or *station;* as, —

Jove nātus, *born of Jupiter.*

Ablative of Agent.

253. The Ablative accompanied by ā (ab) is used with passive verbs to denote the *personal agent;* as, —

ā Caesare accūsātus est, *he was arraigned by Caesar.*

Ablative of Comparison.

254. 1. The Ablative is often used with Comparatives in the sense of *than;* as, —

patria mihi vītā cārior est, *my country is dearer to me than life.*

111

2. **Plūs, amplius** (*more*), **minus** (*less*), and **longius** (*further*), are often employed as the equivalents of **plūs quam, minus quam,** *etc.*; as,—

plūs decem hominēs aderant, *more than ten men were present.*

255. VOCABULARY.

ā, ab, *by,* prep. with abl.
amplius, *more.*
amplus, a, um, *great, glorious.*
Catilīna, ae, m., *Catiline.*
commeātus, ūs, m., *supplies.*
dissēnsiō, ōnis, f., *disagreement.*
expellō, ere, pulī, pulsus, *I drive out.*
genus, eris, n., *stock, family.*
locus, ī, m., *place; family.*
nāscor, ī, nātus sum, *I am born.*

obsidiō, ōnis, f., *siege.*
occīdō, ere, cīdī, cīsus, *I kill.*
possessiō, ōnis, f., *possession.*
repellō, ere, reppulī, repulsus, *I drive back, repel.*
septingentī, ae, a, *seven hundred.*
Ubiī, ōrum, m., *Ubii,* a Gallic tribe.
Usipetēs, um, m., *Usipetes,* a German tribe.
vīgintī, *twenty,* indecl.

EXERCISES.

256. 1. Caesar Ubiōs obsidiōne līberāvit. 2. Helvētiī fīnibus suīs excessērunt. 3. Usipetēs propter dissēnsiōnēs possessiōnibus suīs expulsī sunt. 4. Hostēs Caesarem commeātū prohibuērunt. 5. Catilīna amplissimō genere nātus est. 6. Hīc adulēscēns summō locō nātus est. 7. Hostēs ā mīlitibus nostrīs repulsī sunt. 8. Nihil est hominibus cārius lībertāte. 9. Amplius vīgintī vīcī incenduntur. 10. In eō proeliō minus septingentī mīlitēs occīsī sunt.

257. 1. The Germans were driven out of their villages. 2. We shall free our fellow-citizens from fear. 3. The Romans drove back the Gauls from the rampart of the camp. 4. We kept the cavalry away from the ford of the river. 5. Caesar was born of a most noble family. 6. More than a hundred towns were captured by Caesar. 7. What is nobler than friendship? 8. Is not virtue better than friendship? 9. Caesar advanced less than ten miles.[1]

---

[1] Lit. 'ten thousands of paces'; § 236, 1.

CHAPTER XLIII.

ABLATIVE (CONTINUED).

INSTRUMENTAL USES.

Ablative of Means.

258. The Ablative is used to denote *means* or *instrument;* as, —

> **Alexander sagittā vulnerātus est,** *Alexander was wounded by an arrow.*

Under this Ablative fall the following uses : —

1. **Ūtor, fruor, fungor, potior, vescor,** and their compounds take the Ablative ; as, —

> **dīvitiīs ūtitur,** *he uses his wealth* (lit. *he benefits himself by his wealth*) ;
> **vītā fruitur,** *he enjoys life* (lit. *he enjoys himself by life*).

2. With **opus est,** *there is need* ; as, —
> **duce nōbīs opus est,** *we need a leader.*

3. With Verbs of *filling* and Adjectives of *plenty* ; as, —

> **fossās virgultīs complēvērunt,** *they filled the trenches with brush.*

Ablative of Cause.

259. The Ablative is used to denote *Cause ;* as, —

> **multa glōriae cupiditāte fēcit,** *he did many things on account of his love of glory.*

1. So especially with verbs denoting mental states ; as, **dēlector, gaudeō, laetor, glōrior, fīdō, cōnfīdō** ; also with **contentus** ; as, —

> **fortūnā amīcī gaudeō,** *I rejoice at the fortune of my friend* (*i.e. on account of it*).

Ablative of Manner.

260. The Ablative with **cum** is used to denote *manner;* as, —

> **cum gravitāte loquitur,** *he speaks with dignity.*

1. The preposition may be omitted when the Ablative is modified by an adjective; as, —

> **māgnā gravitāte loquitur,** *he speaks with great dignity.*

Ablative of Attendant Circumstance.

261. The Ablative (often with **cum**) is used to denote an *attendant circumstance* of an action or an event; as, —

> **bonīs auspiciīs,** *under good auspices;*
> **māgnō cum damnō,** *with great loss.*

262. VOCABULARY.

addūcō, ere, dūxī, ductus, *I lead on, impel.*

celeritās, ātis, f., *speed.*

cōnficiō, ere, fēcī, fectus, *I exhaust.*

dēditiō, ōnis, f., *surrender.*

dētrīmentum, ī, n., *loss, damage.*

dīgnitās, ātis, f., *dignity.*

ēruptiō, ōnis, f., *sally.*

grātia, ae, f., *influence.*

inopia, ae, f., *lack.*

lacessō, ere, lacessīvī, lacessītus, *I harass.*

nocturnus, a, um, *at night.*

opus, n., *need*, indeclinable.

perveniō, īre, vēnī, ventum, *I come, arrive.*

ratiō, ōnis, f., *reason.*

recipiō, ere, cēpī, ceptus, *I take back;* with reflexive **sē,** *to retreat.* .

ūtor, ī, ūsus sum, *I use.*

EXERCISES.

263. 1. Helvētiī inopiā omnium rērum adductī lēgātōs dē dēditiōne ad Caesarem mīsērunt. 2. Equitēs portīs ēruptiōnem faciunt. 3. Hostēs equitēs nostrōs proeliō lacessere coepērunt. 4. Gallī vulneribus cōnfectī sē recēpērunt. 5. Opus est celeritāte. 6. Montem multitūdine hominum complēvērunt. 7. Hōc

eā ratiōne fēcit.   8. Tuā grātiā, dignitāte, ope[1] ūtī volō.
9. Eādem celeritāte nocturnō itinere ad mare pervēnit.   10. Gallī cum māgnō dētrīmentō repulsī sunt.

264. 1. The soldiers had been exhausted by the long march.
2. We shall use the help of the Gauls.   3. The trenches were filled by the soldiers with large stones.   4. We shall need cavalry and infantry.   5. He spoke with great dignity.   6. From fear of danger the envoys withdrew from the camp.   7. The Helvetii were not contented with their narrow boundaries.

---

[1] In Latin the conjunction 'and' is often omitted between the last two members of an enumeration.

CHAPTER XLIV.

ABLATIVE (CONTINUED).

Ablative of Accompaniment.

265. The Ablative with **cum** is used to denote *accompaniment*; as, —

> **cum comitibus profectus est,** *he set out with his attendants.*

Ablative of Degree of Difference.

266. The Ablative is used with comparatives and words involving comparison (as **post, ante, īnfrā, suprā ; superāre,** *surpass*) to denote the *degree of difference*; as, —

> **tribus pedibus altior,** *three feet higher* (lit. *higher by three feet*).

Ablative of Quality.

267. The Ablative, modified by an adjective, is used to denote *quality*; as, —

> **puella eximiā fōrmā,** *a girl of exceptional beauty.*

1. The Ablative of Quality may also be used predicatively ; as, —

> **est māgnā prūdentiā,** *he is (a man) of great wisdom.*

Ablative of Price.

268. With verbs of *buying* and *selling*, price is designated by the Ablative ; as, —

> **servum quīnque minīs ēmit,** *he bought the slave for five minae.*

Ablative of Specification.

269. The Ablative of Specification is used to denote that *in respect to which* something is or is done ; as, —

> **Helvētiī omnibus Gallīs virtūte praestābant,** *the Helvetians surpassed all the Gauls in valor.*

1. Here belongs the use of the Ablative with **dīgnus** and **indīgnus**; as, —

dīgnī honōre, *worthy of honor.*

270. VOCABULARY.

ante, adv., *before.*

antecēdō, ere, cessī, cessūrus, *I precede.*

auctōritās, ātis, f., *authority, influence.*

dīgnus, a, um, *worthy.*

fidēs, eī, f., *confidence.*

nihilō, abl., *by nothing.*

paulō, abl., *by a little.*

post, *afterwards.*

solvō, ere, solvī, solūtus, *I loose;* of ships, *unmoor;* **nāvēs solvere,** *set sail.*

superō, 1, *I surpass.*

talentum, ī, n., *a talent* (about $1200).

vēndō, ere, vēndidī, vēnditus, *I sell.*

EXERCISES.

271. 1. Ipse cum equitātū antecēdit.   2. Paucīs ante diēbus profectī sumus.   3. Paulō post nāvēs solvit.   4. Adversum proelium equestre paucīs ante diēbus factum erat.   5. Haec cīvitās erat māgnā auctōritāte.   6. Nihilō minus Helvētiī id, quod cōnstituerant, facere cōnantur.   7. Hōs agrōs sex talentīs vēndidit.   8. Ille dīgnus est fidē.   9. Omnēs dīgnitāte superat. 10. Turris decem pedibus quam mūnītiō altior fuit.

272. 1. Caesar set out with four legions.   2. He returned home with his brother.   3. A few years before, Caesar had first come into Gaul.   4. A few years after, he returned to Rome. 5. This plan is much better.   6. This house was sold for ten talents.   7. Are we not worthy of the highest honor?   8. This man surpassed the rest in virtue.   9. The enemy were superior in number.

CHAPTER XLV.

Ablative Absolute.

273. The Ablative Absolute is grammatically independent of the rest of the sentence. In its commonest form it consists of a noun or pronoun limited by a participle; as, —

> **urbe captā, Aenēās fūgit,** *when the city had been captured, Aeneas fled* (lit. *the city having been captured*).

1. Instead of a participle we often find an adjective or noun; as, —

> **vīvō Caesare, rēs pūblica salva erat,** *while Caesar was alive the state was safe* (lit. *Caesar being alive*);
> **Centōne et Tuditānō cōnsulibus,** *in the consulship of Cento and Tuditanus* (lit. *Cento and Tuditanus being consuls*).

2. The Ablative Absolute may be equivalent to almost any kind of a subordinate clause in English, *i.e.* to a clause introduced by *when, as, since, if, though, etc.*

LOCATIVE USES OF THE ABLATIVE.

Ablative of Place.

A. *Place where.*

274. The place where is regularly denoted by the *Ablative with a preposition;* as, —

> **in urbe habitat,** *he dwells in the city.*

1. But names of towns — except Singulars of the First and Second Declensions — stand in the Ablative without a preposition; as, —

> **Carthāgine,** *at Carthage.*

B. *Place from which.*[1]

275. Place from which is regularly denoted by the *Ablative with a preposition;* as, —

> **ab Italiā profectus est,** *he set out from Italy.*

1. But names of towns and small islands stand in the Ablative without a preposition; as, —

> **Rōmā profectus est,** *he set out from Rome.*

Ablative of Time.

276. The Ablative is used to denote the time *at which* or *within which;* as, —

> **quārtā hōrā mortuus est,** *he died at the fourth hour;*
> **stella Sāturnī trīgintā annīs cursum cōnficit,** *the planet Saturn completes its orbit within thirty years.*

THE LOCATIVE.

277. The Locative case occurs chiefly in the following words : —

1. Regularly in the Singular of names of towns and small islands of the first and second declensions, to denote the place *in which;* as,—

> **Rōmae,** *at Rome;*   **Corinthī,** *at Corinth* (see § 22, 3).

2. In a few special words, as, —

> **domī,** *at home;*   **humī,** *on the ground.*

278.   VOCABULARY.

Aprīlis, e, adj., *of April.*

cōgō, ere, coēgī, coāctus, *I collect.*

conjūrātiō, ōnis, f., *conspiracy.*

dēspērō, 1, *I despair.*

Kalendae, ārum, f., *Kalends* (first of the month).

M., abbreviation for **Mārcus, Ī, m.,** *Marcus,* a man's name.

Messalla, ae, m., *Messalla,* a man's name.

peditātus, ūs, m., *infantry.*

Pīsō, ōnis, m., *Piso,* a man's name.

Rōma, ae, f., *Rome.*

tempus, oris, n., *time.*

tertius, a, um, *third.*

trīduum, Ī, n., *three days.*

vigilia, ae, f., *watch* (of the night).

---

[1] Place from which, though strictly a " Genuine Ablative" use, is treated here for the sake of convenience.

EXERCISES.

279. 1. Barbarī, māgnā multitūdine peditātūs coāctā,[1] ad castra vēnērunt. 2. Is, M. Messallā et M. Pīsōne cōnsulibus, conjū-rātiōnem fēcit. 3. Hostēs, īnsidiīs in silvīs collocātīs, adventum Rōmānōrum exspectābant. 4. Athēnīs morābāmur. 5. Rōmae erat māgnus tumultus. 6. Rōmā in Galliam contendit. 7. Ā Galliā Rōmam trīduō redībit. 8. Tertiā vigiliā ē castrīs profec-tus est. 9. Eō tempore mīlitēs dē suā salūte dēspērābant. 10. Kalendīs Aprīlibus hās litterās mīsī.

280. 1. In the consulship of Pompey and Crassus the Germans crossed the Rhine. 2. When these tribes had been overcome Caesar returned into winter quarters. 3. In these places were large forests. 4. He remained one day at Geneva. 5. We tarried at Athens. 6. From Athens we returned to Rome. 7. From Rome we hurried into Gaul. 8. We set out in the first watch. 9. You were consul in that year. 10. Within six years I shall be consul.

---

[1] Avoid translating the Ablative Absolute by the English Nominative Absolute. Find a natural English equivalent.

CHAPTER XLVI.

SYNTAX OF ADJECTIVES.

Adjectives used Substantively.

281. 1. PLURAL ADJECTIVES USED SUBSTANTIVELY. Adjectives, including Possessive Pronouns, are quite freely used as Substantives in the Plural. The Masculine denotes persons; the Neuter denotes things; as, —

docti, *learned men;* nostri, *our men;* parva, *small things.*

2. In the Singular, Adjectives are not often used as Substantives.

Adjectives with the Force of Adverbs.

282. The Latin often uses an Adjective where the English idiom employs an Adverb or an adverbial phrase; as, —

inviti abeunt, *they go away unwillingly* (lit. *unwilling*).

Comparatives and Superlatives.

283. 1. The Comparative often corresponds to the English Positive with ' *rather*,' ' *somewhat*,' ' *too*'; as, —

senectūs est loquācior, *old age is rather talkative.*

2. So the Superlative often corresponds to the Positive with '*very*'; as, —

vir fortissimus, *a very brave man.*

Other Peculiarities.

284. 1. Certain Adjectives may be used to denote *a part of an object,* chiefly prīmus, extrēmus, summus, medius, īnfimus, īmus; [1] as, —

summus mōns, *the top of the mountain.*

2. **Prior, prīmus, ultimus,** and **postrēmus** are frequently equivalent to a relative clause; as, —

prīmus eam vīdī, *I was the first who saw her.*

---

[1] In this use the Adjective precedes the Noun.

285.   VOCABULARY.

abeō, īre, iī, itūrus, *go away.*

crēdō, ere, didī, ditum, *believe.*

extrēmus, a, um, *extreme, end of.*

gravis, e, *heavy, difficult.*

hiems, is, f., *winter.*

hortor, ārī, ātus sum, *I exhort.*

invītus, a, um, *unwilling.*

laetus, a, um, *glad.*

nox, noctis, f., *night.*

plērīque, aeque, aque, *most.*

prōcēdō, ere, cessī, cessūrus,
   I advance.

respondeō, ēre, spondī, spōn-
   sus, *I answer, reply.*

EXERCISES.

286.   1. Caesar suōs hortātus est.   2. Plērīque haec crēdunt.
3. Mihi pauca respondit.   4. Invītus haec fēcī.   5. Laetī abiē-
runt.   6. Via gravior erat.   7. Numerus lēgātōrum erat māximus.   8. Usipetēs extrēmā hieme Rhēnum trānsiērunt.   9. Gallī
mediā nocte ex castrīs ēgressī sunt.   10. Galba prīmus prōcessit.
11. Plērōsque lēgātōs ab hōc colloquiō invītōs abeuntēs vīdimus.

287.   1. Our (men)[1] withstood the onset of the barbarians.
2. I said all these (things) in the senate.   3. He remembers
many (things).[2]   4. Most (persons) heard this.   5. We
glad(ly) remained.   6. I replied unwilling(ly).   7. Our
(men) seized the top of the mountain.   8. In the last (part of
the) summer we were informed of these things.[3]   9. We were the
first to set out.   10. The march was somewhat difficult.

---

[1] Words in parenthesis are not to be translated.   .

[2] See § 242, footnote.

[3] The substantive use of neuter pronouns and adjectives is regularly confined to
the Nominative and Accusative Cases; rēs must be used here.

CHAPTER XLVII.

SYNTAX OF PRONOUNS.

Personal Pronouns.

288. 1. The Personal Pronouns as subjects of verbs are, as a rule, not expressed except for the purpose of *emphasis, contrast,* or *clearness.* Thus ordinarily : —

videō, *I see ;*   amat, *he loves.*

But **ego tē videō, et tū mē vidēs,** *I see you, and you see me.*

2. The Genitives **meī, tuī, nostrī, vestrī** are used only as Objective Genitives ; **nostrum** and **vestrum** as Genitives of the Whole. Thus : —

memor tuī, *mindful of you ;*

nēmō vestrum, *no one of you.*

Possessive Pronouns.

289. The Possessive Pronouns, as a rule, are not employed except for the purpose of *clearness.* Thus : —

patrem amō, *I love my father.*

But —   patrem tuum amō, *I love your father.*

Reciprocal Pronouns.

290. The Latin has no special reciprocal pronoun ('*each other*'), but expresses the reciprocal notion by the phrases : **inter nōs, inter vōs, inter sē,** or by the simple **nōs, vōs, sē ;** as, —

Belgae obsidēs inter sē dedērunt, *the Belgae gave each other hostages* (lit. *among themselves*).

Demonstrative Pronouns.

Hīc, Ille, Iste.

291. 1. Where **hīc** and **ille** are used in contrast, **hīc** usually refers to the latter of two objects, and **ille** to the former.

2. **Iste** frequently involves contempt ; as, **iste homō,** *that fellow !*

Ipse.

292. 1. **Ipse,** literally *self,* acquires its special force from the context; as, —

> eŏ ipsŏ diě, *on that very day;*
> ad ipsam rīpam, *close to the bank;*
> ipsŏ terrŏre, *by mere fright.*

Pronominal Adjectives.

293. 1. **Alius,** *another,* and **alter,** *the other,* are often used correlatively; as, —

> aliud loquitur, aliud sentit, *he says one thing, he thinks another;*
> alter exercitum perdidit, alter věndidit, *one ruined the army, the other sold it.*

294. VOCABULARY.

cědŏ, ere, cessī, cessūrus, *I yield, withdraw.*

coniciŏ, ere, conjēcī, conjectus, *I hurl.*

differŏ, ferre, distulī, dīlātus, *I differ.*

exitus, ūs, m., *exit, passage.*

fīdūcia, ae, f., *confidence.*

Institūtum, ī, n., *institution.*

laus, laudis, f., *praise.*

mereor, ěrī, meritus sum, *I deserve.*

misericordia, ae, f., *pity.*

premŏ, ere, pressī, pressus, *I press, crowd.*

subeŏ, īre, iī, itūrus, *I approach.*

EXERCISES.

295. 1. Tua nostrī fīdūcia mihi grāta est. 2. Multī vestrum laudem meritī sunt. 3. Misericordiā vestrī movēbar. 4. Hostēs in exitū portārum sēsē premēbant. 5. Gallī īnstitūtīs atque lēgibus inter sē differunt. 6. Nostrī ipsā multitūdine nāvium perterrēbantur. 7. Ipsa locī nātūra perīculum repellēbat. 8. Nē eō quidem tempore quisquam locō cessit. 9. Hārum fīliārum altera occīsa,[1] altera capta est. 10. Aliī tēla coniciunt, aliī vāllum subeunt.

---

[1] Supply **est** from the following **capta est.**

296. 1. I was touchéd by your recollection of me. 2. Part of us went away. 3. Your pity of us touched my father. 4. He was driven out by his own[1] fellow-citizens. 5. They had long contended with[2] each other. 6. We have long contended with each other. 7. Some fought with swords, others with javelins. 8. One was killed, another fled. 9. The one fled, the other was captured.

---

[1] *his own :* use the proper form of **suus**.
[2] Compare the fifth sentence in the Latin exercise.

CHAPTER XLVIII.

THE SUBJUNCTIVE IN INDEPENDENT SENTENCES.

297. The Subjunctive is used in Independent Sentences to express something —

   1. **As willed — Volitive Subjunctive ;**
   2. **As desired — Optative Subjunctive ;**
   3. **Conceived of as possible — Potential Subjunctive.**

Volitive Subjunctive.

298. The Volitive Subjunctive has the following varieties : —

A. HORTATORY SUBJUNCTIVE.

299. The Hortatory Subjunctive expresses *an exhortation*. This use is confined to the first person plural of the Present. The negative is **nē**. Thus : —

    eāmus, *let us go ;*
    nē dēspērēmus, *let us not despair.*

B. JUSSIVE SUBJUNCTIVE.

300. The Jussive Subjunctive expresses a *command*. The Jussive stands regularly in the Present Tense, and is used, —

   1. Most frequently in the third singular and third plural ; as, —
    dīcat, *let him tell.*

   2. Negative commands, *i.e. prohibitions*, are rarely expressed by the Subjunctive, but usually by means of **nōlī (nōlīte)**, with a following infinitive ; as, —
    nōlī hōc facere, *don't do this* (lit. *be unwilling to do*) !

C. DELIBERATIVE SUBJUNCTIVE.

301. The Deliberative Subjunctive is used *in questions and exclamations implying doubt or indignation.* The

Present is used referring to present time, the Imperfect referring to past. The negative is **nōn.** Thus: —

> **quid faciam,** *what shall I do ?*
> **quid facerem,** *what was I to do ?*
> **hunc ego nōn dīligam,** *shall I not cherish this man ?*

a. These Deliberative Questions are usually purely Rhetorical in character, and do not expect an answer.

302.   **VOCABULARY.**

accēdō, ere, cessī, cessūrus, *I draw near.*
cōnsīdō, ere, sēdī, *I settle.*
cūrō, 1, *I care for, take care of.*
dēsistō, ere, dēstitī, *I cease.*
dīmittō, ere, mīsī, missus, *I let go.*

disciplīna, ae, f., *discipline.*
mōs, mōris, m., *custom.*
nē, *not.*
retineō, ēre, uī, tentus, *I retain.*
sūmō, ere, sūmpsī, sūmptus, *I take.*

EXERCISES.

303. 1. Mōrēs atque disciplīnam majōrum retineāmus ! 2. Hanc occāsiōnem nē dīmittāmus ! 3. Omnēs proeliō dēsistant ! 4. Haec cūrentur ! 5. Ille accēdat ! 6. Nōlī discēdere ! 7. Nōlīte, mīlitēs, officia vestra dēserere ! 8. Hunc virum nōn dēfenderem ? 9. Quārē nōn hīc cōnsīdāmus ? 10. Quid sūmam ! 11. Nēmō incolās hūjus īnsulae lacessat.

304. 1. Let us withstand the onset of the enemy ! 2. Let us not abandon our duty ! 3. Let Ariovistus return home ! 4. Let the Germans not ravage the fields of the Gauls ! 5. Were we not to keep the Germans away from Gaul ! 6. Do not go away ! 7. Do not join battle ! 8. What are we to do?

CHAPTER XLIX.

305. The Optative Subjunctive occurs in expressions of *wishing*. The negative is regularly **nē**. The use of tenses is as follows : —

1. The Present Tense, often accompanied by **utinam**, is used where the wish is conceived of *as possible*.

> **dī istaeo prohibeant,** *may the gods prevent that!*
> **nē veniant,** *may they not come!*

2. The Imperfect expresses, in the form of a wish, the *regret that something is not so now;* the Pluperfect, that something *was not so in the past.* The Imperfect and Pluperfect are regularly accompanied by **utinam**; as, —

> **utinam istud ex animō dīcerēs,** *would that you were saying that in earnest!* (*i.e.* I regret that you are not saying it in earnest);
> **utinam vēnisset,** *would that he had come.*

Potential Subjunctive.

306. The force of the Potential Subjunctive is expressed by the English auxiliaries *should, would*. Both the Present and Perfect tenses occur, and without appreciable difference of meaning, as, —

> **fortūnam facilius reperiās quam retineās,** *you would find Fortune more easily than you would hold her.*

1. The negative of the Potential Subjunctive is **nōn**.

2. *May* and *can*-Potentials are so rare that the student should not venture to use these auxiliaries in rendering the Latin Potential.

The Imperative.

307. The Imperative is used in *commands, admonitions,* and *entreaties* (negative **nē**); as, —

> ēgredere ex urbe, *depart from the city ;*
> mihi ignōsce, *pardon me ;*
> valē, *farewell.*

1. The Present is the tense of the *Imperative* most commonly used.

2. Except with the Future Imperative the negative is not used in classical prose.

308. **VOCABULARY.**

aestās, ātis, f., *summer.*

āvertō, ere, vertī, versus, *I avert.*

consūmō, ere, sūmpsī, sūmptus, *I use up.*

dō, dăre, dedī, datus, *I give, render.*

facilis, e, *easy.*

intellegō, ere, lēxī, lēctus, *I know, understand.*

jūs, jūris, n., *right, power.*

opera, ae, f., *assistance.*

patior, ī, passus sum, *I suffer.*

utinam, affirmative particle.

vincō, ere, vīcī, victus, *I conquer.*

EXERCISES.

309. 1. Haec suspiciō āvertātur ! 2. Utinam pater meus haec intellegeret ! 3. Utinam hanc aestātem in hīs operibus nē consūmpsissēmus ! 4. Illī nē vincant. 5. Nēmō haec supplicia patiātur. 6. Hōc facilius videātur. 7. Auxilium ā tē nōn postulem. 8. Vestrō ducī, mīlitēs, operam date. 9. Cōnsulēs summum jūs habentō. 10. Hī lēgātī laetī discēdant.

310. 1. Would that we had better defended the lives and fortunes of our fellow-citizens ! 2. May our country not suffer any harm ! 3. Would that these soldiers were braver ! 4. Would we had not abandoned our duty ! 5. What would seem better? 6. I should scarcely believe this. 7. Defend, fellow-citizens, the common safety.

CHAPTER L.

Clauses of Purpose.

311. 1. Clauses of Purpose are introduced most commonly by **ut (utī), quŏ** (*that, in order that*), **nĕ** (*in order that not, lest*), and stand in the Subjunctive ; as, —

> **edimus, ut vīvāmus,** *we eat that we may live.*
> **adjūtā mĕ quŏ hŏc fīat facilius,** *help me, in order that this may be done more easily.*
> **portās clausit, nĕ quam oppidānī injūriam acciperent,** *he closed the gates, lest the townspeople should receive any injury.*

> *a*) **Quŏ,** as a rule, is employed only when the purpose clause contains a comparative.

2. A Relative Pronoun (**quī**) or Adverb (**ubi, unde, quŏ**) is frequently used to introduce a Purpose Clause ; as, —

> **Helvĕtiī lĕgātŏs mittunt quī dīcerent,** *the Helvetii sent envoys to say* (lit. *who should say*).

Sequence of Tenses.

312. 1. In all dependent clauses, the tenses of the Subjunctive usually conform to the so-called 'Sequence of Tenses.' By the Sequence of Tenses, Principal Tenses of the Indicative are followed by Principal Tenses of the Subjunctive, Historical by Historical.

2. The Principal Tenses of the Indicative are: Present, Future, Present Perfect, Future Perfect.

The Historical Tenses are: Imperfect, Historical Perfect, Pluperfect.

3. In the Subjunctive the Present and Perfect are Principal tenses, the Imperfect and Pluperfect, Historical,

EXAMPLES OF SEQUENCE.

PRINCIPAL SEQUENCE, —

   video quid faciās, *I see what you are doing.*

   vidēbō quid faciās, *I shall see what you are doing.*

   vīderō quid faciās, *I shall have seen what you are doing.*

   video quid fēceris, *I see what you have done.*

   vidēbō quid fēceris, *I shall see what you have done.* ·

   vīderō quid fēceris, *I shall have seen what you have done.*

HISTORICAL SEQUENCE, —

   vidēbam quid facerēs, *I saw what you were doing.*

   vīdī quid facerēs, *I saw what you were doing.*

   vīderam quid facerēs, *I had seen what you were doing.*

   vidēbam quid fēcissēs, *I saw what you had done.*

   vīdī quid fēcissēs, *I saw what you had done.*

   vīderam quid fēcissēs, *I had seen what you had done.*

4. The Present and Imperfect Subjunctive denote incomplete action, the Perfect and Pluperfect completed action.

313.   VOCABULARY.

Aquītānia, ae, f., *Aquitania*, a district of Gaul.

conjungō, ere, jūnxī, jūnctus, *I unite.*

Crassus, ī, m., *Crassus*, a man's name.

exsistō, ere, exstitī, *I arise.*

mōtus, ūs, m., *revolt.*

nē, *lest, that* . . . *not.*

quō, *in order that.*

remaneō, ēre, mānsī, mānsūrus, *I remain.*

ut, *that, in order that.*

EXERCISES.

314. 1. Crassus in Aquītāniam proficīscitur, nē tantae nātiōnēs conjungantur.   2. Locum castrīs idōneum dēlēgit nē commeātū prohibērētur.   3. Caesar cum equitātū proficīscitur nē quis[1] mōtus exsistat.   4. Nōnnūllī remanēbant ut suspīciōnem timōris vītārent.   5. Quō iter expedītius faceret, impedīmenta relīquit. 6. Lēgātōs mīsit quī haec nūntiārent.   7. Castra in locīs superiōribus posuit nē quis[1] ea oppūgnāret.

---

[1] In Latin we regularly find nē quis = *in order that no* (*one*); nē ūllus = *in order that no*, etc.

315. 1. We did these (things) that we might be free.   2. We do these (things) that we may be free.   3. Caesar chose men to fortify the camp.   4. We put Galba in charge of the captives in order that none[1] should flee.   5. We fortified the camp with a trench in order that we might more easily defend it.   6. Caesar joined battle, in order that greater armies might not assemble.

CHAPTER LI.

CLAUSES OF CHARACTERISTIC.—RESULT CLAUSES.—CAUSAL CLAUSES.

Clauses of Characteristic.

316. 1. A relative clause used *to express some quality or characteristic of an indefinite or general antecedent* is called a Clause of Characteristic, and stands in the Subjunctive; as,—

> **multa sunt, quae mentem acuant,** *there are many things which sharpen the wits.*

2. Clauses of Characteristic are used especially after such expressions as, **est quī; sunt quī; nēmō est quī; ūnus est quī; quis est quī;** *etc.* Thus:—

> **sunt quī dīcant,** *there are (some) who say;*
> **nēmō est quī putet,** *there is nobody who thinks.*

Result Clauses.

317. Clauses of Result are usually introduced by **ut** (*that, so that*), negative **ut nōn** (*so that not*), and take the Subjunctive. Thus:—

> **mōns altissimus impendēbat, ut perpaucī prohibēre possent,** *a very high mountain overhung, so that a very few could stop them.*

---

[1] Translate: 'lest any.'

Causal Clauses.

318. Causal Clauses are introduced chiefly by the following particles: 1. **quod, quia, quoniam**; 2. **cum**.

319. The use of moods is as follows:—

1. **Quod, quia, quoniam** take the Indicative when the reason is *that of the writer or speaker;* they take the Subjunctive when the reason is viewed *as that of another.* Thus:—

> **Parthōs timeō quod diffīdō cōpiīs nostrīs,** *I fear the Parthians, because I distrust our troops.*
> **Sōcratēs accūsātus est quod corrumperet juventūtem,** *Socrates was arraigned on the ground that he was corrupting the young.* (Here the reason is not that of the writer but of the accuser. Hence the Subjunctive.)

2. **Cum** causal regularly takes the Subjunctive; as,—

> **quae cum ita sint,** *since this is so.*

320. VOCABULARY.

accidit, ere, accidit, *it happens.*
appropinquō, 1, *I approach.*
barbarus, a, um, *barbarous.*
commūtātiō, ōnis, f., *change.*
cōnsistō, ere, cōnstitī, *I consist.*
cum, *because, since.*
dēspiciō, ere, exī, ectus, *I despise.*
jūrō, 1, *I swear, take oath.*
obsideō, ēre, sēdī, sessus, *I blockade.*

paucitās, ātis, f., *fewness, small number.*
quod, *because.*
quoniam, *inasmuch as,* conj.
renovō, 1, *I renew.*
sciō, scīre, scīvī, scītus, *I know.*
sublevō, 1, *I relieve.*
tam, *so* (of degree).
ūnus, a, um, *alone.*

EXERCISES.

321. 1. Nēmō erat quī nōn jūrāret.   2. Multī sunt quī haec sciant.   3. Nūlla via erat quae nōn obsidērētur.   4. Caesaris adventū tanta commūtātiō rērum facta est ut nostrī proelium renovārent.   5. Nōn tam barbarus sum, ut haec nōn sciam.

6. Caesar Gallōs accūsat quod ab eīs nōn sublevētur.　7. Hōc acciderat quod Gallī legiōnem nostram propter paucitātem dēspiciēbant.　8. Quoniam Germānī appropinquant, castra movēbimus.　9. Hostēs ācriter pūgnāvērunt, cum in ūnā virtūte omnis spēs salūtis cōnsisteret.

322. 1. Who is there that[1] says these (things)?　2. These soldiers were so brave that they feared no one.　3. The enemy were so terrified that they fled into the forests.　4. This place was such that our (men) could easily defend it.　5. Inasmuch as these (things) are so, we shall remain in this place.　6. Because no one else was present, he accused us.　7. He accused you because (= on the ground that) you did not resist the enemy.

---

[1] Observe that this is the relative *that.*

CHAPTER LII.

TEMPORAL CLAUSES.

Temporal Clauses introduced by *Postquam, Ut, Ubi, Simul Ac, etc.*

323. 1. **Postquam,** *after;* ut, ubi, *when;* simul ac (simul atque), *as soon as,* when used to refer *to a single past occurrence,* regularly take the Perfect Indicative; as, —

> **Epamīnōndās postquam audīvit vīcisse Boeōtiōs, 'Satis' inquit 'vīxī,'** *Epaminondas, after he heard that the Boeotians had conquered, said, 'I have lived enough.'*

2. In English we often use the Pluperfect after the corresponding particles, but the Latin holds regularly to the Perfect.

Temporal Clauses introduced by *Cum.*

A. Cum REFERRING TO THE PAST.

324. **Cum,** when referring to the past, takes —

A. The Indicative (Imperfect, Historical Perfect, or Pluperfect) to denote *the point of time at which* something occurs.

B. The Subjunctive (Imperfect or Pluperfect) to denote *the situation or circumstances under which* something occurs.

Examples: —

INDICATIVE.

> **erās cōnsul, cum mea domus ārdēbat,** *you were consul at the time when my house burned up.*

SUBJUNCTIVE.

> **cum hōc dīxisset, omnēs abiērunt,** *when he had said this, all went away.*

135

325. When **cum** refers to the Present or Future, it regularly takes the Indicative ; as, —

> tum tua rēs agitur, pariēs cum proximus ārdet, *your own interests are at stake when your neighbor's house is burning.*

326. VOCABULARY.

animadvertō, ere, vertī, versus, *I notice.*

cognōscō, ere, nōvī, nitus, *I learn, become acquainted with.*

comperiō, īre, perī, pertus, *I find out.*

cum, *when,* conj.

ēiciō, ere, ējēcī, ējectus, *I thrust out* ; sē ēicere, *rush forth.*

exeō, īre, iī, exitūrus, *I go out, go forth.*

factiō, ōnis, f., *faction.*

postquam, *after,* conj.

quaerō, ere, quaesīvī, quaesītus, *I inquire.*

simul ac (atque), *as soon as.*

subdūcō, ere, dūxī, ductus, *I withdraw.*

ubi, *when.*

EXERCISES.

327. 1. Postquam id animadvertit, Caesar cōpiās suās in collem proximum subdūxit. 2. Caesar ubi id comperit, sē in Galliam recēpit. 3. Simul ac tē vīdī, hōc sēnsī. 4. Cum Caesar in Galliam vēnit, duae factiōnēs erant. 5. Caesar cum ex captīvīs quaereret, hanc causam reperiēbat. 6. Cum ad id oppidum accessisset, puerī mulierēsque pācem petīvērunt. 7. Ut equitātus noster sē in agrōs ējēcit, hostēs ex silvīs exībant. 8. Cum veniēs, cognōscēs.

328. 1. After Caesar had made the bridge, he marched into Germany. 2. When he had heard these (things), he went away. 3. As soon as I saw you, I entreated your help. 4. On that day when you spoke in the senate, very many were present. 5. When the Gauls had seen our (men), they fled into the forests.

CHAPTER LIII.

Clauses introduced by *Antequam* and *Priusquam*.

A. With the Indicative.

329. **Antequam** and **priusquam** (often written **ante . . . quam, prius . . . quam**) take the Indicative to denote *an actual fact.*

1. Sometimes the Present or Future Perfect; as, —

   prius respondēs quam rogō, *you answer before I ask.*
   nihil contrā disputābō priusquam dīxerit, *I will say nothing in opposition, before he speaks.*

2. Sometimes the Perfect, especially after negative clauses; as, —

   nōn prius jugulandī fīnis fuit, quam Sulla omnēs suōs dīvitiīs explēvit, *there was no end of murder until Sulla satisfied all his henchmen with wealth.*

B. With the Subjunctive.

330. **Antequam** and **priusquam** take the Subjunctive to denote an act as *anticipated.*

   priusquam tēlum adicī posset, omnis aciēs terga vertit, *before a spear could be hurled, the whole army fled.*

Clauses introduced by *Dum, Dōnec, Quoad.*

331. I. **Dum,** *while,* regularly takes the Present Indicative with the force of an Imperfect; as, —

   Alexander, dum inter prīmōrēs pūgnat, sagittā ictus est, *Alexander, while he was fighting in the van, was struck by an arrow.*

II. **Dum, dōnec,** and **quoad,** *as long as,* take the Indicative; as, —

   dum anima est, spēs est, *as long as there is life there is hope.*

III. **Dum, dōnec,** and **quoad,** *until,* take —

1. The Indicative, to denote *an actual event;* as, —

dōnec rediit, fuit silentium, *there was silence till he came.*

2. The Subjunctive, to denote *anticipation* or *expectancy;* as, —

exspectāvit Caesar dum nāvēs convenīrent, *Caesar waited for the ships to assemble.*

332. VOCABULARY.

adversārius, iī, m., *adversary.*
agō, ere, ēgī, āctus, *I do.*
antequam, *before.*
commūniō, īre, īvī (iī), ītus, *strongly fortify.*
Domitius, ī (iī), m., *Domitius, a man's name.*
dōneo, *until.*

dum, *while; as long as ; until.*
magistrātus, ūs, m., *magistrate.*
Massilia, ae, f., *Marseilles.*
perficiō, ere, fēcī, fectus, *I accomplish.*
priusquam, *before.*
silentium, ī (iī), n., *silence.*
tamen, *nevertheless, yet.*

EXERCISES.

333. 1. Hunc collem occupat priusquam ab adversāriīs sentiātur. 2. Antequam haec perficerem, abiit. 3. Antequam ad causam redeō, dē mē pauca dīcam. 4. Nōn prius fugā dēstitērunt quam ad Rhēnum pervēnērunt. 5. Dum haec inter eōs aguntur, Domitius Massiliam pervēnit. 6. Huic magistrātuī restitī, dum potuī. 7. Dōnec rediit, fuit tamen silentium. 8. Caesar exspectāvit dum haec mandāta ad hostēs perferrentur.

334. 1. Before he set out for[1] Britain, Caesar fitted his ships out with all things. 2. We did not set out, before we informed you of our plan. 3. Before I set out, I shall inform the senate of my plans. 4. While the troops were assembling, Caesar consulted with the tribunes. 5. As long as Caesar was in Gaul, he was waging war. 6. We waited six days till you should come.

---

[1] *I.e. into.*

CHAPTER LIV.

SUBSTANTIVE CLAUSES.

335. A Substantive Clause is one which as a whole serves as the Subject or Object of a verb, or denotes some other case relation.

Substantive Clauses developed from the Jussive.

336. These are generally used as object-clauses, and occur especially with the following classes of verbs : —

1. With verbs signifying *to admonish, request, command* (conjunctions ut, nē) ; as, —

> postulō ut fīat, *I demand that it be done* (dependent form of the Jussive fīat, *let it be done !*) ;
> ōrat, nē abeās, *he begs that you will not go away.*
>
> > Jubeō, *command, order,* regularly takes the Infinitive.

2. With verbs signifying *to grant, concede* (conjunction ut) ; as, —

> huic concēdō ut ea praetereat, *I allow him to pass that by* (dependent form of the Jussive ea praetereat, *let him pass that by*).

3. With verbs of *deciding, resolving, etc.* (conjunctions ut, nē) ; as, —

> dēcrēvit senātus ut Opīmius vidēret, *the senate decreed that Opimius should see to it* (dependent form after an historical tense of the Jussive, Opīmius videat, *let Opimius see*).

Substantive Clauses after Verbs of *hindering.*

337. These are introduced by nē, quōminus, or quīn ; as, —

> nē lūstrum perficeret, mors prohibuit, *death prevented him from finishing the lustrum.*
> prohibuit quōminus in ūnum coīrent, *he prevented them from coming together.*

338.   VOCABULARY.

Bōjī, ōrum, *Boji*, an ancient tribe.

concēdō, ere, cessī, cessūrus, *I grant.*

dēcernō, ere, crēvī, crētus, *I decree.*

imperō, 1, *I command.*

itaque, *accordingly.*

omnīnō, *at all* (with negatives).

permittō, ere, mīsī, missus, *I permit.*

praecipiō, ere, cēpī, ceptus, *I enjoin.*

quōminus, *from* (with verbs of hindering).

reddō, ere, reddidī, redditus, *I return, give back.*

rēiciō, ere, rējēcī, rējectus, *I hurl back.*

restituō, ere, uī, ūtus, *I restore.*

sequor, I, secūtus sum, *I seek.*

trānsportō, 1, *I set across.*

EXERCISES.

339. 1. Equitibus imperat ut hostibus terrōrem īnferant. 2. Itaque Caesar suīs praecēpit nē quod omnīnō tēlum in hostēs rēicerent.   3. Hās cīvitātēs hortātur, ut populī Rōmānī fidem sequantur.   4. Haeduīs concessit ut Bōjōs in fīnibus suīs collocārent.   5. Sēquanīs permīsit ut hōs obsidēs redderent. 6. Dēcrēvimus ut hae legiōnēs Rhēnum trānsportārentur.   7. Eōs prohibuī nē excēderent.   8. Mē prohibuit quōminus haec restituerem.

340. 1. I commanded the soldiers[1] to attack this town. 2. Caesar commands the soldiers[1] to attack this town.   3. He commands them[1] not to cross the river.   4. Ariovistus permitted his cavalry[1] to ravage the fields of the Gauls.   5. The senate decreed that the soldiers should march forth.   6. We hindered the enemy from crossing this river.

---

[1] Use the Dative.

CHAPTER LV.

Substantive Clauses developed from the Optative.

341. Here belong clauses : —

1. With verbs of *wishing, desiring*, especially **optō, volō, mālō** (conjunctions **ut, nē**) ; as, —

> **optō ut in hōc jūdiciō nēmō improbus reperiātur,** *I hope that in this court no bad man may be found* (here **ut reperiātur** represents a simple optative of direct statement, *viz.* **nēmō improbus reperiātur,** *may no bad man be found!*).

2. With verbs of *fearing* (**timeō, metuō, vereor**). Here **nē** means *that, lest,* and **ut** means *that not* ; as, —

> **timeō nē veniat,** *I fear that he will come* (originally : *may he not come! I'm afraid [he will]*);
> **timeō ut veniat,** *I fear that he will not come* (originally : *may he come! I'm afraid [he won't]*).

Substantive Clauses of Result.

342. Substantive Clauses of Result (introduced by **ut, ut nōn**) are a development of pure Result clauses, and occur with the following classes of words : —

1. As object clauses after verbs of *doing, accomplishing*. Thus : —

> **gravitās morbī facit ut medicīnā egeāmus,** *the severity of disease makes us need medicine* (lit. *makes that we need*).

2. As the subject of several impersonal verbs ; for example, **fit,** *it happens,* **efficitur, accidit,** *etc.* Thus : —

> **ex quō efficitur, ut voluptās nōn sit summum bonum,** *from which it follows that pleasure is not the greatest good.*

Indirect Questions.

343. Indirect Questions are Substantive Clauses used after verbs of *asking, inquiring, telling,* and the like. They

take their verb in the Subjunctive. Like Direct Questions
(see § 203) they may be introduced —

   a) By Interrogative Pronouns or Adverbs; as, —

      dīc mihi ubi fueris, quid fēceris, *tell me where you were, what
you did.*

   b) By num or -ne, without distinction of meaning; as, —

      Epamīnōndās quaesīvit num salvus esset clipeus, or **sal-
vusne esset clipeus,** *Epaminondas asked whether his shield
was safe.*

344.   **VOCABULARY.**

contrōversia, ae, f., *controversy.*

ēdūcō, ere, dūxī, ductus, *I lead
forth.*

ita, *so* (of manner).

lēgātiō, ōnis, f., *embassy.*

lūna, ae, f., *moon.*

optō, 1, *I desire.*

ōrātiō, ōnis, f., *speech.*

plēbs, is, f., *common people.*

praetereā, *besides.*

prīmō, *first, firstly.*

rescindō, ere, scidī, scissus, *I
tear down.*

sīc, *so* (of manner).

tergum, I, n., *back.*

vertō, ere, vertī, versus, *I turn;*

terga vertere, *flee.*

EXERCISES.

345. 1. Optō ut haec ōrātiō plēbī placeat.   2. Optāmus nē
ūllās contrōversiās habeāmus.   3. Praetereā verēbātur nē hostēs
pontem rescinderent.   4. Veritus sum ut legiōnēs ex castrīs
ēdūcerentur.   5. Ita factum est ut hostēs statim terga verterent.
6. Sīc effēcit ut rēgem in potestāte suā habēret.   7. Eādem
nocte accidit ut lūna plēna esset.   8. Ab hīs quaesīvit quae et
quantae cīvitātēs in armīs essent.   9. Prīmō ā tē quaerō hūjusne
lēgātiōnis prīnceps sīs.

346. 1. I fear that our (men) will flee.   2. Caesar feared
that his (men) would flee.   3. We fear that the soldiers will
not withstand the onset of the barbarians.   4. We desire that
we may be free.   5. It happened that ships were lacking.
6. We brought it about that you were informed of these things.
7. I asked the envoys what they wished. .   8. I asked them
whether the Germans had crossed the Rhine.

CHAPTER LVI.

CONDITIONAL SENTENCES. — CLAUSES WITH *quamvīs* AND *quamquam*.

347. Conditional Sentences are compound sentences consisting of two parts, the Protasis (or *condition*), usually introduced by **sī, nisi**, or **sīn**, and the Apodosis (or *conclusion*). We distinguish the following types of Conditional Sentences : —

First Type. — Nothing Implied as to the Reality of the Supposed Case.

348. Here we regularly have the Indicative in both Protasis and Apodosis. Any tense may be used ; as, —

> **sī hōc crēdis, errās,** *if you believe this, you are mistaken ;*
> **nātūram sī sequēmur, numquam aberrābimus,** *if we follow Nature, we shall never go astray ;*
> **sī hōc dīxistī, errāvistī,** *if you said this, you were in error.*

Second Type. — 'Should' . . . 'would' Type.

349. Here we regularly have the Subjunctive (of the Present or Perfect tense) in both Protasis and Apodosis ; as, —

> **sī hōc dīcās, errēs,**   } *if you should say this, you would*
> **sī hōc dīxeris, errāveris,** }   *be mistaken.*

Third Type. — Supposed Case represented as Contrary to Fact.

350. Here we regularly have the Subjunctive in both Protasis and Apodosis, the Imperfect referring *to present time*, and the Pluperfect referring *to past* ; as, —

> **sī amīcī meī adessent, opis nōn indigērem,** *if my friends were here, I should not lack assistance.*
> **sī hōc dīxissēs, errāvissēs,** *if you had said this, you would have erred.*

Clauses with *quamvīs, quamquam*, etc., '*although.*'

351. 1. **Quamvīs**, *however much, although,* does not introduce a statement of fact, but represents an act merely as conceived. It is followed by the Subjunctive, usually of the present tense; as, —

> **nōn est potestās opitulandī reī pūblicae quamvīs ea premātur perīculīs,** *there is no opportunity to succor the state, though it be beset by dangers.*

2. **Quamquam, etsī, tametsī,** *although,* introduce a statement of fact, and are followed by the Indicative (of any tense); as, —

> **quamquam festīnās, nōn est mora longa,** *although you are in haste, the delay is not long.*

3. **Cum,** *although,* is followed by the Subjunctive; as, —

> **mē nōn adjūvit, cum posset,** *he did not help me, though he was able.*

352.   VOCABULARY.

animus, ī, m., *soul, heart.*
Atticus, ī, m., *Atticus,* the friend of Cicero.
cum, *though.*
honor, ōris, m., *honor.*
immortālis, e, *immortal.*
incertus, a, um, *uncertain.*
līber, era, erum, *free.*
mandō, ī, *I assign.*
mors, mortis, f., *death.*
nisi, *unless.*

opprimō, ere, pressī, pressus, *I overwhelm.*
pateō, ēre, patuī, *lie open.*
prōvideō, ēre, vīdī, vīsus, *I provide, take care.*
quamquam, *although.*
quamvīs, *though, although.*
valeō, ēre, uī, itūrus, *avail, prevail.*
vīs, vis, f., *violence*; plu. **vīrēs, ium,** *strength.*

EXERCISES.

353. 1. Mors nōn est timenda, sī animus immortālis est. 2. Sī vim facere cōnābiminī, vōs prohibēbō. 3. Sī ille nōbīs hōc negōtium mandet, quid respondeās? 4. Sī auctōritās mea valuisset, nōs nunc līberī essēmus. 5. Rēs pūblica oppressa esset, nisi cōnsul prōvīdisset. 6. Sī haec cōnsilia probārēs, laetus essem. 7. Atticus honōrēs nōn petiit, cum eī patērent. 8. Rōmānī, quamquam vulneribus cōnfectī erant, impetum hostium sustinēbant. 9. Quamvīs victōria incerta sit, ducem nē dēserāmus.

354. 1. If the soldiers are of good heart,[1] there is hope of victory. 2. If you come[2] to Rome, you will see me. 3. If you should come to Rome, you would see us. 4. If you had told me this, I should not have set out. 5. If our fleet were at hand, we should wish nothing else. 6. Although boats were lacking, Caesar decided to cross the Rhine. 7. Though no one should come, I shall remain.

CHAPTER LVII.

INDIRECT DISCOURSE (*Ōrātiō Oblīqua*).

355. When the language or thought of any person is quoted without change, that is called Direct Discourse (*Ōrātiō Rēcta*); as, —

Caesar said, 'The die is cast.'

When, on the other hand, one's language or thought is made to depend upon a verb of *saying, thinking, etc.*, that is called Indirect Discourse (*Ōrātiō Oblīqua*); as, —

Caesar said that the die was cast;
Caesar thought that his troops were victorious.

Moods in Indirect Discourse.

356. Declaratory Sentences upon becoming Indirect change their main clause to the Infinitive with Subject Accusative, while all subordinate clauses take the Subjunctive; as, —

Rēgulus dīxit,[3] **quam diū jūre jūrandō hostium tenērētur, nōn esse sē senātōrem,** *Regulus said that as long as he was held by his pledge to the enemy he was not a senator.* (Direct: **quam diū teneor, nōn sum senātor.**)

---

[1] § 267.

[2] Observe that *come* really equals *shall come.* Hence the future must be used. In conditional sentences the English present often has the force of the future, and must be so rendered in Latin.

[3] The verb of *saying, etc.*, regularly precedes the Indirect Discourse.

Tenses in Indirect Discourse.

A. Tenses of the Infinitive.

357. The tenses of the Infinitive denote time not absolutely, but *with reference to the verb on which they depend.* Thus : —

a) The Present Infinitive represents an act as *contemporaneous with* the time of the verb on which it depends; as, —

> dīcit sē facere, *he says he is doing;*
> dīxit sē facere, *he said he was doing.*

b) The Perfect Infinitive represents an act as *prior to* the time of the verb on which it depends; as, —

> dīcit sē fēcisse, *he says he has done;*
> dīxit sē fēcisse, *he said he had done.*

c) The Future Infinitive represents an act as *subsequent to* that of the verb on which it depends; as, —

> dīcit sē factūrum esse, *he says he will do;*
> dīxit sē factūrum esse, *he said he would do.*

B. Tenses of the Subjunctive.

358. These follow the regular principle for the Sequence of Tenses, being Principal, if the verb of *saying* is Principal; Historical, if it is Historical; as, —

> dīcit sē lēgātōs vidēre, quī vēnerint, *he says he sees the envoys who have come;*
> dīxit sē lēgātōs vidēre, quī vēnissent, *he said he saw the envoys who had come.*

359.   VOCABULARY.

adveniō, īre, vēnī, ventum, *I arrive.*

arbitror, ārī, ātus sum, *I consider.*

exīstimō, 1, *I think.*

incolō, ere, uī, cultus, *I inhabit.*

Inferior, us, *inferior* (§ 74, 2).

Infīrmus, a, um, *weak.*

modo, *just, just now.*

neque (nec), *nor.*

onerārius, a, um, *burden-bearing;* nāvēs onerāriae, *transports.*

pellō, ere, pepulī, pulsus, *rout, defeat.*

posterus, a, um, *following* (§ 74, 2).

putō, 1, *I think.*

EXERCISES.

360. 1. Existimō hās legiōnēs, quae modo advēnerint, īnfīrmās esse. 2. Neque arbitror hostēs sine injūriā trānsitūrōs esse. 3. Intellegimus māximās nātiōnēs ā Caesare pulsās esse. 4. Caesar intellēxit cōpiās quās habēret nōn esse īnferiōrēs. 5. Num putāvistis eōs quī hōs agrōs incolerent discessūrōs esse? 6. Posterō diē Caesar certior factus est nāvēs onerāriās, quās coēgisset, captās esse. 7. Nūntius dīxit montem, quem Caesar occupārī voluisset, ab hostibus tenērī.

361. 1. It is reported that the Gauls are fortifying the hill which they have seized. 2. It is reported that the Gauls will fortify the hill which they have seized. 3. It is reported that the Gauls have fortified the hill which they have seized. 4. It was reported that the Gauls were fortifying the hill which they had seized. 5. It was reported that the Gauls would fortify the hill which they had seized. 6. It was reported that the Gauls had fortified the hill which they had seized.

CHAPTER LVIII.

THE INFINITIVE.

Infinitive without Subject Accusative.

362. This may be used either as Subject or Object.

A. *As Subject.*

363. The Infinitive without Subject Accusative is used as the Subject of **esse** and various impersonal verbs, particularly **opus est, necesse est, oportet, licet, pudet,** *etc.*; as, —

> **dulce et decōrum est prō patriā morī,** *it is sweet and noble to die for one's country.*

B. *As Object.*

364. 1. The Infinitive without Subject Accusative is used as the Object of many verbs, to denote another action of the same subject, particularly after —

volō, cupiō, mālō, nōlō;	**cōgitō, meditor,** *purpose, intend;*
dēbeō, *ought;*	**audeō,** *dare;*
statuō, cōnstituō, *decide;*	**vereor, timeō,** *fear;*

and many others.

2. A predicate Noun or Adjective with these Infinitives is attracted into the Nominative; as, —

> **beātus esse sine virtūte nēmō potest,** *no one can be happy without virtue.*

Infinitive with Subject Accusative.

365. This may be used either as Subject or Object.

A. *As Subject.*

366. The Infinitive with Subject Accusative (like the simple Infinitive) appears as Subject with **esse** and Impersonal verbs, particularly with **ūtile est, oportet, cōnstat,** *etc.*; as, —

> **nihil in bellō oportet contemnī,** *nothing ought to be despised in war* (lit. *nothing to be despised, is fitting*).

B. *As Object.*

367. The Infinitive with Subject Accusative is used as Object after the following classes of verbs : —

I. Most frequently after verbs of *saying, thinking, knowing, perceiving,* and the like. This is the regular construction of Principal Clauses of Indirect Discourse, and has received full illustration in the preceding chapter (LVII).

II. With **jubeō,** *order,* and **vetō,** *forbid;* as, —

> **Caesar mīlitēs pontem facere jussit,** *Caesar ordered the soldiers to make a bridge.*

Historical Infinitive.

368. The Infinitive is often used in historical narrative instead of the Imperfect Indicative. The Subject stands in the Nominative; as, —

> **interim cottīdiē Caesar Haeduōs frūmentum flāgitāre,** *meanwhile Caesar was daily demanding grain of the Haedui.*

369.   VOCABULARY.

comparō, 1, *I get ready.*

cōnstat, stāre, stitit, *it is evident.*

dispōnō, ere, posuī, positus, *I distribute.*

jubeō, ēre, jussī, jussus, *I order.*

lapis, idis, m., *stone.*

licet, ēre, licuit, *it is permitted.*

nancīscor, ī, nactus sum, *I procure.*

necesse est, *it is necessary.*

oportet, *it behooves; it is fitting.*

opus est, *it is necessary.*

ōrdō, inis, m., *rank.*

servō, 1, *I preserve.*

statuō, ere, uī, ūtus, *decide.*

EXERCISES.

370. 1. Opus est cōpiam frūmentī nancīscī.   2. Necesse est castra vāllō mūnīre.   3. Nōn licet in urbem revertī.   4. Gallia lībera esse dēbet.   5. Statuī praesidia dispōnere.   6. Cōnstat māgnum numerum barbarōrum ad castra vēnisse.   7. Hōs vīcōs incendī oportet.   8. Caesar mīlitēs jussit ōrdinēs servāre. 9. Jussit nāvēs comparārī.   10. Hostēs ex omnibus partibus lapidēs in vāllum conicere.   11. Hae legiōnēs ex hībernīs ēgredī nōn ausae sunt.

371. 1. It was necessary to do many (things) at the same time. 2. It is necessary to be brave in battle. 3. We wish to be brave. 4. Endeavor to be good. 5. It behooves us to set out at once. 6. It is necessary (for) us to fortify this camp. 7. It behooves us to be brave. 8. I ordered you to summon the tribunes. 9. We ordered the messengers to be dismissed.

CHAPTER LIX.

PARTICIPLES.

372. 1. TENSES OF THE PARTICIPLE. The tenses of the Participle, like those of the Infinitive, express time not absolutely, but with reference to the verb upon which the Participle depends.

2. The Present Participle denotes action *contemporary with* that of the verb. Thus: —

> **audiō tē loquentem** = *you* ARE *speaking, and I hear you;*
> **audiēbam tē loquentem** = *you* WERE *speaking, and I heard you;*
> **audiam tē loquentem** = *you* WILL BE *speaking, and I shall hear you.*

3. The Perfect Passive Participle denotes action *prior to* that of the verb. Thus: —

> **locūtus taceō** = *I* HAVE *spoken and am silent;*
> **locūtus tacuī** = *I had spoken and then was silent;*
> **locūtus tacēbō** = *I shall speak and then shall be silent.*

a. The Future Participle, as a rule, is not used except in the Active Periphrastic Conjugation.

4. The **absolute** time of the action of a participle, therefore, is determined entirely by the finite verb with which it is connected.

5. Participles are often equivalent to an English subordinate clause, relative, temporal, causal, conditional, *etc.*; as, —

> **omne malum nāscēns facile opprimitur,** *every evil is easily crushed at birth;*
> **mente ūtī nōn possumus cibō et pōtiōne complētī,** *if gorged with food and drink, we cannot use our intellects.*

6. Often, too, the participle is equivalent to a coördinate clause; as, —

Ahāla Maelium occupātum interēmit, *Ahala surprised and killed Maelius* (lit. *killed Maelius having been surprised*).

373.   VOCABULARY.

Ardea, ae, f., *Ardea,* a Latin town.
cāsus, ūs, m., *chance, hazard.*
cernō, ere, *I perceive.*
Conōn, ōnis, m., *Conon,* a Greek general.
cōnspiciō, ere, spexī, spectus, *I see.*
dīruō, ere, uī, tus, *I tear down.*
experior, īrī, pertus sum, *I try, test.*
labōrō, 1, *I toil;* in battle, *be hard pressed.*

Lysander, drī, m., *Lysander,* a Spartan commander.
mūrus, ī, m., *wall.*
oculus, ī, m., *eye.*
perdō, ere, didī, ditus, *I lose.*
persequor, ī, secūtus sum, *I follow up.*
reficiō, ere, fēcī, fectus, *I rebuild.*
submittō, ere, mīsī, missus, *I send, dispatch.*
Tarquinius, ī (iī), m., *Tarquin,* a Roman king.
tueor, ērī, *I guard, watch.*

EXERCISES.

374. 1. Eīs quōs labōrantēs cōnspexit subsidium submīsit. 2. Conōn mūrōs ā Lysandrō dīrutōs refēcit. 3. Tarquinius Ardeam oppūgnāns rēgnum perdidit. 4. Virtūtem vestram multīs proeliīs expertus vōs nunc ad aliōs cāsūs vocō. 5. Oculus sē nōn vidēns alia cernit. 6. Caesar hōs pulsōs persequitur. 7. Turrim mīlitibus tuendam trādidit. 8. Mīlitēs jam vulneribus cōnfectōs bonō animō esse jubet. 9. Nostrī hostīs ex castrīs ēgredientēs adortī sunt.

375. 1. This soldier was killed (while) fighting in the first line of battle. 2. (Though) exhausted with many wounds, we did not abandon our leader. 3. When he had been summoned he came at once. 4. We put to flight the cavalry (who had been) driven back. 5. Caesar left these captives to be guarded.

CHAPTER LX.

GERUND AND GERUNDIVE. — SUPINE.

376. Of the four cases in which the Gerund occurs, only the Genitive, Accusative, and Ablative are in common use.

1. The Genitive admits the same constructions as nouns; as, —

   cupidus audiendī, *desirous of hearing.*

2. The Accusative occurs only with prepositions; as, —

   ad agendum nātus, *born for action.*

3. The Ablative is used both alone and with prepositions; as, —

   mēns discendō alitur, *the mind is fed by learning.*

4. As a rule, only the Genitive of the Gerund and the Ablative (without a preposition) admit a Direct Object.

Gerundive Construction instead of the Gerund.

377. 1. Instead of the Genitive or Ablative of the Gerund with a Direct Object, another construction *may be, and very often is, used.* This consists in putting the Direct Object in the case of the Gerund (Gen. or Abl.) and using the Gerundive in agreement with it. This is called the Gerundive Construction. Thus: —

GERUND CONSTRUCTION.	GERUNDIVE CONSTRUCTION.
cupidus urbem videndī, *desirous of seeing the city;*	**cupidus urbis videndae;**
dēlector ōrātōrēs legendō, *I am charmed with reading the orators.*	**dēlector ōrātōribus legendīs.**

2. The Gerundive Construction *must also be used* to avoid a Direct Object with the Dative of the Gerund, or with a case dependent upon a Preposition; as, —

   locus castrīs mūniendīs aptus, *a place adapted to fortifying a camp;*

   ad pācem petendam vēnērunt, *they came to ask peace.*

3. The commonest use of the Gerundive Construction is with **ad** to denote purpose, as in the second of the two preceding examples.

The Supine.

378. 1. The Supine in -um is used after Verbs of motion to express *purpose*; as, —

> lēgātī ad Caesarem grātulātum convēnērunt, *envoys came to Caesar to congratulate him.*

2. The Supine in -ū is used as an Ablative of Specification with facilis, difficilis, incrēdibilis, jūcundus, optimus, *etc.*; as, —

> haec rēs est facilis cognitū, *this thing is easy to learn.*

379. VOCABULARY.

ad, *for* (denoting purpose), prep. with acc.

administrō, 1, *I perform.*

aliēnus, a, um, *unfavorable.*

causā, abl., *for the sake of*; the dependent genitive precedes.

cōnsector, ārī, ātus sum, *I follow up.*

explōrō, 1, *I examine.*

ōrātor, ōris, m., *orator, envoy.*

praedō, ōnis, m., *robber.*

reddō, ere, reddidī, redditus, *I render.*

spatium, ī (iī), n., *space, time.*

Themistoclēs, is, m., *Themistocles,* an Athenian statesman.

tūtus, a, um, *safe.*

versor, ārī, ātus sum, *be engaged in.*

EXERCISES.

380. 1. Nūlla fuit causa colloquendī. 2. Spatium sūmāmus ad cōgitandum. 3. Themistoclēs maritimōs praedōnēs cōnsectandō mare tūtum reddidit. 4. Caesar in hīs locīs nāvium parandārum causā morātur. 5. Multī rēgēs bellōrum gerendōrum cupidī fuērunt. 6. Tempus ad proelium committendum aliēnum fuit. 7. Ipse antecēdit ad itinera explōranda. 8. In hīs rēbus administrandīs versābātur. 9. Pācem petītum ōrātōrēs mittit. 10. Hōc est optimum factū.

381. 1. (There) was no opportunity of withdrawing. 2. The envoys came for (the purpose of) conferring with Caesar. 3. By saying these (things) he made the soldiers more eager for fighting.

4. For the sake of saving the city we have given much[1] money.
5. He marches out from camp for (the purpose of) attacking this town.   6. No place is easier to approach.[2]   7. We have come to announce this victory.

---

[1] Use **măgnus.**
[2] Use the proper form of **adeŏ.**

ENGLISH–LATIN EXERCISES

ON

CHAPTERS III–XXXIV.

―――――◆―――――

CHAPTER III.*

382. 1. You[1] summon the farmers. 2. We praise Galba's[2] daughter. 3. Galba's daughters encourage the farmers. 4. He praises the troops. 5. The inhabitants of the island accuse Galba. 6. Galba praises the farmers.

[1] Unless it is clear that the Plural is meant, *you* is to be regarded as the sign of the Singular.

[2] *I.e.* the daughter *of Galba*.

CHAPTER IV.

383. 1. Dangers; by danger; of dangers. 2. To a friend; of friends. 3. The towns; of the town. 4. We are farmers. 5. We attack the towns of the Sequani. 6. He is a friend of the farmers. 7. The troops avoid battle. 8. I entreat the help of the Germans. 9. He harasses the Gauls in battle.

CHAPTER V.

384. 1. Of great victories; by a great victory. 2. Many dangers; of many dangers. 3. To the Roman people; of the Roman people. 4. Many islands; many villages; many towns. 5. We get ready many beasts of burden. 6. We praise Galba, the Roman lieutenant. 7. Many Gauls and Germans contend in battle. 8. The beasts of burden are small.

―――――――――――――――――

* The numbers correspond to those in the body of the book.

CHAPTER VI.

385. 1. Of a high rampart; with a high rampart. 2. The great valor of the Roman soldiers. 3. To the father of the consul. 4. Of the cavalry; to the cavalry. 5. We praise Galba the consul. 6. Caesar demands many hostages. 7. The Roman soldiers contend with[1] the Helvetii. 8. The Gauls attack the rampart of the Roman camp.

[1] Unless *with* is equivalent to *by*, it is regularly to be rendered by **cum** in Latin.

CHAPTER VII.

386. 1. High trees; of high towers; in[1] deep rivers. 2. In the River Rhine. 3. The fears of the soldiers. 4. To the enemy; the camp of the enemy. 5. The cavalry of the enemy contend with the Romans. 6. Caesar establishes peace with many states. 7. The rivers are deep. 8. The cavalry of Caesar harass the enemy.

[1] To denote location in a place the Preposition is regularly necessary in Latin. The simple Ablative does not suffice.

CHAPTER VIII.

387. 1. Of the senate; to the senate; concerning the senate. 2. In the harbors of the island; of the harbors. 3. Many hopes. 4. The remaining legions. 5. With the remaining legions Caesar attacks the town. 6. In the harbors are many islands. 7. The senate is in doubt concerning the loyalty of the legions. 8. He announces many things to the senate.

CHAPTER IX.

388. 1. Of the whole cohort; whole cohorts. 2. Of another hill; other hills; on other hills. 3. Of one battle; in one battle. 4. By a cavalry battle; of cavalry battles; in cavalry battles. 5. The soldiers contend without any hope of victory. 6. The legions attack another town. 7. We avoid the dangers of another battle. 8. We are in doubt concerning many other things.

CHAPTER X.

389. 1. In a fertile field; of fertile fields. 2. Of very many young men; with very many young men. 3. Of the common council; with noble envoys; in naval battles. 4. The young man is unharmed. 5. All the fields of the Haedui are fertile. 6. All the envoys of the Gauls entreat Caesar's help. 7. He praises all the tribunes of the legion.

CHAPTER XI.

390. 1. Braver soldiers; of braver soldiers; with the bravest soldiers. 2. The most difficult approaches; by the most difficult approaches; by a more difficult approach. 3. Of the first legion; with the first legion. 4. The larger camp; in the smaller camp. 5. The soldiers of the first legion attack the smaller camp. 6. We avoid the greatest dangers. 7. Galba is the bravest leader. 8. The approaches are most difficult.

CHAPTER XII.

391. 1. More fiercely; most fiercely; most courageously. 2. Most easily. 3. Of three cities, in three battles, two daughters. 4. With three hundred soldiers. 5. Two thousand cavalry. 6. The Belgians fight more bravely than the Sequani. 7. The Romans overcome the Gauls most easily. 8. We contend with three thousand Gauls. 9. Three hundred Romans retard the onset of the Gauls.

CHAPTER XIII.

392. 1. Of us; to you; to himself; to themselves. 2. My father; our father; our fathers. 3. Of your friend; of your friends; to my friends. 4. To this commander; of these commanders;

of these trees.　5.. We call these soldiers to us.　6. With all these legions Caesar attacks the town.　7. No other commander blames his soldiers.　8. My daughter calls me.

CHAPTER XIV.

393.　1. The same causes ; of the same armies ; concerning the same duties.　2. That gate : of those gates ; of those armies.　3. Of the slave himself ; concerning the slaves. themselves.　4. That slave (of yours) ; of those six slaves.　5. I call him ; I call her ; I call them ; I call his[1] father ; I call their[1] father.　6. The leaders of these armies are cowardly.　7. These duties are most difficult.

[1] *I.e.* ' the father of him,' ' the father of them ' ; **suus** cannot be used ; § 87, 1.

CHAPTER. XV.

394.　1. A certain man ; of certain men ; concerning certain things.　2. Any cause you please ; some causes ; some men.　3. What man ? What battle ?　4. Of each army ; concerning each slave.　5. This commander arms certain legions.　6. Booty delights some soldiers.　7. What towns (do)[1] the soldiers attack ?　8. They attack a certain town of the Belgians.

[1] This word is not to be translated.

CHAPTER XVI.

395.　1. We were ; we shall be ; we had been.　2. I have been ; he will have been ; he will be.　3. You have been ; you were ; they will have been.　4. I have not yet been consul.　5. These consuls were cowardly.　6. Where had your father been ?　7. He had been in the camp of the enemy.　8. We have been in many towns of the Gauls.　9. Before this camp was a deep trench.

CHAPTER XVII.

396. 1. Let them be; I should have been; they would have been. 2. To have been; be thou; they shall be. 3. May he be; he would have been. 4. May there be friendship between you and me. 5. May we be happy.' 6. Let this law be brief. 7. I should have been glad. 8. Under another leader the soldiers would have been braver.

CHAPTER XVIII.

397. 1. I have summoned you; I was summoning you. 2. You summoned me; we shall summon you; they had summoned you. 3. We praised him; they had praised him; I was praising him. 4. The soldiers will fight; they have fought; we have fought. 5. Caesar had got ready many ships. 6. He will station two legions in that place. 7. I have not yet approved these plans. 8. Who had approved those words?

CHAPTER XIX.

398. 1. Let the soldiers contend; the soldiers would have contended. 2. To have contended; about to contend; by contending. 3. May he approve our words; he would have approved your words. 4. Who would have praised this man? 5. The soldiers try to seize that hill. 6. Praise all these soldiers. 7. We are about to attack another town. 8. All the Gauls are fond of fighting.

CHAPTER XX.

399. 1. We shall be praised; we have been praised; we had been praised. 2. She was praised; she will be praised; she had been praised. 3. You are expected; you will be expected; they will be expected. 4. Who was being praised? 5. All these towns will be attacked. 6. The Gauls had often been overcome. 7. These six ships have been got ready. 8. On the following day many soldiers were wounded.

CHAPTER XXI.

400. 1. Let them be called together; they would have been called together. 2. The senate must be (= is to be) called together at once. 3. We should easily have been overcome. 4. You would scarcely have been praised. 5. These towns would have been taken by storm most easily. 6. Your words would not have been approved. 7. The onset of the enemy must be retarded.

CHAPTER XXII.

401. 1. We have seen you; we shall see you; he had seen you. 2. We were fearing; you had feared; he will fear. 3. To have feared, to have seen; fearing, seeing. 4. May he have; we should have had; he shall have. 5. You ought to remain in this place. 6. We had seen the standards of the enemy. 7. We should easily have kept the enemy away.

CHAPTER XXIII.

402. 1. We seem; he seemed; you had seemed. 2. They will be terrified; we had been terrified. 3. Your suspicions were increased. 4. The camp had been moved. 5. Our soldiers seem to have filled up the trench of the enemy. 6. The onset of the barbarians will be bravely withstood. 7. The Gauls must be kept away. 8. These trenches would have been quickly filled up.

CHAPTER XXIV.

403. 1. We defended the city; they had defended the city; they will defend the city. 2. I sent a letter; we shall send a letter; they had sent a letter. 3. Let us defend; we should have defended; let him defend. 4. To send; to have sent. 5. I shall leave a garrison in this place. 6. Caesar sent two legions into Spain. 7. He had decided to defend the camp. 8. War will be waged in Gaul.

CHAPTER XXV.

404. 1. Hostages had been sent; hostages will be sent; hostages have been sent. 2. We shall be defended; he had been defended; she had been defended. 3. These legions have been led to the other camp. 4. A garrison has been left here. 5. You would have been compelled to remain. 6. Many wars will be waged. 7. Two legions were sent against the enemy. 8. These ships will be fitted out with all things.

CHAPTER XXVI.

405. 1. We were fortifying; we have fortified; they will fortify. 2. They were assembling; they have assembled; they would have assembled. 3. He came; he will have come; let him come. 4. Fortify this camp, soldiers![1] 5. The enemy hindered the march of our army![2] 6. The Germans assembled on all sides from the forests. 7. We have heard the report of that battle. 8. I afterwards discovered these things.

[1] The Vocative ordinarily stands second in the sentence.
[2] Use *agmen*.

CHAPTER XXVII.

406. 1. We were surrounded; they had been surrounded; they will be surrounded. 2. He was heard; we had been heard; she will be heard. 3. Let him be heard; they would have been heard; to be heard. 4. These captives were surrounded with two cohorts of soldiers. 5. Nothing has been discovered. 6. No other voice will be heard. 7. The larger camp ought to be fortified.

CHAPTER XXVIII.

407. 1. We were taking; I had taken; they will take. 2. Let us take; let him take; taking. 3. They would have fled; he would have been killed. 4. They will be killed; they were killed.   5. Let us make a bridge !   6. This camp was plundered.   7. The envoys of the king were received. 8. We received your commands.   9. We shall flee from these dangers.

CHAPTER XXIX.

408. 1. He was marching forth ; they marched forth ; let us march forth.   2. We ought to return.   3. We have tarried ; you were tarrying ; they had tarried.   4. I set out ; he will set out ; they would have set out.   5. No one dared to march forth.   6. We have not yet endeavored to send this letter. 7. Who will dare to resist?   8. The troops advanced a little. 9. We shall return.

CHAPTER XXX.

409. 1. We had been about to speak.   2. The soldiers were on the point of attacking (= were about to attack) this town. 3. She was about to set out.   4. That camp must be defended. 5. Peace must be established with other states.   6. Our liberty must be defended.   7. He was about to wage war.   8. We were on the point of surrendering ourselves.[1]

[1] See § 86.

CHAPTER XXXI.

410. 1. He could ;[1] they could ; you can.   2. He will be able ; they had been able ; may he be able.   3. We should have been able ; to have been able.   4. He was in charge ; I had been in charge ; they will be in charge.   5. We were absent ; they would have been absent ; to have been present. 6. Much[2] money had already been given.   7. We shall give much money to you.   8. He would have given much money to you.

[1] *I.e., he was able.*
[2] For *much money*, the Latin regularly has *great money*.

CHAPTER XXXII.

411. 1. We bore; we have borne; he had borne.   2. He would have borne; by bearing; to have borne.   3. Let us bear; we were bearing; they will bear.   4. Let us endure; to have endured; enduring.   5. The standards were brought back. 6. The Helvetii betook themselves to the mountain.   7. We shall bear assistance to you.[1]   8. Who will be able to endure these tortures?

[1] Use the Dative.

CHAPTER XXXIII.

412. 1. We wished; we should have wished; to have wished. 2. I had been unwilling; you were unwilling; you are unwilling. 3. To have preferred; he would have preferred; he had preferred.   4. We had become; may he become; they would have become.   5. He had been unwilling to withdraw.   6. Caesar had been informed of (= concerning) this thing.   7. No one preferred to remain here.

CHAPTER XXXIV.

413. 1. We were returning; we should have returned; to have returned; they will cross.   2. They had crossed; they crossed; he will cross.   3. You will remember; they were remembering; we hate; let us hate; he hated.   4. I had begun to cross the river.   5. Two thousand cavalry[1] perished.   6. The cavalry of the enemy went around the camp of the Romans.   7. This river is crossed[2] by a ford.   8. The soldiers will return.

[1] See § 80, 4.   [2] See § 197, 1.

SELECTIONS FOR READING.

I. FABLES.

THE WOMAN AND THE HEN.

414. Mulier quaedam habēbat gallīnam, quae eī cottīdiē ōvum pariēbat aureum. Hinc suspicārī[1] coepit,[2] illam aurī māssam intus cēlāre,[3] et gallīnam occīdit. Sed nihil in eā repperit, nisi quod in aliīs gallīnīs reperīrī[4] solet. Itaque dum mājōribus[5] dīvitiīs[6] inhiat,[7] etiam minōrēs[8] perdidit.

THE OXEN.

415. In eōdem prātō pāscēbantur trēs[9] bovēs in māximā concordiā, et sīc ab omnī ferārum incursiōne[10] tūtī erant. Sed dissidiō[11] inter illōs ortō, singulī ā ferīs[12] petītī et laniātī sunt.

Fābula docet, quantum bonī[13] sit[14] in concordiā.

THE DOG IN THE MANGER.

416. Canis jacēbat in praesaepī bovēsque lātrandō[15] ā pābulō[16] arcēbat. Cuī ūnus boum,[17] " *Quanta ista,*" inquit, " *invidia est, quod nōn pateris ut eō cibō*[18] *vescāmur,*[19] *quem tū ipse capere nec velīs nec possīs !* "

Haec fābula invidiae[20] indolem dēclārat.

The footnotes refer to the sections of this book.

[1] 364.	[6] 220, III.	[11] 273.	[16] 251.
[2] 198.	[7] 331.	[12] 253.	[17] 236.
[3] 356.	[8] 73.	[13] 236.	[18] 258, 1.
[4] 364.	[9] 80, 2.	[14] 343.	[19] 336, 2.
[5] 73.	[10] 251.	[15] 376, 3.	[20] 233.

THE TRAVELLERS AND THE ASS.

417. Duo quī ūnā iter faciēbant, asinum oberrantem in sōlitū-
dine cōnspicātī,[21] accurrunt laetī,[22] et uterque eum sibi vindicāre[23]
coepit, quod eum prior[24] cōnspexisset.[25] Dum vērō contendunt[26]
et rīxantur, nec ā verberibus[27] abstinent, asinus aufūgit et neuter
eō[28] potītur.

THE KID AND THE WOLF.

418. Haedus, stāns in tēctō domūs, lupō[29] praetereuntī[30] male-
dīxit. Cui lupus, "*Nōn tū,*" inquit, "*sed tēctum mihi maledīcit.*"
Saepe locus et tempus hominēs[31] timidōs audācēs[32] reddit.

THE PEASANT AND THE MOUSE.

419. Mūs ā rūsticō[33] dēprehēnsus tam ācrī morsū[34] ējus digi-
tōs vulnerāvit, ut ille eum dīmitteret,[35] dīcēns : "*Nihil, mehercule,
tam pusillum est, quod dē salūte dēspērāre dēbeat,*[36] *modo sē dēfendere velit.*

THE WOLF AND THE CRANE.

420. In faucibus lupī os inhaeserat. Mercēde[37] igitur con-
dūcit gruem, quī illud extrahat.[38] Hōc grūs longitūdine[39] collī
facile effēcit. Cum autem mercēdem postulāret,[40] subrīdēns lupus
et dentibus[41] īnfrendēns, "*Num tibi,*" inquit, "*parva mercēs vidētur, quod caput incolume ex lupī faucibus extrāxistī?*"

THE TRUMPETER.

421. Tubicen ab hostibus captus,[42] "*Nōlīte[43]*" mē, inquit,
"*interficere; nam inermis sum, neque quidquam habeō praeter hanc
tubam.*" At hostēs, "*Propter hōc ipsum,*" inquiunt, "*te interimē-*

---

[21] 172.	[27] 251.	[33] 253.	[39] 258.
[22] 282.	[28] 258, 1.	[34] 258.	[40] 324, *B.*
[23] 364.	[29] 220, II, *a.*	[35] 317.	[41] 258.
[24] 284, 2.	[30] 197.	[36] 317.	[42] 372, 5.
[25] 319.	[31] 209.	[37] 268.	[43] 300, 2.
[26] 331.	[32] 209, 2.	[38] 311, 2.	

mus, quod, cum ipse pūgnandī[44] *sīs*[45] *imperītus, aliōs ad pūgnam incitāre*[46] *solēs.*[47] "

Fābula docet, nōn sōlum maleficōs esse pūniendōs[48] sed etiam eōs, quī aliōs ad male faciendum[49] irrītent.[50]

The Farmer and his Sons.

422. Agricola senex, cum mortem sibi[1] appropinquāre[2] sentīret,[3] fīliōs convocāvit, quōs,[4] ut fierī[5] solet, interdum discordāre[6] nōverat, et fascem virgulārum afferrī[7] jubet. Quibus[8] allātīs, fīliōs hortātur, ut hunc fascem frangerent.[9] Quod cum facere nōn possent,[10] distribuit singulās virgās, eīsque[11] celeriter frāctīs, docuit illōs, quam fīrma rēs[12] esset[13] concordia, quamque imbēcillis discordia.

The Mice.

423. Mūrēs aliquandō habuērunt cōnsilium, quō modō ā fēle cavērent.[14] Multīs aliīs[15] prōpositīs, omnibus[16] placuit[17] ut eī[18] tintinnābulum annecterētur[19]; sīc enim ipsōs sonitū[20] admonitōs eam fugere[21] posse.[22] Sed cum jam inter mūrēs quaererētur,[23] quī fēlī[24] tintinnābulum annecteret,[25] nēmō repertus est.

Fābula docet, in suādendō plūrimōs esse[26] audācēs,[27] sed in ipsō perīculō timidōs.

The Tortoise and the Eagle.

424. Testūdō aquilam māgnopere ōrābat, ut sēsē volāre docēret.[28] Aquila eī ostendēbat quidem, eam rem petere[29] nātūrae[30] suae contrāriam; sed illa nihilō[31] minus īnstābat, et obsecrābat

---

[44] 376, 1; 241.	[4] 364.	[14] 343.	[23] 324, *B.*
[45] 351, 3.	[5] 193.	[15] 273.	[24] 220, III.
[46] 364.	[6] 364.	[16] 220, II, *a.*	[25] 343.
[47] 319.	[7] 367, II.	[17] 202.	[26] 356.
[48] 356.	[8] 273.	[18] 220, III.	[27] 32, 1; 2.
[49] 376, 2.	[9] 336, I.	[19] 336, 3.	[28] 336, I.
[50] 356.	[10] 324, *B.*	[20] 258.	[29] 356.
[1] 220, III.	[11] 273.	[21] 364.	[30] 228.
[2] 364.	[12] 24, I.	[22] 356.	[31] 266.
[3] 324, *B.*	[13] 343.		

aquilam, ut sē[32] volucrem[33] facere[34] vellet.[35]   Itaque ungulīs[36] arreptam[37] aquila sustulit in sublīme, et dēmīsit illam, ut per aërem ferrētur.[38]   Tum in saxa incidēns comminūta[39] interiit.

Haec fābula docet, multōs cupiditātibus[40] suīs occaecātōs cōnsilia prūdentiōrum respuere,[41] et in exitium ruere stultitiā[42] suā.[43]

THE LION.

425. Societātem jūnxerant leō, juvenca, capra, ovis.   Praedā[44] autem, quam cēperant, in quattuor partēs aequālēs dīvīsā, leō, *"Prīma,"* ăit, *" mea est; dēbētur enim haec praestantiae meae. Tollam et secundam, quam merētur rōbur meum.   Tertiam vindicat sibi ēgregius labor meus.   Quārtam quī sibi arrogāre voluerit, is sciat,*[45] *sē habitūrum mē inimīcum sibi."*[46]   Quid facerent[47] imbēcillēs bēstiae, aut quae sibi leōnem īnfēstum habēre[48] vellet?[47]

II. ROMAN HISTORY.

1. *The Regal Period,* 753–510 B.C.

SATURN.

426. Antīquissimīs temporibus[1] Sāturnus in Italiam vēnisse dīcitur.   Ibi haud procul ā Jāniculō arcem condidit, eamque[2] Sāturniam[3] appellāvit.   Hīc Italōs[4] prīmus[5] agricultūram[6] docuit.

LATINUS AND AENEAS.

427. Posteā Latīnus in illīs regiōnibus imperāvit.   Sub hōc rēge Trōja in Asiā ēversa est.   Hinc Aenēās, Anchīsae fīlius, cum multīs Trōjānīs, quibus[7] ferrum Graecōrum pepercerat, aufūgit et

[32] 209.	[38] 311.	[44] 273.	[2] 209.
[33] 209, 2.	[39] 372, 6.	[45] 300.	[3] 209.
[34] 364.	[40] 258.	[46] 228.	[4] 213.
[35] 336, 1.	[41] 356.	[47] 301.	[5] 284, 2.
[36] 258.	[42] 259.	[48] 364.	[6] 213.
[37] 372, 6.	[43] 90, footnote 1.	[1] 276.	[7] 220, II, *a.*

in Italiam pervēnit. Ibi Latīnus rēx eī benīgnē receptō fīliam
Lāvīniam in mātrimōnium dedit. Aenēās urbem condidit, quam [8]
in honōrem conjugis Lāvīnium [9] appellāvit.

Founding of Alba Longa by Ascanius.

428. Post Aenēae mortem Ascanius, Aenēae fīlius, rēgnum
accēpit. Hīc sēdem rēgnī in alium locum trānstulit, urbemque
condidit in monte Albānō, eamque Albam Longam nuncupāvit.
Eum secūtus est Silvius, quī post Aenēae mortem ā Lāvīniā [10]
genitus erat. Ējus posterī omnēs ūsque ad Rōmam conditam
Albae [11] rēgnāvērunt.

Other Kings of Alba.

429. Ūnus hōrum rēgum, [12] Rōmulus Silvius, sē Jove [13] mājōrem [14]
esse [15] dīcēbat, et, cum tonāret, [16] mīlitibus [17] imperāvit, ut clipeōs
hastīs [18] percuterent, [19] dīcēbatque hunc sonum multō [20] clāriōrem [21]
esse [22] quam tonitrum. Fulmine [23] ictus et in Albānum lacum
praecipitātus est.

Silvius Procās, rēx Albānōrum, duōs fīliōs relīquit Numitōrem
et Amūlium. Hōrum minor nātū, [24] Amūlius, frātrī optiōnem dedit,
utrum rēgnum habēre [25] vellet, [26] an bona, quae pater relīquisset. [27]
Numitor paterna bona praetulit ; Amūlius rēgnum obtinuit.

Birth of Romulus and Remus.

430. Amūlius, ut rēgnum fīrmissimē possidēret, [28] Numitōris
fīlium per īnsidiās interēmit et fīliam frātris Rheam Silviam [29]
Vestālem virginem [30] fēcit. Nam hīs Vestae sacerdōtibus [31] non

[8] 209.	[14] 32, 1 ; 2.	[20] 266.	[26] 343.
[9] 209.	[15] 356.	[21] 31, 1 ; 2.	[27] 356.
[10] 252.	[16] 324, *B.*	[22] 356.	[28] 311.
[11] 277.	[17] 220, II, *a.*	[23] 258.	[29] 209.
[12] 236.	[18] 258.	[24] 269.	[30] 209.
[13] 254.	[19] 336, 1.	[25] 364.	[31] 220, II, *a.*

licet virō[32] nūbere.[33]   Sed haec ā Marte geminōs fīliōs, Rōmulum
et Remum, peperit.   Hōc cum Amūlius comperisset,[34] mātrem
in vincula conjēcit, puerōs[35] autem in Tiberim[36] abicī[37] jussit.

431. Forte Tiberis aqua ultrā rīpam sē effūderat, et, cum
puerī in vadō essent positī,[38] aqua refluēns eōs in siccō relīquit.
Ad eōrum vāgītum lupa accurrit, eōsque ūberibus[39] suīs aluit.
Quod vidēns Faustulus quīdam, pāstor illīus regiōnis, puerōs sustulit, et uxōrī Accae Lārentiae nūtriendōs dedit.

FOUNDATION OF ROME, 753 B.C.

432. Sīc Rōmulus et Remus pueritiam inter pāstōrēs trānsēgērunt.   Cum adolēvissent,[40] et forte comperissent, quis ipsōrum
avus, quae māter fuisset,[41] Amūlium interfēcērunt, et Numitōrī avō
rēgnum restituērunt.   Tum urbem condidērunt in monte Aventīnō,
quam[42] Rōmulus ā suō nōmine Rōmam[43] vocāvit.   Haec cum
moenibus[44] circumdarētur,[45] Remus occīsus est, dum frātrem
irrīdēns moenia trānsilit.[46]

SEIZURE OF THE SABINE WOMEN.

433. Rōmulus, ut cīvium numerum augēret,[47] asȳlum patefēcit,
ad quod multī ex cīvitātibus suīs pulsī accurrērunt.   Sed novae
urbis cīvibus conjugēs deerant.   Itaque fēstum Neptūnī et lūdōs
īnstituit.   Ad hōs cum multī ex fīnitimīs populīs cum mulieribus
et līberīs vēnissent,[48] Rōmānī inter ipsōs lūdōs spectantēs virginēs
rapuērunt.

WAR WITH THE SABINES.

434. Populī illī quōrum[49] virginēs raptae erant bellum adversus
raptōrēs suscēpērunt.   Cum Rōmae appropinquārent,[50] forte in

---

[32] 220, I.
[33] 363.
[34] 324, B.
[35] 367, II.
[36] 48.

[37] 367, II.
[38] 319, 2.
[39] 258.
[40] 324, B.
[41] 343.

[42] 209.
[43] 209.
[44] 258.
[45] 324, B.
[46] 331, 1.

[47] 311.
[48] 324, B.
[49] 233.
[50] 324, B.

Tarpēiam virginem incidērunt quae in arce sacra[1] prōcūrābat. Hanc rogābant, ut viam in arcem mōnstrāret,[2] eīque permīsērunt, ut mūnus sibi posceret.[3] Illa petiit, ut sibi darent,[4] quod in sinistrīs manibus gererent, ānulōs aureōs et armillās sīgnificāns. At hostēs in arcem ab eā perductī scūtīs[5] Tarpēiam obruērunt ; nam et ea in sinistrīs manibus gerēbant.

TREATY WITH THE SABINES.

435. Tum Rōmulus cum hoste, quī montem Tarpēium tenēbat, pūgnam cōnseruit in eō locō, ubi nunc Forum Rōmānum est.   In mediā[6] caede raptae prōcessērunt, et hinc patrēs hinc conjugēs et socerōs complectēbantur, et rogābant, ut caedis fīnem facerent.[7] Utrīque hīs precibus[8] commōtī sunt.   Rōmulus foedus īcit et Sabīnōs in urbem recēpit.

INSTITUTIONS OF ROMULUS. — HIS DEATH.

436. Posteā cīvitātem discrīpsit.   Centum senātōrēs lēgit eōsque[9] cum ob aetātem tum ob reverentiam eīs dēbitam patrēs[10] appellāvit.   Plēbem in trīgintā cūriās distribuit, eāsque raptārum nōminibus[11] nuncupāvit. Annō[12] rēgnī trīcēsimō septimō, cum exercitum lūstrāret,[13] inter tempestātem ortam repente oculīs hominum subductus est.   Hinc aliī[14] eum ā senātōribus interfectum,[15] aliī[14] ad deōs sublātum esse[15] exīstimāvērunt.

REIGN OF NUMA POMPILIUS.

437. Post Rōmulī mortem ūnīus annī interrēgnum fuit.   Quō[16] ēlāpsō, Numa Pompilius, Curibus,[17] urbe in agrō Sabīnōrum, nātus, rēx[18] creātus est.   Hīc vir bellum quidem nūllum gessit ; nec

---

[1] 281, 1.	[6] 284, 1.	[11] 258.	[15] 356.
[2] 336, 1.	[7] 336, 1.	[12] 276.	[16] 273.
[3] 336, 2.	[8] 258.	[13] 324, B.	[17] 274, 1.
[4] 336, 1.	[9] 209.	[14] 293.	[18] 209, 3.
[5] 258.	[10] 209.		

minus tamen cīvitātī[19] prōfuit. Nam et lēgēs dedit, et sacra[20] plūrima īnstituit, ut populī barbarī et bellicōsī mōrēs mollīret.[21] Omnia[22] autem, quae faciēbat, sē nymphae Ēgeriae, conjugis suae, monitū[23] facere[24] dīcēbat. Morbō[25] dēcessit quadrāgēsimō tertiō imperiī annō.[26]

Tullus Hostilius.

438. Numae[27] successit Tullus Hostīlius, cūjus avus sē[28] in bellō adversus Sabīnōs fortem et strēnuum virum[29] praestiterat. Rēx[30] creātus bellum Albānīs[31] indīxit, idque trigeminōrum, Horātiōrum et Cūriātiōrum, certāmine[32] fīnīvit. Albam propter perfidiam Mettiī Fufetiī dīruit. Cum trīgintā duo annōs[33] rēgnāsset,[34] fulmine[35] ictus[36] cum domō suā ārsit.

Ancus Marcius.

439. Post hunc Ancus Mārcius, Numae ex fīliā nepōs, suscēpit imperium. Hīc vir aequitāte[37] et religiōne avō[38] similis, Latīnōs bellō[39] domuit, urbem ampliāvit, et nova eī[40] moenia circumdedit. Carcerem prīmus[41] aedificāvit. Ad Tiberis ōstia urbem condidit, Ōstiamque vocāvit. Vīcēsimō quārtō annō[42] imperiī morbō[43] obiit.

Lucius Tarquinius Priscus.

440. Deinde rēgnum Lūcius Tarquinius Priscus accēpit, Dēmarātī fīlius, quī tyrannōs patriae Corinthī fugiēns in Etrūriam vēnerat. Ipse Tarquinius, quī nōmen ab urbe Tarquiniīs accēpit, aliquandō Rōmam[44] profectus erat.

441. Cum Rōmae[45] commorārētur,[46] Ancī rēgis familiāritātem

---

[19] 220, II, *a*.	[26] 276.	[33] 215.	[40] 220, III.
[20] 281, 1.	[27] 220, III.	[34] 324, *B*.	[41] 284, 2.
[21] 311.	[28] 209.	[35] 258.	[42] 276.
[22] 281, 1.	[29] 209.	[36] 372, 6.	[43] 259.
[23] 259.	[30] 209, 3.	[37] 269.	[44] 216.
[24] 356.	[31] 220, III.	[38] 228.	[45] 277.
[25] 259.	[32] 258.	[39] 258.	[46] 324, *B*.

cōnsecūtus est, quī eum [47] fīliōrum suōrum tūtōrem [48] relīquit. Sed
is pūpillīs [49] rēgnum intercēpit. Senātōribus, quōs Rōmulus creā-
verat, centum aliōs addidit, quī minōrum gentium sunt appellātī.
Plūra bella fēlīciter gessit, nec paucōs agrōs, hostibus adēmptōs,
urbis territōriō [50] adjūnxit. Prīmus [1] triumphāns urbem intrāvit.
Cloācās fēcit; Capitōlium incohāvit. Trīcēsimō octāvō imperiī
annō [2] per Ancī fīliōs, quibus rēgnum ēripuerat, occīsus est.

SERVIUS TULLIUS.

442. Post hunc Servius Tullius suscēpit imperium, genitus ex
nōbilī fēminā, captīvā tamen et famulā. Cum adolēvisset,[3] rēx
eī fīliam in mātrimōnium dedit.

443. Cum Prīscus Tarquinius occīsus esset,[4] Tanaquil dē su-
periōre parte domūs populum allocūta est, dīcēns: *rēgem [5] grave
quidem, sed nōn lētāle vulnus accēpisse;* [6] *eum petere, ut populus,
dum convaluisset,[6] Serviō Tulliō [7] oboedīret.* [8] Sīc Servius rēgnāre
coepit, sed bene imperium administrāvit. Montēs trēs urbī adjūnxit. Prīmus omnium cēnsum ōrdināvit. Sub eō Rōma habuit
octōgintā tria mīlia cīvium cum hīs, quī in agrīs erant.

444. Hīc rēx interfectus est scelere [9] fīliae Tulliae et Tarquiniī
Superbī, fīliī ējus rēgis, cui [10] Servius successerat. Nam ab ipsō
Tarquiniō [11] interfectus est. Tullia in forum properāvit, et prīma [12]
conjugem [13] rēgem [14] salūtāvit. Cum domum [15] redīret,[16] aurīgam
super patris corpus, in viā jacēns, carpentum agere [17] jussit.

TARQUINIUS SUPERBUS.

445. Tarquinius Superbus cognōmen mōribus [18] meruit. Bellō [19]

---

[47] 209.	[3] 324, *B.*	[9] 258.	[15] 216.
[48] 209.	[4] 324, *B.*	[10] 220, III.	[16] 324, *B.*
[49] 224.	[5] 356.	[11] 253.	[17] 367, II.
[50] 220, III.	[6] 356; 331, III, 2.	[12] 284, 2.	[18] 259.
[1] 284, 2.	[7] 220, II, *a.*	[13] 209.	[19] 269.
[2] 276.	[8] 336, 1.	[14] 209.	

tamen strēnuus plūrēs fīnitimōrum populōrum [20] vīcit. Templum
Jovis in Capitōliō aedificāvit. Posteā, dum Ardeam oppūgnat,[21]
urbem Latiī, imperium perdidit. Nam cum fīlius ējus Lucrētiae,
nōbilissimae fēminae, conjugī [22] Tarquiniī Collātīnī, vim fēcisset,[23]
haec sē ipsa occīdit in cōnspectū marītī, patris, amīcōrumque,
postquam eōs obtestāta est [24] ut hanc injūriam ulcīscerentur.[25]

446. Hanc ob causam L. Brūtus, Collātīnus, aliīque nōnnūllī
in exitium rēgis conjūrārunt, populōque [26] persuāsērunt, ut eī portās
urbis clauderet.[27] Exercitus quoque, quī cīvitātem Ardeam cum
rēge oppūgnābat, eum relīquit. Itaque fūgit cum uxōre et līberīs
suīs. Ita Rōmae septem rēgēs rēgnāvērunt annōs [28] ducentōs
quadrāgintā trēs.

2. *The Early Republic*, 510-241 B.C.

INSTITUTION OF THE REPUBLIC, 510 B.C.

447. Hinc cōnsulēs coepēre [29] prō ūnō rēge duo creārī,[30] ut sī
ūnus malus esset, alter eum coërcēret.[31] Annuum eīs imperium
tribūtum est, nē per diūturnitātem potestātis īnsolentiōrēs redderentur.[32] Fuērunt igitur annō [33] prīmō, expulsīs rēgibus,[34] cōnsulēs
L. Jūnius Brūtus, ācerrimus lībertātis vindex, et Tarquinius Collātīnus marītus Lucrētiae sed Collātīnō [35] paulō [36] post dignitās
adēmpta est. Placuerat enim, nē quis ex Tarquiniōrum familiā
Rōmae manēret.[37] Ergō cum omnī patrimōniō suō ex urbe mi-
grāvit, et in ējus locum Valerius Pūblicola cōnsul [38] factus est.

DEATH OF BRUTUS.

448. Commōvit bellum urbī rēx Tarquinius. In prīmā pūgnā
Brūtus cōnsul, et Arrūns, Tarquiniī fīlius, inter sēsē [39] occīdērunt.

---

[20] 236.	[25] 336, 1.	[80] 364.	[85] 224.
[21] 331, I.	[26] 220, II, *a*.	[81] 311.	[86] 266.
[22] 220, I.	[27] 336, 1.	[82] 311.	[87] 336, 3.
[23] 324, *B*.	[28] 215.	[88] 276.	[88] 209, 3.
[24] 323.	[29] 198.	[84] 273.	[39] 290.

Rōmānī tamen ex eā pūgnā victōrēs recessērunt. Brūtum Rōmānae mātrōnae, quasi commūnem patrem, per annum lūxērunt. Valerius Pūblicola Spurium Lucrētium,[40] collēgam[41] sibi fēcit; cum morbō exstīnctus esset,[42] Pūblicola Horātium Pulvīllum sibi collēgam sūmpsit. Itaque prīmus annus quīnque cōnsulēs habuit.

WAR WITH PORSENA, 508 B.C.

449. Secundō quoque annō[43] iterum Tarquinius bellum Rōmānīs[44] intulit, Porsenā,[45] rēge Etrūscōrum, auxilium eī ferente. In illō bellō Horātius Cocles sōlus pontem līgneum dēfendit et hostēs cohibuit, dum pōns ā tergō ruptus esset.[46] Tum sē cum armīs in Tiberim conjēcit, et ad suōs[47] trānsnāvit.

450. Dum Porsena urbem obsidet,[48] Quīntus Mūcius Scaev,ola, juvenis fortis animī,[49] in castra hostium sē contulit eō cōnsiliō, ut rēgem occīderet.[50] At ibi scrībam rēgis prō ipsō rēge interfēcit. Tum ā rēgiīs satellitibus[1] comprehēnsus et ad rēgem dēductus, cum Porsena eum īgnibus[2] allātīs terrēret,[3] dextram ārae[4] accēnsae imposuit, dum flammīs cōnsūmpta esset.[5] Hōc facinus rēx mīrātus juvenem dīmīsit incolumem. Tum hīc, quasi beneficium referēns, äit, *trecentōs aliōs juvenēs*[6] *in eum conjūrāsse.*[6] Hāc rē[7] territus Porsena pācem cum Rōmānīs fēcit, Tarquinius autem Tusculum[8] sē contulit, ibique prīvātus cum uxōre cōnsenuit.

SECESSION OF THE PLEBS, 494 B.C.

451. Sextō decimō annō[9] post rēgēs exāctōs, populus Rōmae[10] sēditiōnem fēcit, questus quod tribūtīs[11] et mīlitiā ā senātū exhaurīrētur.[12] Māgna pars plēbis urbem relīquit, et in montem

---

[40] 209.
[41] 209.
[42] 324, *B.*
[43] 276.
[44] 220, III.
[45] 273.
[46] 331, III, 2.
[47] 281, 1.
[48] 331, I.
[49] 237.
[50] 311.
[1] 253.
[2] 273.
[3] 324, *B.*
[4] 220, III.
[5] 331, III, 2.
[6] 356.
[7] 258.
[8] 216.
[9] 276.
[10] 277.
[11] 258.
[12] 319.

trāns Aniēnem amnem sēcessit. Tum patrēs turbātī Menēnium
Agrippam mīsērunt ad plēbem quī eam senātuī conciliāret.[13] Hīc
eīs inter alia [14] fābulam nārrāvit dē ventre et membrīs hūmānī
corporis; quā [15] populus commōtus est, ut in urbem redīret.[16]
Tum prīmum tribūnī plēbis creātī sunt, quī plēbem adversum
nōbilitātis superbiam dēfenderent.[17]

TREASON OF CORIOLANUS, 492 B.C.

452. Octāvō decimō annō [18] post exāctōs rēgēs Q. Mārcius,
Coriolānus [19] dictus ab urbe Volscōrum Coriolīs, quam bellō
cēperat, plēbī [20] invīsus fierī coepit. Quārē urbe [21] expulsus ad
Volscōs, ācerrimōs Rōmānōrum hostēs, contendit, et ab eīs [22]
dux [23] exercitūs factus Rōmānōs saepe vīcit. Jam ūsque ad
quīntum milliārium urbis accesserat, nec ūllīs cīvium suōrum lēgā-
tiōnibus flectī poterat, ut patriae parceret.[24] Dēnique Veturia
māter et Volumnia uxor ex urbe ad eum vēnērunt; quārum flētū [25]
et precibus commōtus est, ut exercitum removēret.[26] Quō [27] factō
ā [28] Volscīs ut prōditor occīsus esse dīcitur.

BATTLE OF THE CREMERA, 477 B.C.

453. Cum Rōmānī adversum Vējentēs bellum gererent,[29] familia
Fabiōrum sōla hōc bellum suscēpit. Profectī sunt trecentī sex
nōbilissimī hominēs, duce [30] Fabiō cōnsule. Cum saepe hostēs
vīcissent, apud Cremeram fluvium castra posuērunt. Ibi, cum
Vējentēs dolō [31] ūsī eōs in īnsidiās pellexissent, in proeliō exortō
omnēs periērunt. Ūnus superfuit ex tantā familiā quī propter
aetātem puerīlem dūcī nōn potuerat ad pūgnam. Hīc genus

---

[13] 311, 2.   [18] 276.   [23] 209, 3.   [28] 253.
[14] 281, 1.   [19] 209, 3.   [24] 336, 1.   [29] 324, *B.*
[15] 258.   [20] 228.   [25] 258.   [30] 273.
[16] 336, 1.   [21] 251.   [26] 336, 1.   [31] 258, 1.
[17] 311, 2.   [22] 253.   [27] 273.

prōpāgāvit ad Quīntum Fabium Māximum illum, quī Hannibalem prūdentī cunctātiōne dēbilitāvit.

THE DECEMVIRS.

454. Annō trecentēsimō et alterō ab urbe conditā decemvirī creātī sunt, quī cīvitātī lēgēs scrīberent.[32] Hī prīmō annō bene ēgērunt; secundō autem dominātiōnem exercēre[33] coepērunt. Sed cum ūnus eōrum, Appius Claudius, virginem ingenuam, Virginiam, Virginiī centuriōnis fīliam, corrumpere vellet, pater eam occīdit. Tum ad mīlitēs profūgit eōsque ad sēditiōnem commōvit. Adēmpta est decemvirīs[34] potestās, ipsīque omnēs aut morte[35] aut exsiliō pūnītī sunt.

THE SIEGE OF VEII.

455. In bellō contrā Vējentānōs Fūrius Camillus urbem Faleriōs obsidēbat. In quā obsidiōne cum lūdī litterāriī magister prīncipum fīliōs ex urbe in castra hostium dūxisset, Camillus hōc dōnum nōn accēpit, sed scelestum hominem, manibus[36] post tergum vinctīs, puerīs Faleriōs redūcendum trādidit; virgāsque eīs dedit, quibus prōditōrem in urbem agerent.[37] Hāc tantā animī nōbilitāte commōtī Faliscī urbem Rōmānīs trādidērunt. Camillō autem apud Rōmānōs crīminī[38] datum est, quod albīs equīs triumphāsset[39] et praedam inaequē dīvīsisset; damnātus ob eam causam et cīvitāte[40] expulsus est.

ROME CAPTURED BY THE GAULS, 390 B.C.

456. Paulō[41] post Gallī Senonēs ad urbem vēnērunt, Rōmānōs ad flūmen Alliam vīcērunt, et urbem etiam occupārunt. Jam nihil praeter Capitōlium dēfendī potuit. Et jam praesidium famē[42] labōrābat, et in eō erant, ut pācem ā Gallīs aurō[43]

[32] 311, 2.	[35] 258.	[38] 227.	[41] 266.
[33] 364.	[36] 273.	[39] 319.	[42] 259.
[34] 224.	[37] 311, 2.	[40] 251.	[43] 268.

emerent,[44] cum Camillus cum manū mīlitum superveniēns hostēs
māgnō proeliō [45] superāvit.

ACHIEVEMENT OF TITUS MANLIUS TORQUATUS, 361 B.C.

457. Annō trecentēsimō nōnāgēsimō tertiō post urbem conditam Gallī iterum ad urbem accesserant, et quārtō mīlliāriō trāns
Aniēnem fluvium cōnsēderant. Contrā eōs missus est Titus
Quīnctius. Ibi Gallus quīdam eximiā corporis māgnitūdine [46] for-
tissimum Rōmānōrum ad certāmen singulāre prōvocāvit. Titus
Mānlius, nōbilissimus juvenis, prōvocātiōnem accēpit, Gallum occīdit, eumque torque [47] aureō spoliāvit, quō ōrnātus erat. Hinc
et ipse et posterī ējus Torquātī [48] appellātī sunt. Gallī fugam ca-
pessīvērunt.

MARCUS VALERIUS CORVINUS, 348 B.C.

458. Novō bellō [49] cum Gallīs exortō, annō urbis quadringentēsimō sextō, iterum Gallus prōcessit rōbore atque armīs īnsīgnis,
et prōvocāvit ūnum ex Rōmānīs ut sēcum armīs dēcerneret.[50] Tum
sē M. Valerius, tribūnus mīlitum, obtulit; et, cum prōcessisset
armātus, corvus eī [1] suprā dextrum bracchium sēdit. Mox, commissā pūgnā,[2] hīc corvus ālīs [3] et unguibus Gallī oculōs verberāvit.
Ita factum est ut Gallus nūllō negōtiō ā Valeriō interficerētur,[4] quī
hinc Corvīnī nōmen accēpit.

WAR WITH THE SAMNITES, 323 B.C.

459. Posteā Rōmānī bellum gessērunt cum Samnītibus, ad
quod L. Papīrius Cursor cum honōre dictātōris profectus est.
Quī cum negōtiī cūjusdam causā Rōmam [5] rediisset, praecēpit
Q. Fabiō Rulliānō,[6] magistrō equitum, quem apud exercitum relīquit, nē pūgnam cum hoste committeret.[7] Sed ille, occāsiōnem

---

[44] 342.	[48] 209, 3.	[2] 273.	[5] 216.
[45] 258.	[49] 273.	[3] 258.	[6] 220, II, *a*.
[46] 267.	[50] 336, 1.	[4] 342, 2.	[7] 336, 1.
[47] 251.	[1] 224.		

nactus, fēlīcissimē dīmicāvit, et Samnītēs dēlēvit.   Ob hanc rem ā
dictātōre capitis [8] damnātus est.   At ille in urbem cōnfūgit, et ingentī favōre [9] mīlitum et populī līberātus est ; in Papīrium autem
tanta exorta est sēditiō, ut paene ipse interficerētur.[10]

Battle of the Caudine Forks, 321 b.c.

460. Duōbus annīs [11] post T. Veturius et Spurius Postumius cōnsulēs bellum adversum Samnītēs gerēbant.   Hī ā Pontiō Tele-
sīnō,[12] duce hostium, in īnsidiās inductī sunt.   Nam ad Furculās
Caudīnās Rōmānōs pellexit in angustiās, unde sēsē expedīre nōn
poterant.   Ibi Pontius patrem suum Herennium rogāvit, quid
faciendum putāret.[13]   Ille respondit, *aut omnēs occīdendōs esse* [14]
ut Rōmānōrum vīrēs frangerentur,[15] *aut omnēs dīmittendōs, ut
beneficiō obligārentur.*   Pontius utrumque cōnsilium improbāvit,
omnēsque sub jugum mīsit.   Samnītēs dēnique post bellum ūndēquīnquāgintā annōrum superātī sunt.

War with Pyrrhus, 281 b.c.

461. Dēvictīs Samnītibus,[16] Tarentīnīs [17] bellum indictum est,
quia lēgātīs Rōmānōrum injūriam fēcissent.[18]   Hī Pyrrhum,[19]
Ēpīrī rēgem, contrā Rōmānōs auxilium [20] poposcērunt.   Is mox in
Italiam vēnit, tumque prīmum Rōmānī cum trānsmarīnō hoste
pūgnāvērunt.   Missus est contrā eum cōnsul Pūblius Valerius
Laevīnus.   Hīc, cum explōrātōrēs Pyrrhī cēpisset, jussit eōs per
castra dūcī, tumque dīmittī, ut renūntiārent [21] Pyrrhō, quaecumque
ā Rōmānīs [22] agerentur.

462. Pūgnā [23] commissā, Pyrrhus auxiliō [24] elephantōrum vīcit.
Nox proeliō fīnem dedit.   Laevīnus tamen per noctem fūgit.

---

[8] 244.	[13] 343.	[17] 220, III.	[21] 311.
[9] 259.	[14] 356.	[18] 319.	[22] 253.
[10] 317.	[15] 311.	[19] 213.	[23] 273.
[11] 266.	[16] 273.	[20] 213.	[24] 258.
[12] 253.			

Pyrrhus Rōmānōs mille octingentōs cēpit, eōsque summō honōre [25] trāctāvit. Cum eōs, quī in proeliō interfectī erant, omnēs adversīs vulneribus [26] et trucī vultū [26] etiam mortuōs jacēre [27] vidēret, tulisse ad caelum manūs dīcitur cum hāc vōce : *"Ego cum tālibus virīs brevī [28] orbem terrārum subigam."*

463. Posteā Pyrrhus Rōmam [29] perrēxit ; omnia ferrō īgnīque vāstāvit ; Campāniam dēpopulātus est, atque ad Praeneste vēnit, mīlliāriō ab urbe octāvō decimō. Mox terrōre [30] exercitūs, quī cum cōnsule [31] sequēbātur, in Campāniam sē recēpit. Lēgātī ad Pyrrhum dē captīvīs redimendīs [32] missī honōrificē ab eō [33] susceptī sunt ; captīvōs sine pretiō reddidit. Ūnum ex lēgātīs, Fabricium sīc admīrātus est ut eī quārtam partem rēgnī suī prōmitteret, [34] sī ad sē trānsīret, [35] sed ā Fabriciō contemptus est.

464. Cum jam Pyrrhus ingentī Rōmānōrum admīrātiōne [36] tenērētur, lēgātum mīsit Cīneam, praestantissimum virum quī pācem peteret [37] eā condiciōne, ut Pyrrhus eam partem Italiae quam armīs [38] occupāverat obtinēret. Rōmānī respondērunt, *eum cum Rōmānīs pācem habēre nōn posse [39] nisi ex Italiā recessisset.* [40] Cīneās cum rediisset, Pyrrhō eum interrogantī, quālis ipsī Rōma vīsa esset, [41] respondit, sē rēgum patriam vīdisse.

INTEGRITY OF FABRICIUS.

465. In alterō proeliō Pyrrhus vulnerātus est, elephantī interfectī, vīgintī mīlia hostium caesa sunt. Pyrrhus Tarentum [42] fūgit. Interjectō annō, Fabricius contrā eum missus est. Ad hunc medicus Pyrrhī nocte [43] vēnit prōmittēns, sē Pyrrhum venēnō occīsūrum sī mūnus sibi darētur. [44] Hunc Fabricius vinctum

---

[25] 260.
[26] 267.
[27] 356.
[28] 276.
[29] 216.

[30] 259.
[31] 265.
[32] 377, 1.
[33] 253.
[34] 317.

[35] 356.
[36] 258.
[37] 311, 2.
[38] 258.
[39] 356.

[40] 356.
[41] 343.
[42] 216.
[43] 276.
[44] 356.

redūcī[45] jussit ad dominum. Tunc rēx admīrātus illum dīxisse fertur: "*Ille est Fabricius, quī difficilius ab honestāte quam sōl ā cursū suō āvertī potest.*" Paulō post Pyrrhus tertiō etiam proeliō fūsus ā Tarentō recessit, et, cum in Graeciam rediisset, ad Argōs, Peloponnēsī urbem, interfectus est.

FIRST PUNIC WAR, 264 B.C.

466. Annō quadringentēsimō nōnāgēsimō post urbem conditam Rōmānōrum exercitūs prīmum in Siciliam trājēcērunt, rēgemque Syrācūsārum Hierōnem, Poenōsque, quī multās cīvitātēs in eā īnsulā occupāverant, superāvērunt. Quīntō annō hūjus bellī, quod contrā Poenōs gerēbātur, prīmum Rōmānī, Gāiō Duīliō, Gnaeō Cornēliō Asinā cōnsulibus,[46] marī dīmicāvērunt. Duīlius Carthāginiēnsēs vīcit, trīgintā nāvēs occupāvit, quattuordecim mersit, septem mīlia hostium[47] cēpit, tria mīlia occīdit. Nūlla victōria Rōmānīs[48] grātior fuit.

THE ROMANS INVADE AFRICA, 256 B.C.

467. Paucīs annīs interjectīs, bellum in Āfricam est trānslātum. Hamilcar, Carthāginiēnsium dux, pūgnā[49] nāvālī superātus est; nam, perditīs sexāgintā quattuor nāvibus, sē recēpit; Rōmānī vīgintī duās āmīsērunt. Cum in Āfricam vēnissent, Poenōs in plūribus proeliīs vīcērunt, māgnam vim hominum cēpērunt, septuāgintā quattuor cīvitātēs in fidem accēpērunt. Tum victī Carthāginiēnsēs pācem ā Rōmānīs[50] petiērunt. Quam cum Mārcus Atīlius Rēgulus, Rōmānōrum dux, dare nōllet nisi dūrissimīs condiciōnibus, Carthāginiēnsēs auxilium petiērunt ā Lacedaemoniīs. Hī Xanthippum mīsērunt, quī Rōmānum exercitum māgnō proeliō vīcit. Rēgulus ipse captus et in vincula conjectus est.

---

[45] 367, II.
[46] 273, I.
[47] 236.
[48] 228.
[49] 258.
[50] 213, 2.

PATRIOTISM OF REGULUS, 250 B.C.

468. Nōn tamen ubique fortūna Carthāginiēnsibus[1] fāvit. Cum aliquot proeliīs[2] victī essent, Rēgulum rogāvērunt, ut Rōmam proficīscerētur,[3] et pācem captīvōrumque permūtātiōnem ā Rōmānīs obtinēret. Ille cum Rōmam[4] vēnisset, inductus in senātum dīxit, *sē dēsiisse[5] Rōmānum esse ex illā diē, quā[6] in potestātem Poenōrum vēnisset.*[5] Tum Rōmānīs[7] suāsit, nē pācem cum Carthāginiēnsibus facerent :[8] illōs enim tot cāsibus frāctōs spem nūllam nisi in pāce habēre : *tantī nōn esse,[9] ut tot mīlia captīvōrum propter sē ūnum et paucōs, quī ex Rōmānīs captī essent,[9] redderentur.* Haec sententia obtinuit. Regressus igitur in Āfricam crūdēlissimīs suppliciīs exstīnctus est.

CLOSE OF THE FIRST PUNIC WAR, 241 B.C.

469. Tandem C. Lutātiō Catulō, A. Postumiō cōnsulibus,[10] annō bellī Pūnicī vīcēsimō tertiō māgnum proelium nāvāle commissum est contrā Lilybaeum, prōmunturium Siciliae. In eō proeliō septuāgintā trēs Carthāginiēnsium nāvēs captae, centum vīgintī quīnque dēmersae, trīgintā duo mīlia hostium[11] capta, tredecim mīlia occīsa sunt. Statim Carthāginiēnsēs pācem petiērunt, eīsque pāx tribūta est. Captīvī Rōmānōrum, quī tenēbantur ā Carthāginiēnsibus redditī sunt. Poenī Siciliā,[12] Sardiniā, et cēterīs īnsulīs, quae inter Italiam Āfricamque jacent, dēcessērunt, omnemque Hispāniam quae citrā Hibērum est, Rōmānīs permīsērunt.

---

[1] 220, II, *a.*	[4] 216.	[7] 220, II, *a.*	[10] 273, 1.
[2] 258.	[5] 356.	[8] 336, 1.	[11] 236.
[3] 336, 1.	[6] 276.	[9] 356.	[12] 251.

NOTES ON THE SELECTIONS FOR READING.

414. eī: *for her.*   **pariēbat**: notice the imperfect tense, which is regularly used to denote a customary or repeated action.   **illam**: this is the subject of *cēlāre; mōssam* is the object.   **repperit**: from *reperiō.*   **nisi quod**: *except what;* the antecedent of *quod* is *id* understood.   **minōrēs**: *i.e. lesser riches;* understand *dīvitiās.*

415. pāscēbantur: *used to graze.*   **dissidiō ... ortō**: *when discord arose* or *since discord arose,* lit. *discord having arisen.*   In rendering the ablative absolute, pains should be taken to translate it by an equivalent English idiom.   **quantum bonī**: *how great advantage,* lit. *how much of good.*

416. Cui: indirect object of *inquit.*   **boum**: gen. plu. of *bōs.*   **ista**: *your,* lit. *that, that of yours.*   **quod**: *in that;* the clause *quod pateris* is explanatory of *invidia.*   **pateris**: from *patior.*   **nec ... nec**: *neither ... nor.*   **velīs, possīs**: these verbs are in the subjunctive by attraction.   In Latin, a clause dependent upon a subjunctive is regularly attracted into the same mood.

417. Duo: *two men.*   **ūnā**: the adv., *together.*   **iter faciēbant**: *were travelling,* lit. *were making a journey.*   **nec**: *and ... not.*

418. praetereuntī: *who was passing by;* pres. participle of *praetereō.*

419. ille: *i.e.* the farmer.   **eum**: the mouse.   **quod dēspērāre dēbeat**: *that it ought to despair; quod* is the relative; clauses of result are sometimes introduced by relatives.   **modo ... velit**: *provided it wishes; modo* in this sense is regularly followed by the subjunctive.

420. quī ... extrahat: *to pull it out.*   **Hōc**: *i.e.* the removal of the bone.   **parva mercēs**: this is the predicate nominative with *vidētur,* the subject of *vidētur* being the clause *quod ... extrāxistī, that you took your head out unharmed.*

421. inquiunt: 3d plu. of *inquit;* its subject is *hostēs.*   **hōc ipsum**: *this very thing.*   **cum**: *though.*

422. Agricola senex: *an old farmer.*   **mortem sibi appropinquāre**: *that death was approaching him,* lit. *death to approach himself.*   **ut**

182

fierī solet: *as is wont to happen.* **nōverat**: *knew;* the perfect of *nōscō* has the force of the present in the sense, *I know,* and the pluperfect similarly has the force of the imperfect. **ut frangerent**: *to break.* Observe that *frangerent* is in the imperfect, although *hortātur* is in the present. At first sight this seems to violate the principle for the sequence of tenses; but *hortātur* is what is called an Historical Present, *i.e.* it really refers to the past; and hence is treated as an historical tense. **Quod cum facere nōn possent**: *and when they could not do this,* lit. *when they could not do which;* it is very common in Latin to introduce a sentence by a relative, where in English we should employ a demonstrative or personal pronoun with a conj., — *and he, but he, and this, but this, etc.* **frāctīs**: *i.e.* by the sons. **quamque**: *and how; que* is the enclitic.

423. **quō modō . . . cavērent**: *as to how they should guard against the cat.* **multīs aliīs prōpositīs**: *when many other things had been proposed.* **posse**: this infinitive depends upon the idea of *thinking* involved in *placuit, etc.* **cum jam quaererētur**, *etc.*: *when it came to asking who would fasten,* lit. *when it was already asked, etc.;* **quī** is the interrogative; this form (instead of *quis*) often occurs in indirect questions.

424. **sēsē**: *it, i.e.* the tortoise. **eam, rem**: *eam* is subject of *petere;* *rem* is the object. **arreptam sustulit**: *snatched up and carried.*

425. **Prīma**: understand *pars.* **āit**: third sing. of pres. ind. of *ājō.* **et**: *also.* **quī**: its antecedent is the following *is.* **inimīcum**: *as an enemy.* **Quid facerent,** *etc.*: *what were the beasts to do?* **quae**: *which one?*

426. **Sāturnus**: the god Saturn. **Jāniculō**: the Janiculum was a hill on the right bank of the Tiber, directly opposite the seven hills on which Rome was built.

427. **Trōja**: the famous city in northwestern Asia Minor. The mythical date of its overthrow is 1184 B.C. **Hinc**: *i.e.* from Troy. **pepercerat**: from *parcō.* **eī benīgnē receptō dedit**: *received him kindly and gave him,* lit. *gave to him having been kindly received.* **in mātrimōnium, in honōrem**: *in marriage, in honor;* the Latin says *into.*

428. **monte Albānō**: in Latium about twenty miles S.E. of Rome. **Alba Longa**: lit. *the long white (town);* so called from the fact that its white buildings stretched for a long distance over the ridge of the hill. **genitus erat**: from *gignō.* **ūsque ad Rōmam conditam**: *up to the very founding of Rome,* lit. *even up to Rome founded.*

429. **tonāret**: impersonal. **minor nātū**: *the younger,* lit. *the lesser as to birth.* **praecipitātus est**: *fell headlong.* **relīquisset**: inasmuch as the preceding indirect question is indirect discourse, *relīquisset* is a subordinate clause in indirect discourse; hence the subjunctive.

430. Vestālem virginem: there were six Vestal virgins; their duty was to watch the fire which was kept constantly burning on the hearth of Vesta's temple.   **ā Mārte**: *by* (lit. *from*) *Mars*.   **peperit**: from *pariō*.

431. ultrā rīpam, *etc.*: *i.e. had overflowed its banks*, lit. *had poured itself beyond the bank.*   *effūderat* is from *effundō*.   **essent positī**: = *positī essent;* from *pōnō*.   **in siccō**: *on dry land; siccō* is used substantively. **Quod**: *this*, lit. *which;* another illustration of the use of the relative pronoun, where in English we naturally employ the demonstrative.   **sustulit**: from *tollō*.   **nūtriendōs**: *to be cared for.*

432. trānsēgērunt: from *trānsigō*.   **adolēvissent**: from *adolēscō*. **frātrem irrīdēns**: *in ridicule of his brother*, lit. *ridiculing.*

433. populīs: the pupil should bear in mind that this means *tribes*, not *people* in the ordinary English sense.   **ipsōs**: *very*.   **spectantēs**: *as they were looking on.*

434. raptōrēs: *those who had seized* (*the maidens*).   **quod**: *what* (*that which*); as antecedent, understand *id*, object of *darent*.   **et ea**: *those also, those too; et* is here an adverb.

435. Forum Rōmānum: the Forum was situated on level ground surrounded by six of the seven hills of Rome.   **raptae**: *the* (*women who had been*) *seized.*   **hinc ... hinc**: *on the one side ... on the other.*

436. discrīpsit: *i.e.* organized different political and social classes. **cum ... tum**: *not only ... but also*, lit. *when ... then* (*while ... at the same time*).   **ortam**: from *orior*.   **oculīs**: *from the eyes; oculīs* is really dative; verbs of *taking away* at times take the dative in the sense of *from*.   **aliī ... aliī**: *some ... others.*

437. interrēgnum: *interregnum, i.e.* a period between reigns.   **Curibus**: this limits *nātus*.   **quidem**: *to be sure;* observe that *quidem* always lays stress upon the word immediately preceding it (here *bellum*); frequently it is best to attempt no special translation of *quidem*, but to bring out its force in English by the arrangement of words or by oral emphasis.   **gessit**: from *gerō*.   **nec minus tamen prōfuit**: *and yet he was none the less of advantage.*   **et ... et**: *both ... and.*   **sē nymphae, etc.**: *he said he did at the advice of the nymph Egeria, his wife.*

438. praestiterat: from *praestō*.   **rēgnāsset**: = *rēgnāvisset*.   **ārsit**: remember that *ārdeō* is intransitive.

439. nova eī moenia circumdedit: *surrounded it with new walls,* lit. *surrounded new walls to it.* **ad Tiberis ōstia:** Rome was some twenty miles from the mouth of the Tiber by the course of the river. **obiit:** *died,* lit. *met (death).*

441. pūpillīs: *from his wards.* **minōrum gentium:** understand *senātōrēs, i.e. senators of the lesser gentes (tribes).* **nec paucōs agrōs:** *and not a few lands.* **hostibus:** *from the enemy;* dative. **adēmptōs:** from *adimō.* **triumphāns:** *in a triumphal procession,* lit. *triumphing.* **Cloācās:** several of the ancient Roman sewers still exist and are in use to-day. **Capitōlium:** the magnificent temple on the summit of the Capitoline Hill. It was dedicated to Jupiter, Juno, and Minerva. **per Ancī fīliōs:** *i.e.* at their instigation; they hired assassins to perform the deed. **quibus:** *from whom;* dative.

443. grave quidem: *serious, to be sure.* **eum petere:** *that he requested.* **dum convaluisset:** *until he should recover.*

444. in agrīs: *in the country.* **jacēns:** *(which was) lying.*

445. Templum Jovis: the one begun by Tarquinius Priscus. **ipsa:** *with her own hand.*

446. Hanc ob causam: when a noun is limited by an adjective or a pronoun, the preposition very often stands between the two. **in exitium:** *for the destruction.* **eī:** *i.e.* against him.

447. sī . . . esset: *esset* is in the subjunctive as the result of attraction to the subjunctive *coërcēret.* **īnsolentiōrēs:** *too arrogant.* **expulsīs rēgibus:** *after the expulsion of the kings.* **Collātīnō:** *from Collatinus* (dative). **Placuerat:** *they had ordained,* lit. *it had pleased (them).* **in ējus locum:** *in his place.*

448. urbī: *against the city.* **inter sēsē occīdērunt:** *killed each other.* **Rōmānī . . . victōrēs recessērunt:** *the Romans retired as victors; victōrēs* is the predicate nominative. **lūxērunt:** from *lūgeō.*

449. Horātius Cocles: read Macaulay's *Horatius at the Bridge* (*Lays of Ancient Rome*) for a spirited account of Horatius's achievement. **ad suōs:** *to his friends.*

450. eō cōnsiliō, *etc.:* *with this design,* viz. *to kill the king;* the clause *ut . . . occīderet* is in apposition with *cōnsiliō.* **Ignibus allātīs:** *by bringing in fires; allātīs* is from *afferō.* **terrēret:** *i.e. endeavored to frighten him.* **accēnsae:** *burning,* lit. *kindled.* **cōnsūmpta esset:** this loss of his right hand was the origin of the name Scaevola, 'the left-handed.' **conjūrāsse:** a shortened form for *conjūrāvisset.* **prīvātus:** *as a private citizen.*

451. post rēgēs exāctōs: *after the expulsion of the kings.*   **trāns Aniēnem**: hardly more than three or four miles from the city.   **fābulam dē ventre**, *etc.:* according to the fable, the limbs of the body once rebelled and refused longer to furnish food for the stomach.   Menenius pointed out that the governing class at Rome was really just as essential to the welfare of the state, as was the stomach to the welfare of the body.   **tribūnī**: at first two in number, later five, and ultimately ten.   By their power of intercession they could protect plebeians from the unjust treatment of which the patrician magistrates were often guilty.

452. quīntum mīlliārium urbis: *fifth milestone from the city.*   **Quō factō**: *and when this had been done.*   **ut prōditor**: *as a traitor.*

453. duce Fabiō: *under the leadership of Fabius.*   **hostēs**: obj. of *vīcissent.*   **dolō ūsī**: *having employed strategy.*   **exortō**: from *exorior.*   **Ūnus**: *one only.*

454. trecentēsimō et alterō: *the three hundred and second.*   **ab urbe conditā**: *from the founding of the city.*

455. lūdī litterāriī: the two words together mean *school*, lit. *a school for letters* (reading and writing), as opposed, for example, to a gladiatorial school, where gladiators were trained.   **prīncipum fīlios**: as hostages.   **in castra hostium**: *i.e.* of the Romans.   **manibus . . . vinctīs**: *with his hands tied behind his back.*   **quibus . . . agerent**: *with which to drive.*   **Camillō crīminī . . . datum est**: lit. *it was set against Camillus for a charge, i.e.* Camillus was accused.   **triumphāsset**: = *triumphāvisset.* **damnātus**: understand *est* from *expulsus est.*

456. Paulō post: *post* is here an adverb.   **Gallī Senonēs**: a tribe from northern Italy.   **ad Alliam**: the Allia was a small river flowing into the Tiber about eleven miles from Rome.   **occupārunt**: = *occupāvērunt.* **in eō**, *etc.:* *were on the point of purchasing*, lit. *were in this, (viz.) that they should purchase; ut . . . emerent* explains *eō.*

457. quārtō mīlliāriō: *at the fourth milestone;* abl. of place, without the prep.

458. sēcum: = *cum sē;* the preposition *cum* is always thus appended to the personal and reflexive pronouns.   **obtulit**: from *offerō.*   **armātus**: *in arms.*   **eī suprā dextrum**,* etc.:* *perched above his right arm*, lit. *above the right arm to him.*   **Ita factum est**: *thus it happened.*   **nūllō negōtiō**: *with no difficulty, i.e. without difficulty.*

459. dictātōris: on occasions of great public danger, the Romans often appointed a dictator, who had absolute power.   His period of office was limited to six months.   **Quī cum**: *when he.*   **magister equitum**: the master of the horse was appointed by the dictator and ranked next to him. **nactus**: from *nanciscor.* **capitis damnātus est**: *was condemned to death*, lit. *of his head (i.e. of his life).*

460. post: adv. **faciendum**: *i.e. faciendum esse.* **aut ... aut**: *either ... or.* **dīmittendōs**: understand *esse.* **sub jugum**: in token of submission; the yoke was made by setting two spears in the ground and laying a third across the top.

461. poposcērunt: from *posco.* **agerentur**: subjunctive by attraction to *renūntiārent.*

462. per noctem: *by night.* **adversīs vulneribus**: *with wounds in front.* **etiam mortuōs**: *even in death.* **Ego cum tālibus virīs ... subigam**: this is equivalent to a conditional sentence of the second type, *If I should have such soldiers, I should subdue.*

463. perrēxit: from *pergo.* **ad Praeneste**: *to the vicinity of Praeneste;* to say: *to Praeneste*, the accusative alone would have sufficed. **mīliāriō**, *etc.:* *at the eighteenth milestone;* abl. of place, without the prep. **exercitūs**: objective gen. depending upon *terrore; fear of the army.* **dē captīvīs redimendīs**: *with regard to ransoming the captives.* **sī trānsīret**: this is virtually a subordinate clause in indirect discourse, since *prōmitteret* is practically equivalent to *said he would give him.*

464. admīrātiōne tenērētur: in English, we say: *to be filled with admiration.* **eā condiciōne**: explained by the following *ut*-clause. **nisi recessisset**: *unless he should withdraw.*

465. interjectō annō: *after the lapse of a year,* lit. *a year having been put between.* "**Ille est Fabricius quī**": *Fabricius is one who.* **ā Tarentō**: *from the vicinity of Tarentum;* to say: *from Tarentum*, the ablative alone would have sufficed. **ad Argōs**: *near Argi (Argos).*

466. trājēcērunt: here intransitive, — *crossed over.*

467. Paucīs annīs interjectīs: *after the lapse of a few years.* **in fidem**: *into allegiance.* **Quam cum**, *etc.:* *when Regulus was unwilling to grant this.* **nisi dūrissimīs condiciōnibus**: *except on very hard terms.* **captus**: for *captus est.*

468. dēsiisse: from *dēsino.* **nē ... facerent**: *not to make.* **illōs ... habēre**: indirect discourse dependent on the idea of *saying* involved in *suāsit.* **tantī nōn esse**: *that it was not worth while,* lit. *of so great account; tantī* is a predicate genitive of quality, with some such word as *pretī (of value)* understood. **ut ... redderentur**: this substantive clause of result is the logical subject of *esse.*

469. captae, dēmersae, capta: understand *sunt* with these.

GENERAL LATIN-ENGLISH VOCABULARY.

A.

A., abbreviation for **Aulus**, *Aulus.*

ā, ab, prep. w. abl., *from ; by.*

abeō, īre, iī, itūrus, *go away.*

abiciō, ere, jēcī, jectus, *throw away, cast.*

absēns (pres. participle of **absum**), entis, *absent.*

abstineō, ēre, tinuī, *abstain from.*

absum, esse, āfuī, āfutūrus, *be absent, be distant* (§ 182).

ac (atque), *and, and also ;* ac is not used before vowels.

Acca Lārentia, ae, f., *Acca Larentia,* a woman's name.

accēdō, ere, cessī, cessūrus, *draw near.*

accendō, ere, cendī, cēnsus, *kindle.*

accidō, ere, idī, *happen.*

accipiō, ere, ēpī, eptus, *receive.*

accurrō, ere, cucurrī, cursum, *run to, run up ; hasten.*

accūsō, 1, *accuse.*

ācer, ācris, ācre, *sharp, vigorous, keen, severe.*

aciēs, ēī, f., *line of battle.*

ācriter, *sharply, fiercely.*

ad, prep. w. acc., *to, towards, for* (denoting purpose) ; *near.*

addō, ere, idī, itus, *add.*

addūcō, ere, dūxī, ductus, *lead on, impel.*

adeō, īre, iī, itūrus, *go to, visit.*

adimō, ere, ēmī, ēmptus, *take away.*

aditus, ūs, m., *approach.*

adjungō, ere, jūnxī, jūnctus, *join to ; annex.*

administrō, 1, *perform.*

admīrātiō, ōnis, f., *admiration.*

admīror, ārī, ātus sum, *admire.*

admodum, *quite, very much.*

admoneō, ēre, uī, itus, *remind, warn.*

adolēscō, ere, lēvī, *grow up.*

adorior, īrī, ortus sum, *attack.*

adsum, adesse, adfuī, *be present, be at hand* (§ 182).

adulēscēns, centis, m., *young man.*

adveniō, īre, vēnī, ventum, *arrive.*

adventus, ūs, m., *arrival.*

adversārius, iī, m., *adversary.*

adversum, adversus, prep. w. acc., *against.*

adversus, a, um, *adverse ; in front* (of wounds).

aedificium, ī (iī), n., *building.*

aedificō, 1, *build.*

Aenēās, ae, m., *Aeneas,* a man's name.

aequālis, e, *equal.*

aequitās, tātis, f., *justice.*

aequus, qua, quum, *level.*

āēr, āëris, m., *air.*

aestās, tātis, f., *summer.*

aetās, tātis, f., *age, time of life.*

188

afferŏ, ferre, attulī, allātus, *bring* (§ 188).

Āfrica, ae, f., *Africa.*

ager, agrī, m., *field, land.*

agger, eris, m., *embankment, rampart.*

agmen, minis, n., *army (on the march), column.*

agō, ere, ēgī, āctus, *do ; drive.*

agricola, ae, m., *farmer.*

agricultūra, ae, f., *agriculture.*

Agrippa, ae, m., *Agrippa,* a man's name.

ājŏ, defective, *say ;* pres. and perf. 3d sing. ăit.

āla, ae, f., *wing.*

alacer, cris, cre, *eager.*

Alba Longa, Albae Longae, f., *Alba Longa,* name of a town.

Albānus, a, um, *Alban.*

albus, a, um, *white.*

aliēnus, a, um, *unfavorable.*

aliquandō, *once upon a time ; formerly.*

aliquis, aliquid, *some one, something* (§ 102).

aliquī, aliqua, aliquod, adj., *some* (§ 102).

aliquot, indecl., *several, some.*

alius, a, ud, *other, another, else* (§ 61).

Allia, ae, f., *Allia,* name of a river.

Allobrogēs, um, *the Allobroges,* a Gallic tribe.

alloquor, loquī, locūtus sum, *address, speak to.*

alŏ, ere, aluī, altus, *nourish.*

alter, era, erum, *the other ; second* (§ 61).

altitūdŏ, inis, f., *height ; depth.*

altus, a, um, *high ; deep.*

amīcē, adv., *in a friendly manner.*

amīcitia, ae, f., *friendship.*

amīcus, ī, m., *friend.*

āmittŏ, ere, mīsī, missus, *lose.*

amnis, is, m., *river.*

amŏ, 1, *love.*

ampliŏ, 1, *enlarge.*

amplius, adv., *more.*

amplus, a, um, *ample, glorious.*

Amūlius, ī (iī), m., *Amulius,* a man's name.

an, interrog. particle, *or, whether.*

Anchīsēs, ae, m., *Anchises,* a man's name.

ancora, ae, f., *anchor.*

Ancus Mārcius, gen. Ancī Mārcī (iī), m., *Ancus Marcius,* fourth king of Rome.

angustiae, ārum, f. pl., *a narrow pass.*

angustus, a, um, *narrow.*

animadvertŏ, ere, vertī, versus, *notice.*

animal, mālis, n., *animal.*

animus, ī, m., *mind, soul ; courage, heart.*

Aniŏ, Aniēnis, m., *Anio,* name of a river.

annectŏ, ere, nexuī, nexus, *tie to.*

annus, ī, m., *year.*

annuus, a, um, *for one year.*

ante, prep. w. acc., *before, in front of;* adv., *before.*

anteā, *previously, before.*

antecēdŏ, ere, cessī, cessūrus, *precede.*

antequam, conj., *before.*

antīquus, a, um, *ancient.*

ānulus, ī, m., *ring.*

apertus, a, um, *open.*

appellŏ, 1, *name, call.*

Appius, ī (iī), m., *Appius,* a man's name.

appropinquŏ, 1, *approach.*

Aprīlis, e, adj., *of April.*

apud, prep. w. acc., *among, at, with, at the home of.*

aqua, ae, f., *water.*

aquila, ae, f., *eagle.*

Aquītānia, ae, f., *Aquitania*, a district of Gaul.

āra, ae, f., *altar.*

arbitror, trārī, trātus sum, *consider.*

arbor, oris, f., *tree.*

arceō, ēre, uī, *keep off; keep away.*

arcessō, ere, īvī, ītus, *summon.*

Ardea, ae, f., *Ardea*, a Latin town.

ārdeō, ēre, ārsī, ārsūrus, *burn.*

Argī, ōrum, m., *Argos*, name of a town.

Ariovistus, ī, m., *Ariovistus*, a king of the Germans.

arma, ōrum, n. pl., *arms.*

armātūra, ae, f., *equipment.*

armilla, ae, f., *bracelet.*

armō, I, *arm.*

arripiō, ere, uī, eptus, *seize.*

arrogō, I, *lay claim to.*

Arrūns, runtis, m., *Arruns*, a man's name.

arx, arcis, f., *citadel.*

Ascanius, ī (iī), m., *Ascanius*, son of Aeneas.

Asia, ae, f., *Asia.*

Asina, ae, m., *Asina*, a man's name.

asinus, ī, m., *ass.*

asȳlum, ī, n., *place of refuge.*

at, *but.*

Athēnae, ārum, f. pl., *Athens.*

Atīlius, ī (iī), *Atilius*, a man's name.

atque, *and, and also;* see ac.

Atticus, ī, m., *Atticus*, a friend of Cicero.

attulī, perf. of afferō.

auctōritās, tātis, f., *authority, influence.*

audācter, *courageously.*

audāx, gen. audācis, *courageous.*

audeō, ēre, ausus sum; semi-dep., *dare.*

audiō, īre, īvī, ītus, *hear.*

aufugiō, ere, fūgī, fugitūrus, *flee.*

augeō, ēre, auxī, auctus, *increase* (tr.).

Aulus, ī, m., *Aulus*, a man's name.

aureus, a, um, *golden.*

aurīga, ae, m., *charioteer.*

aurum, ī, n., *gold.*

aut, *or;* aut … aut, *either … or.*

autem, *however; but.*

auxilium, ī (iī), n., *aid, help;* in pl. auxilia, ōrum, n., *auxiliary troops, auxiliaries.*

Avāricum, ī, n., *Avaricum*, a Gallic town.

Aventīnus, ī, *Aventine*, a hill of Rome.

āvertō, ere, tī, versus, *avert, turn aside.*

avus, ī, m., *grandfather.*

Bacēnis, is, f., *Bacenis*, a forest in Germany.

barbarus, ī, m., *a barbarian;* adj., us, a, um, *barbarian.*

beātus, a, um, *happy.*

Belgae, ārum, m. pl., *Belgians*, a Gallic tribe.

bellicōsus, a, um, *warlike.*

bellō, I, *make war, carry on war.*

bellum, ī, n., *war.*

bene, adv., *well* (§ 79).

beneficium, ī (iī), n., *kindness.*

benīgnē, *kindly, graciously.*

bēstia, ae, f., *beast.*

Bibulus, ī, m., *Bibulus*, a man's name.

bīduum, ī, n., *two days.*

Bōjī, ōrum, m. pl., *the Boji*, an ancient tribe.

bonus, a, um, *good;* in pl. bona, ōrum, n., *property.*

bōs, bovis, m., *ox;* gen. pl. boum.

bracchium, ī (iī), n., *arm.*

brevis, e, *short, brief;* brevī, *within a short time.*

Britannia, ae, f., *Britain.*

Brūtus, ī, m., *Brutus*, a man's name.

C., abbreviation for Gāius, *Gaius.*

caedēs, is, f., *slaughter.*

caedō, ere, cecīdī, caesus, *cut, slay, kill.*

caelum, ī, n., *heaven.*

Caesar, aris, m., *Caesar.*

calamitās, tātis, f., *calamity.*

Camillus, ī, m., *Camillus,* a man's name.

Campānia, ae, f., *Campania.*

canis, is, c., *dog.*

capessō, ere, īvī, ītus, *take;* fugam capessere, *flee.*

capiō, capere, cēpī, captus, *take; adopt; capture.*

Capitōlium, ī (iī), n., *the Capitol.*

capra, ae, f., *she-goat.*

captīva, ae, f., *captive.*

captīvus, ī, m., *captive, prisoner.*

caput, itis, n., *head.*

carcer, is, m., *prison.*

carpentum, ī, n., *chariot.*

Carthāginiēnsis, e, *Carthaginian;* Carthāginiēnsēs, ium, m., *Carthaginians.*

cārus, a, um, *dear.*

castellum, ī, n., *fort.*

castra, ōrum, n. pl., *a camp.*

cāsus, ūs, m., *chance, misfortune.*

Catilīna, ae, m., *Catiline.*

Catulus, ī, m., *Catulus,* a man's name.

causa, ae, f., *cause, condition;* causā, abl., *for the sake of;* the dependent genitive precedes causā.

caveō, ēre, cāvī, cautūrus, *be on one's guard.*

cēdō, ere, cessī, cessūrus, *yield, withdraw.*

celer, eris, e, *swift.*

celeritās, tātis, f., *speed.*

celeriter, *quickly.*

cēlō, 1, *conceal.*

cēnsus, ūs, m., *census.*

centum, *hundred,* indecl.

centuriō, ōnis, m., *centurion.*

cernō, ere, *perceive.*

certāmen, inis, n., *contest.*

certus, a, um, *sure;* comp. certior in phrase certior fierī, *be informed;* certiōrem facere, *inform.*

cēterī, ae, a, *the rest; the others.*

cibus, ī, m., *food.*

Cīneās, ae, m., *Cineas,* a man's name.

circiter, adv., *about.*

circumdō, dăre, dedī, dătus, *surround, place around.*

circumeō, īre, iī, itus, *go around, surround.*

circumveniō, īre, vēnī, ventus, *surround.*

citerior, ius, comp. adj., *nearer, hither.*

citrā, prep. w. acc., *this side of.*

cīvis, is, c., *citizen, fellow-citizen.*

cīvitās, tātis, f., *state.*

clam, *secretly.*

clārus, a, um, *clear, loud; distinguished.*

classis, classis, f., *fleet.*

Claudius, ī (iī), m., *Claudius,* a man's name.

claudō, ere, clausī, clausus, *shut, close.*

clēmēns, gen. entis, *merciful.*

clipeus, ī, m., *shield.*

cloāca, ae, f., *sewer.*

Cn., abbreviation of Gnaeus, *Gnaeus,* a man's name.

Cocles, itis, m., *Cocles,* a man's name.

coepī, coepisse, *began, have begun* (§ 198).

coërceō, ēre, uī, itus, *hold in check, confine.*

cōgitō, 1, *think.*

cognōmen, inis, n., *name, surname.*

cognōscō, ere, nōvī, nitus, *learn.*

cōgō, ere, coēgī, coāctus, *force, compel; collect.*

cohibeō, ēre, uī, itus, *check, restrain.*

cohors, cohortis, f., *cohort* (division of a legion).

Collātīnus, ī, m., *Collatinus*, a man's name.

collātus, perf. pass. ptc. of cōnferō.

collēga, ae, m., *colleague.*

collis, is, m., *hill.*

collocō, 1, *place, arrange, station.*

colloquium, ī (iī), n., *conference.*

colloquor, ī, locūtus sum, *confer.*

collum, ī, n., *neck.*

commeātus, ūs, m., *supplies.*

comminuō, ere, uī, ūtus, *dash to pieces.*

committō, ere, mīsī, missus, *bring together;* with proelium or pūgnam, *to join battle.*

commoror, ārī, ātus sum, *delay, sojourn.*

commoveō, ēre, mōvī, mōtus, *move, stir up, excite; induce.*

commūniō, īre, iī, ītus, *strongly fortify.*

commūnis, e, *common.*

commūtātiō, ōnis, f., *change.*

comparō, 1, *get ready.*

comperiō, īre, perī, pertus, *find out.*

complector, ī, plexus sum, *embrace.*

compleō, ēre, plēvī, plētus, *fill up.*

complūrēs, plūra, gen. ium, *very many.*

comprehendō, ere, endī, ēnsus, *arrest.*

concēdō, ere, cessī, cessūrus, *grant.*

conciliō, 1, *reconcile, win over.*

concilium, ī (iī), n., *council.*

concordia, ae, f., *harmony.*

concurrō, ere, ī, cursum, *run together.*

concursus, ūs, m., *a running together.*

condiciō, ōnis, f., *condition, terms.*

condō, ere, didī, ditus, *found, build.*

condūcō, ere, dūxī, ductus, *hire.*

cōnferō, ferre, tulī, collātus, *bring together;* sē cōnferre, *betake one's self* (§ 188).

cōnficiō, ere, fēcī, fectus, *exhaust.*

cōnfīdō, ere, fīsus sum, *trust,* semidep. (§ 220, II, *a*).

cōnfīrmō, 1, *establish, confirm.*

cōnfugiō, ere, fūgī, fugitūrus, *flee for refuge.*

coniciō, ere, jēcī, jectus, *hurl; cast; put.*

conjungō, ere, jūnxī, jūnctus, *unite.*

conjūnx, jugis, c., *husband; wife.*

conjūrātiō, ōnis, f., *conspiracy.*

conjūrō, 1, *conspire.*

Conōn, ōnis, m., *Conon,* a Greek general.

cōnor, ārī, ātus sum, *endeavor, attempt.*

cōnsector, ārī, ātus sum, *follow up.*

cōnsenēscō, ere, senuī, *grow old.*

cōnsequor, ī, secūtus sum, *acquire.*

cōnserō, ere, uī, tus, *join.*

cōnservō, 1, *preserve.*

cōnsīdō, ere, ēdī, essus, *settle.*

cōnsilium, ī (iī), n., *plan; council; advice.*

cōnsistō, ere, stitī, *consist.*

cōnspectus, ūs, m., *view, sight.*

cōnspiciō, ere, spexī, spectus, *see.*

cōnspicor, ārī, ātus sum, *catch sight of, observe.*

cōnstat, impers., *it is evident* (§ 202).

cōnstituō, ere, uī, ūtus, *decide, determine.*

cōnsul, ulis, m., *consul.*

cōnsūmō, ere, sūmpsī, sūmptus, *use up, consume.*

contemnō, ere, tempsī, temptus, *despise.*

contendō, ere, tendī, tentum, *hurry, hasten; contend.*

contentus, a, um, *contented.*

contineō, ēre, uī, *confine, hold in check.*

contrā, prep. w. acc., *against, opposite.*

contrārius, a, um, *contrary to, opposite.*

contrōversia, ae, f., *controversy.*

contumēlia, ae, f., *insult.*

convalēscō, ere, valuī, *recover, regain strength.*

conveniō, īre, vēnī, ventum, *come together, assemble.*

convocō, 1, *call together.*

cōpia, ae, f., *plenty;* in pl. cōpiae, ārum, *troops, forces.*

Corinthus, ī, m., *Corinth,* a city of Greece.

Coriolānus, ī, m., *Coriolanus,* a man's name.

Coriolī, ōrum, m., *Corioli,* a Latin town.

Cornēlius, ī (iī), *Cornelius,* a man's name.

cornū, ūs, n., *horn;* in military sense, *wing* of an army.

corpus, oris, n., *body.*

corrumpō, ere, rūpī, ruptus, *ruin.*

Corvīnus, ī, m., *Corvinus,* a man's name.

corvus, ī, m., *raven.*

cottīdiē, *every day, daily.*

Crassus, ī, m., *Crassus,* a man's name.

crēber, bra, brum, *frequent.*

crēdō, ere, didī, ditum, *believe* (§ 220, II, *a*).

Cremera, ae, f., *Cremera,* a river in Etruria.

creō, 1, *make; elect.*

crīmen, inis, n., *charge, accusation.*

crūdēlis, e, *cruel.*

culpō, 1, *blame.*

1. cum, prep. w. abl., *with.*

2. cum, conj., *when; because, since; though;* cum . . . tum, *not only . . . but also.*

cunctātiō, ōnis, f., *delay.*

cupiditās, tātis, f., *desire, eagerness.*

cupidus, a, um, *fond, eager.*

Curēs, ium, f., *Cures,* a Sabine town.

cūria, ae, f., *ward.*

Cūriātius, ī (iī), m., pl. Cūriātiī, ōrum, m., *Curiatii,* an Alban family.

cūrō, 1, *care for, take care of.*

Cursor, ōris, m., *Cursor,* a man's name.

cursus, ūs, m., *course.*

cūstōdia, ae, f., *custody.*

damnō, 1, *condemn;* capitis damnāre, *condemn to death.*

dē, prep. w. abl., *concerning; of.*

dēbeō, dēbēre, dēbuī, dēbitus, *owe;* with another verb, *ought;* pass., *to be due.*

dēbilitō, 1, *weaken.*

dēcēdō, ere, cessī, cessūrus, *withdraw; die.*

decem, indecl., *ten.*

decemvirī, ōrum, m., *decemvirs,* a board of ten men.

dēcernō, cernere, crēvī, crētus, *decree; decide* (by combat), *fight.*

decimus, a, um, *tenth.*

dēclārō, 1, *make clear, show.*

dēditiō, ōnis, f., *surrender.*

dēdō, dere, didī, dēditus, *give up, surrender.*

dēdūcō, ere, dūxī, ductus, *lead away.*

dēfectiō, ōnis, f., *revolt.*

dēfendō, ere, fendī, fēnsus, *defend.*

dēfēnsiō, ōnis, f., *defence.*

deinde, *then, afterwards.*

dēlātus, perf. pass. participle of dēferō.

dēlectō, 1, *delight.*

dēleō, ēre, ēvī, ētus, *destroy.*

dēlīberō, 1, *deliberate, consult.*

dēligō, ere, lēgī, lēctus, *choose.*

Dēmarātus, ī, m., *Demaratus,* a man's name.

dēmergō, ere, mersī, mersus, *sink.*

dēmittō, ere, mīsī, missus, *let fall.*

dēnique, *finally.*

dēns, dentis, m., *tooth.*

dēpopulor, ārī, ātus sum, *lay waste.*

dēprehendō, dere, dī, hēnsus, *catch.*

dēserō, ere, seruī, sertus, *abandon, desert.*

dēsinō, ere, siī, situm, *cease.*

dēsistō, ere, stitī, *cease.*

dēspērō, 1, *despair.*

dēspiciō, ere, spexī, spectus, *despise.*

dēsum, dēesse, dēfuī, dēfutūrus, *be wanting, fail* (§ 182).

dētrīmentum, ī, n., *loss, damage, harm.*

deus, ī, m., *god.*

dēvincō, ere, vīcī, victus, *conquer.*

dexter, tra, trum, *right;* as subst. (sc. manus), *right hand.*

dīcō, ere, dīxī, dictus, *say; utter; appoint; call.*

dictātor, ōris, m., *dictator.*

diēs, ēī, m. or f., *day.*

differō, ferre, distulī, dīlātum, *differ* (§ 188).

difficilis, e, *difficult.*

difficulter, adv., from adj. difficilis, *with difficulty.*

digitus, ī, m., *finger.*

dīgnitās, tātis, f., *dignity.*

dīgnus, a, um, *worthy.*

dīligentia, ae, f., *diligence.*

dīmicō, 1, *contend.*

dīmittō, ere, mīsī, missus, *let go, dismiss.*

dīripiō, ere, ripuī, reptus, *plunder.*

dīruō, ere, ruī, rutus, *tear down, destroy.*

discēdō, ere, cessī, cessūrus, *depart, withdraw.*

disciplīna, ae, f., *discipline.*

discordia, ae, f., *strife, discord.*

discordō, 1, *be at variance, quarrel.*

discrībō, ere, scrīpsī, scrīptus, *mark out; divide into classes.*

dispōnō, ere, posuī, positus, *distribute.*

dissēnsiō, ōnis, f., *disagreement.*

dissidium, ī (iī), n., *dissension.*

distribuō, ere, uī, ūtus, *distribute.*

diū, adv., *a long time.*

diūturnitās, tātis, f., *long duration.*

dīvidō, ere, īsī, īsus, *divide.*

dīvitiae, ārum, f. pl., *riches.*

dō, dāre, dedī, dātus, *give, render; put, set.*

doceō, ēre, uī, doctus, *teach.*

dolor, ōris, m., *grief.*

dolus, ī, m., *deceit, cunning.*

dominātiō, ōnis, f., *rule, tyranny.*

dominus, ī, m., *master.*

Domitius, ī (iī), m., *Domitius,* a man's name.

domō, āre, uī, itus, *subdue.*

domus, ūs, f., *house, home.*

dōnec, *until.*

dōnō, 1, *present.*

dōnum, ī, n., *gift.*

dubitō, 1, *doubt, be in doubt; hesitate, waver.*

ducentī, ae, a, *two hundred.*

dūcō, ere, dūxī, ductus, *lead.*

Duilius, ī (iī), m., *Duilius,* a man's name.

dum, *while; as long as; until.*

Dumnorīx, rīgis, m., *Dumnorix,* a chief of the Haedui.

duo, duae, duo, *two* (§ 80, 1).

duodecim, indecl., *twelve.*

dūrus, a, um, *hard, severe.*

dux, ducis, m., *leader.*

ē, ex, prep. w. abl., *out of;* ē is not used before vowels or h.

ēdūcō, ere, dūxī, ductus, *lead forth.*

efficiō, ere, fēcī, fectus, *make, render; do, bring about.*

effundō, ere, fūdī, fūsus, *pour out.*

Ēgeria, ae, f., *Egeria,* name of a nymph.

ego, meī, *I.*

ēgredior, gredī, gressus sum, *march out.*

ēgregius, a, um, *excellent, especial.*

ēiciō, ere, jēcī, jectus, *thrust out;* sē ēicere, *rush forth.*

ējus modī, *of that kind* (§ 237, 1).

ēlābor, lābī, lāpsus sum, *glide away, escape, elapse.*

ēlātus, perf. pass. participle of efferō.

elephantus, ī, m., *elephant.*

emō, ere, ēmī, ēmptus, *buy.*

enim, *for;* cannot begin a sentence.

eō, adv., *thither, to that place.*

eō, īre, īvī (iī), itum, *go* (§ 197).

eōdem, *to the same place.*

Ēpīrus, ī, f., *Epirus.*

eques, itis, m., *horseman;* in pl., *cavalry, horsemen.*

equester, tris, tre, *equestrian.*

equitātus, ūs, m., *cavalry.*

equus, ī, m., *horse.*

ergō, *therefore.*

ēripiō, ere, uī, eptus, *snatch away, take away.*

errō, 1, *err, be mistaken.*

ēruptiō, ōnis, f., *sally.*

et, *and;* et . . . et, *both . . . and;* as adv., *also, even.*

etiam, *also; even.*

Etrūria, ae, f., *Etruria.*

Etrūscus, a, um, *Etruscan.*

etsī, *although.*

ēvertō, ere, tī, sus, *overturn, destroy.*

ex, prep. w. abl., *out of;* see ē.

excēdō, ere, cessī, cessūrus, *leave, depart from.*

excitō, 1, *stir up, rouse.*

exeō, īre, iī, itum, *go forth, go out* (§ 197).

exerceō, ēre, uī, itus, *exercise; practise.*

exercitus, ūs, m., *army.*

exhauriō, īre, hausī, haustus, *drain; impoverish.*

exigō, ere, ēgī, āctus, *drive out, banish.*

eximius, a, um, *extraordinary.*

exīstimō, 1, *think, consider.*

exitium, ī (iī), n., *destruction.*

exitus, ūs, m., *exit, passage.*

exorior, orīrī, ortus sum, *arise.*

expediō, īre, īvī, ītus, *extricate.*

expedītus, a, um, *unencumbered, light-armed; easy.*

expellō, ere, pulī, pulsus, *drive out, banish.*

experior, īrī, pertus sum, *try, test.*

explōrātor, ōris, m., *scout.*

explōrō, 1, *examine.*

expūgnō, 1, *take by storm.*

exsilium, ī (iī), n., *exile.*

exsistō, ere, stitī, *arise.*

exspectō, 1, *expect, await.*

exstinguō, ere, stīnxī, stīnctus, *destroy;* in pass., *be put to death, die.*

extrā, prep. w. acc., *outside, beyond.*

extrahō, ere, trāxī, trāctus, *extract, draw forth.*

extrēmus, a, um, *extreme, outermost; end of.*

Fabius, ī (iī), m., *Fabius,* a man's name; Fabiī, ōrum, m. pl., *Fabii,* a Roman gens.

Fabricius, ī (iī), m., *Fabricius.*

fābula, ae, f., *fable.*

facile, *easily.*

facilis, e, *easy.*

facinus, inoris, n., *crime, deed.*

faciō, ere, fēcī, factus, *make, do,* pass. irreg. (§ 193).

factiō, ōnis, f., *faction.*

facultās, tātis, f., *supply.*

Faleriī, ōrum, m., *Falerii,* a city.

Faliscī, ōrum, m., *Faliscans,* inhabitants of Falerii.

fāma, ae, f., *reputation, report.*

famēs, is, f., *hunger;* abl. sing. irreg. famē.

familia, ae, f., *family.*

familāritās, tātis, f., *intimacy.*

famula, ae, f., *servant; slave.*

fascis, is, m., *bundle.*

faucēs, ium, f. pl., *throat, jaws.*

Faustulus, ī, m., *Faustulus,* a man's name.

faveō, ēre, fāvī, fautūrus, *favor.*

favor, ōris, m., *favor, good will.*

fēlēs, is, f., *cat.*

fēlīciter, *successfully.*

fēlīx, gen. fēlīcis, *fortunate, happy.*

fēmina, ae, f., *woman.*

fera, ae, f., *wild beast.*

ferāx, gen. ferācis, *fertile.*

ferē, *almost, about, practically.*

ferō, ferre, tulī, lātus, *bear, carry, bring; lift, raise; lend* (of help); *say.*

ferrum, ī, n., *iron; sword.*

fēstum, ī, *festival.*

fidēs, eī, f., *fidelity, loyalty, protection; confidence, allegiance.*

fīdūcia, ae, f., *confidence.*

fīlia, ae, f., *daughter.*

fīlius, ī (iī), m., *son.*

fīniō, īre, īvī, ītus, *finish, terminate.*

fīnis, is, m., *end, boundary;* in pl., *territory.*

fīnitimus, a, um, *neighboring.*

fīō, fierī, factus sum, *become, be made; occur, happen;* pass. of faciō (§ 193).

fīrmiter (fīrmius, fīrmissimē), *firmly.*

fīrmus, a, um, *firm, strong.*

flāgitō, 1, *demand.*

flectō, ere, flexī, flexus, *bend, prevail upon.*

flētus, ūs, m., *weeping.*

flūmen, inis, n., *river.*

fluvius, ī (iī), m., *river.*

foedus, eris, n., *treaty.*

fore, fut. infin. of sum (§ 116, footnote 2).

forte, *by chance.*

fortis, e, *brave.*

fortiter, *bravely.*

fortūna, ae, f., *fortune;* pl. fortūnae, ārum, f., *fortune* (possessions).

forum, ī, n., *forum; market-place.*

fossa, ae, f., *ditch, trench.*

frangō, ere, frēgī, frāctus, *break.*

frāter, tris, m., *brother.*

frūmentum, ī, n., *grain.*

frūstrā, adv., *in vain.*

fuga, ae, f., *flight.*

fugiō, ere, fūgī, fugitūrus, *flee, escape from.*

fugō, 1, *put to flight.*

fulmen, inis, n., *thunderbolt.*

funditor, ōris, m., *slinger.*

fundō, ere, fūdī, fūsus, *pour, pour out;* of troops, *to rout.*

furcula, ae, f., *fork;* Furculae Caudīnae, *Caudine Forks.*

Fūrius, ī (iī), m., *Furius,* a man's name.

fūrtum, ī, n., *theft.*

futūrus, a, um, future participle of sum.

Gāius, ī, m., *Gaius,* a man's name. (Abbreviated C.)

Galba, ae, m., *Galba,* a man's name.

Gallī, ōrum, m. pl., *Gauls.*

Gallia, ae, f., *Gaul.*

gallīna, ae, f., *hen.*

geminī, ōrum, m. pl., *twins.*

Genēva, ae, f., *Geneva,* a town of the Allobroges.

gēns, gentis, f., *tribe; gens* (division of the Roman people).

genus, eris, n., *stock, family.*

Germānī, ōrum, m. pl., *Germans.*

gerō, ere, gessī, gestus, *carry, wear, carry on, perform;* with bellum, *to wage.*

gignō, ere, genuī, genitus, *beget, bring forth;* pass., *be born.*

gladius, ī (iī), m., *sword.*

Gnaeus, ī, m., *Gnaeus,* a man's name. (Abbreviated Cn.)

Graecia, ae, f., *Greece.*

Graecus, ī, m., *a Greek.*

grātia, ae, f., *influence.*

grātus, a, um, *pleasing, welcome.*

gravis, e, *heavy, difficult; severe, serious.*

grūs, gruis, f., *crane.*

habeō, ēre, habuī, habitus, *have, possess, hold.*

Haeduī, ōrum, m., *Haedui,* a Gallic tribe.

haedus, ī, m., *kid.*

Hamilcar, caris, m., *Hamilcar,* a man's name.

Hannibal, balis, m., *Hannibal,* a man's name.

hasta, ae, f., *spear.*

haud, *not.*

Helvētiī, ōrum, m., *Helvetii,* a Gallic tribe.

Herennius, ī (iī), m., *Herennius,* a man's name.

hīberna, ōrum, n. pl., *winter quarters.*

Hibērus, ī, m., *the Hiberus* (modern *Ebro*), a river in Spain.

1. hīc, haec, hōc, pron., *this.*

2. hīc, adv., *here, at this place.*

hiemō, 1, *pass the winter.*

hiems, is, f., *winter.*

Hierō, ōnis, m., *Hiero,* ruler of Syracuse.

hinc, *hence;* hinc ... hinc, *on this side ... on that side.*

Hispānia, ae, f., *Spain.*

homō, minis, c., *man.*

honestās, tātis, f., *integrity.*

honor, ōris, m., *honor.*

honōrificē, *honorably, with respect.*

hōra, ae, f., *hour.*

Horātius, ī (iī), m., *Horatius,* a man's name; Horātiī, ōrum, *Horatii,* a Roman family.

hortor, ārī, ātus sum, *exhort, urge.*

Hostīlius, ī (iī), m., *Hostilius,* a man's name.

hostis, is, m., *enemy;* especially frequent in pl., *the enemy.*

hūc, *hither.*

hūmānus, a, um, *human.*

ibi, *there, in that place.*

(icō, ere), īcī, ictus, *strike.*

īdem, eadem, idem, *the same.*

idōneus, a, um, *suitable.*

igitur, *therefore, accordingly; now;* (stands usually after first word in clause).

ignāvus, a, um, *cowardly.*

īgnis, is, m., *fire.*

ignōminia, ae, f., *ignominy, disgrace.*

ille, illa, illud, *that; that one; he, she, it.*

imbēcillis, e, *weak, poor.*

imber, imbris, m., *rain-storm.*

immortālis, e, *immortal.*

impedīmentum, ī, n., *hindrance;* in pl., *baggage.*

impediō, īre, īvī (iī), ītus, *impede, hinder.*

imperātor, tōris, m., *commander.*

imperītus, a, um, *inexperienced.*

imperium, ī (iī), *rule, sway.*

imperō, 1, *command; demand; order; reign; levy.*

impetus, ūs, m., *onset, attack.*

implōrō, 1, *entreat.*

impōnō, ere, posuī, positus, *place upon.*

improbō, 1, *disapprove, reject.*

īmus, a, um, *lowest* (§ 74, 2).

in, prep. w. abl., *in, on,* denoting rest in a place; w. acc., *into, in, against.*

inaequē, *unfairly.*

incendō, ere, cendī, cēnsus, *set on fire.*

incertus, a, um, *uncertain.*

incidō, ere, idī, *fall upon; fall in with.*

incipiō, ere, cēpī, ceptus, *begin.*

incitō, 1, *urge on, encourage.*

incohō, 1, *begin.*

incola, ae, m., *inhabitant.*

incolō, ere, coluī, cultus, *inhabit.*

incolumis, e, *unharmed, uninjured.*

incommodum, ī, n., *disaster.*

incursiō, ōnis, f., *incursion, attack.*

indīcō, ere, dīxī, dictus, *proclaim, appoint;* with bellum, *to declare war.*

indolēs, is, f., *nature; character.*

indūcō, ere, dūxī, ductus, *lead in; draw in; draw.*

ineō, īre, iī, itus, *enter upon;* cōnsilium inīre, *form a plan* (§ 197).

inermis, e, *unarmed.*

īnferō, ferre, tulī, illātus, *bring upon, bring against; produce* (§ 188).

īnferior, us, *lower, inferior* (§ 74, 2).

īnfēstus, a, um, *hostile.*

īnfimus, a, um, superl. of īnferior (§ 74, 2).

īnfīrmus, a, um, *weak.*

īnfrendō, ere, *gnash.*

ingēns, gen. ingentis, *huge.*

ingenuus, a, um, *free-born.*

inhaereō, ēre, haesī, haesūrus, *stick fast.*

inhiō, 1, *be eager for* (lit. *gape for*).

inimīcus, ī, m., *a (personal) enemy.*

initium, ī (iī), n., *beginning.*

injūria, ae, f., *wrong, injustice.*

inopia, ae, f., *lack, need.*

inquam; 3d sing. inquit; 3d pl. inquiunt, *say* (inserted between words of a direct quotation).

īnsidiae, ārum, f. pl., *ambush; plots; treachery.*

īnsīgnis, e, *distinguished.*

īnsolēns, gen. īnsolentis, *insolent.*

īnstāns, pres. participle of īnstō.

īnstituō, ere, uī, ūtus, *institute; appoint.*

īnstitūtum, ī, n., *institution.*

īnstō, āre, itī, *press on, be eager.*

īnstruō, ere, strūxī, strūctus, *draw up, arrange; fit out.*

īnsula, ae, f., *island.*

intellegō, ere, lēxī, lēctus, *know, understand.*

inter, prep. w. acc., *among, between, in the midst of.*

intercipiō, ere, cēpī, ceptus, *take away.*

interdum, *at times, sometimes.*

intereā, *in the meanwhile.*

intereō, īre, iī, itūrus, *perish.*

interest, *it concerns,* impers. from intersum.

interficiō, ere, fēcī, fectus, *kill.*

intericiō, ere, jēcī, jectus, *throw between.*

interim, *in the meanwhile.*

interimō, ere, ēmī, ēmptus, *kill.*

interior, ius, *inner.*

interrēgnum, ī, n., *interregnum.*

interrogō, 1, *ask.*

intersum, esse, fuī, futūrus, *be present at.*

intrā, prep. w. acc., *within.*

intrō, 1, *enter.*

intus, adv., *within.*

inveniō, īre, vēnī, ventus, *find.*

invicem, *in turn.*

invideō, ēre, vīdī, vīsum, *envy.*

invidia, ae, f., *envy.*

invīsus, a, um, *hated, hateful.*

invītus, a, um, *unwilling.*

ipse, a, um, *self.*

irrīdeō, ēre, rīsī, rīsus, *deride, ridicule.*

irrītō, 1, *urge on, tempt.*

is, ea, id, *that; he, she, it;* pl., *they*

iste, a, ud, *that; that of yours.*

ita, *so* (of manner).

Italia, ae, f., *Italy.*

Italus, a, um, *Italian;* as noun, m., *an Italian.*

itaque, *accordingly, and so.*

iter, itineris, n., *journey; march;* iter facere, *to march; travel.*

iterum, *again.*

jaceō, ēre, uī, itūrus, *lie, recline.*

jam, *already.*

Jāniculum, ī, n., the hill *Janiculum.*

jŭbeō, ēre, jussī, jussus, *order.*

jūdicō, I, *judge, adjudge.*

jugum, ī, n., *yoke; ridge* (of mountains).

jūmentum, ī, n., *beast of burden.*

jungō, ere, jūnxī, jūnctus, *join;* societātem jungere, *form a partnership.*

Jūnius, ī (iī), m., *Junius,* a man's name.

Juppiter, Jovis, m., *Jupiter.*

Jūra, ae, f., *the Jura,* chain of mts. on west of Switzerland.

jūrō, I, *swear, take oath.*

jūs, jūris, n., *right, power.*

jūs jūrandum, jūris jūrandī, n., *oath.*

jūstus, a, um, *just.*

juvenca, ae, f., *heifer.*

juvenis, is, m., *a young man.*

Kalendae, ārum, f. pl., *Kalends* (first of the month).

L., abbreviation of Lūcius, *Lucius,* a man's name.

Labiēnus, ī, m., *Labienus,* a famous lieutenant of Caesar.

labor, ōris, m., *labor, exertion.*

labōrō, I, *toil; suffer;* in battle, *be hard pressed.*

Lacedaemonius, a, um, *Spartan.*

lacessō, ere, cessīvī (iī), ītus, *harass.*

lacus, ūs, m., *lake.*

laetus, a, um, *glad, joyful.*

Laevīnus, ī, m., *Laevinus,* a man's name.

laniō, I, *tear in pieces.*

lapis, idis, m., *stone.*

Latīnus, ī, m., *Latinus,* a man's name; also *a Latin.*

Latium, ī (iī), n., *Latium,* a part of Italy.

lātrō, I, *bark.*

laudō, I, *praise.*

laus, laudis, f., *praise.*

Lāvīnia, ae, f., *Lavinia,* wife of Aeneas.

Lāvīnium, ī (iī), *Lavinium,* a town.

lēgātiō, ōnis, f., *embassy.*

lēgātus, ī, m., *lieutenant; envoy.*

legiō, ōnis, f., *legion.*

legō, ere, lēgī, lēctus, *choose.*

Lentulus, ī, m., *Lentulus,* a man's name.

leō, ōnis, m., *lion.*

lētālis, e, *fatal.*

levis, e, *light.*

lēx, lēgis, f., *law.*

līber, lībera, līberum, *free.*

līberī, ōrum, m. pl., *children* (freeborn).

līberō, I, *free; acquit.*

lībertās, tātis, f., *liberty.*

licet, impers., *it is permitted* (§ 202).

līgneus, a, um, *wooden.*

Lilybaeum, ī, n., *Lilybaeum,* a promontory of Sicily.

litterae, ārum, f. pl., *a letter.*

litterārius, a, um, *of* or *belonging to reading and writing.*

lītus, oris, n., *shore.*

locus, ī, m.; pl., loca, ōrum, n., *place; family.*

longē, adv., *far.*

longitūdō, inis, f., *length.*

longus, a, um, *long.*

loquor, loquī, locūtus sum, *speak.*

Lūcius, ī (iī), m., *Lucius*, a man's name.

Lucrētia, ae, f., *Lucretia*, a woman's name.

Lucrētius, ī (iī), m., *Lucretius*, a man's name.

lūdus, ī, m., *game, school;* pl., lūdī, ōrum, m., *(public) games.*

lūgeō, ēre, lūxī, lūctus, *mourn.*

lūna, ae, f., *moon.*

lupa, ae, f., *she-wolf.*

lupus, ī, m., *wolf.*

lūstrō, 1, *review* (an army).

Lutātius, ī (iī), *Lutatius,* a man's name.

Lysander, drī, m., *Lysander,* a Spartan commander.

M., abbreviation for Mārcus, ī, m., *Marcus,* a man's name.

magis, *more, rather,* comp. of māg-·nopere.

magister, trī, m., *master;* magister equitum, *master of the horse.*

magistrātus, ūs, m., *magistrate.*

māgnitūdō, inis, f., *size.*

māgnopere, *greatly, earnestly* (§ 79, 1).

māgnus, a, um, *large, great.*

mājor, *larger, greater,* comp. of māgnus; mājor nātū, *elder* (lit. *greater as to birth).*

mājōrēs, um, m. (sc. nātū), *ancestors.*

male, adv., *badly, ill* (§ 79, 1).

maledīcō, ere, dīxī, dictus, *rail at.*

maleficus, ī, m., *evil doer.*

mālō, mālle, māluī, *prefer* (§ 192).

malus, a, um, *bad.*

mandātum, ī, n., *command, order.*

mandō, 1, *assign.*

maneō, ēre, mānsī, mānsūrus, *remain.*

Mānlius, ī (iī), *Manlius,* a man's name.

manus, ūs, f., *hand;* in military sense, *band, force.*

Mārcellus, ī, m., *Marcellus,* a man's name.

Mārcius, ī (iī), m., *Marcius,* a man's name.

mare, is, n., *sea.*

maritimus, a, um, *of the sea, maritime.*

marītus, ī, m., *husband.*

Mārs, Mārtis, m., the god *Mars.*

māssa, ae, f., *mass.*

Massilia, ae, f., *Marseilles.*

māter, tris, f., *mother.*

mātrōna, ae, f., *matron.*

mātrimōnium, ī (iī), n., *marriage;* in mātrimōnium dare, *to give in marriage* (of the father); in mātrimōnium dūcere, *to take in marriage* (of the husband).

māximē, *especially,* sup. of māgnopere.

māximus, a, um, *greatest,* superl. of māgnus.

medicus, ī, m., *physician.*

medius, a, um, *middle, the middle of.*

mehercule, *gracious !, I tell you,* lit. *(so help) me Hercules !*

melior, ius, *better,* comp. to bonus.

membrum, ī, n., *member* (of the body).

meminī, isse, *remember* (§ 198).

memoria, ae, f., *memory, recollection.*

Menēnius, ī (iī), m., *Menenius,* a man's name.

mēns, mentis, f., *mind.*

mercēs, ēdis, f., *price, reward.*

mereō, ēre, meruī, meritus, *deserve.*

mereor, ērī, itus sum, *deserve.*

mergō, ere, mersī, mersus, *sink.*

Messalla, ae, m., *Messalla,* a man's name.

Mettius Fufetius, Mettī (iī) Fufetī (iī), m., *Mettius Fufetius,* a man's name.

meus, a, um, *my*.

migrō, 1, *move, move away*.

mīles, itis, m., *soldier*.

mīlitāris, e, *military*.

mīlitia, ae, f., *military service*.

mīlle, indecl.; pl., mīlia, ium, *thousand* (§ 80, 4).

mīlliārium, ī (iī), n., *milestone*.

minimē, *least* (§ 79, 1).

minimus, a, um, superl. to parvus.

minor, *less*, comp. to parvus ; minor nātū, *younger*.

minus, adv., *less*.

mīror, ārī, ātus sum, *wonder, admire*.

misericordia, ae, f., *pity*.

mittō, ere, mīsī, missus, *send*.

modo, *only ; just, just now ;* as conj., *provided that*.

modus, ī, m., *manner, kind*.

moenia, ium, n. pl., *walls* (of a city).

molliō, īre, īvī, ītus, *soften*.

moneō, ēre, monuī, monitus, *advise, warn*.

monitus, ūs, m., *advice*.

mōns, montis, m., *mountain, hill*.

mōnstrō, 1, *show*.

mora, ae, f., *delay*.

morbus, ī, m., *disease*.

moror, ārī, morātus sum, *tarry, delay*.

mors, mortis, f., *death*.

morsus, ūs, m., *bite*.

mortuus, a, um, *dead*.

mōs, mōris, m., *custom ;* pl., mōrēs, *character*.

Mosa, ae, f., the river *Meuse*.

mōtus, ūs, m., *revolt*.

moveō, ēre, mōvī, mōtus, *move ; touch*.

mox, *presently ; soon ; afterwards*.

Mūcius, ī (iī), m., *Mucius*, a man's name.

mulier, mulieris, f., *woman*.

multitūdō, inis, f., *multitude*.

multō, *by much*, abl. of multum.

multus, a, um, *much ;* pl., *many*.

mūniō, īre, īvī(iī), ītus, *fortify*.

mūnītiō, ōnis, f. *fortification*.

mūnus, eris, n., *reward*.

mūrus, ī, m., *wall*.

mūs, mūris, c., *mouse*.

nam, *for*.

nancīscor, ī, nactus sum, *procure*.

nārrō, 1, *tell*.

nāscor, ī, nātus sum, *be born*.

nātiō, ōnis, f., *nation, tribe*.

nātūra, ae, f., *nature*.

(nātus, ūs), m., only in the Abl. sing., nātū, *as to birth* (in phrases expressing age).

nāvālis, e, *naval*.

nāvis, is, f., *ship, boat*.

nē, *not ; lest ; that . . . not ; from* (after verbs of *hindering*) ; nē . . . quidem, *not even*, emphatic negative, emphasizing the expression placed between nē and quidem.

-ne, enclitic interrog. particle, asking for information.

nec (neque), *nor*.

necesse est, impers., *it is necessary*.

neglegō, ere, lēxī, lēctus, *neglect*.

negōtium, ī (iī), n., *business ; trouble*.

nēmō, c., defective noun, *no one ;* acc. nēminem, dat. nēminī; other cases lacking.

nepōs, ōtis, m., *grandson*.

Neptūnus, ī, m., the god *Neptune*.

neque (nec), *nor, and not*.

neuter, tra, trum, *neither* (§ 61).

nihil, indecl., *nothing*.

nihilō, abl., *by nothing ;* nihilō minus, *none the less*.

nisi, *unless, except*.

nōbilis, e, *noble*.

nōbilitās, tātis, f., *nobility*.

noceō, ēre, nocuī, nocitūrus, *injure, harm.*

nocturnus, a, um, *at night.*

nōlō, nōlle, nōluī, *be unwilling* (§ 192).

nōmen, inis, n., *name.*

nōn, *not;* nōn sōlum . . . sed etiam, *not only . . . but also.*

nōnāgēsimus, a, um, *ninetieth.*

nōndum, *not yet.*

nōnne, interrog. particle expecting answer "yes."

nōnnūllus, a, um, *some.*

nōscō, ere, nōvī, *become acquainted with;* the perfect has present meaning: *I know.*

noster, tra, trum, *our.*

novus, a, um, *new.*

nox, noctis, f., *night.*

nūbō, ere, nūpsī, nūpta, *veil one's self* (for the bridegroom); *marry,* used only of the woman.

nūllus, a, um, no (§ 61).

num, interrog. particle expecting answer "no."

Numa Pompilius, Numae Pompilī (iī), *Numa Pompilius,* second king of Rome.

numerus, ī, m., *number.*

Numitor, ōris, m., *Numitor,* grandfather of Romulus and Remus.

nunc, *now.*

nuncupō, I, *name, call.*

nūntiō, I, *announce, report.*

nūntius, ī (iī), m., *messenger.*

nūtriō, īre, īvī, ītus, *nurse, take care of.*

nympha, ae, f., *nymph.*

ob, prep. w. acc., *on account of.*

obeō, īre, iī, itus, *meet;* also used for mortem obīre (lit., *meet death*), *die.*

oberrō, I, *wander about.*

obligō, I, *lay under obligation.*

oblīvīscor, ī, oblītus sum, *forget.*

oboediō, īre, īvī, ītum, *obey.*

obruō, ere, ruī, rutus, *overwhelm.*

obsecrō, I, *entreat.*

obses, idis, c., *hostage.*

obsideō, ēre, sēdī, sessus, *blockade.*

obsidiō, ōnis, f., *siege.*

obtestor, ārī, ātus sum, *adjure.*

obtineō, ēre, uī, tentus, *occupy, hold, obtain, secure; prevail.*

occaecō, I, *blind.*

occāsiō, ōnis, f., *occasion, opportunity.*

occīdō, ere, occīdī, occīsus, *kill.*

occupō, I, *take possession of, seize; occupy.*

octāvus, a, um, *eighth;* octāvus decimus, *eighteenth.*

octingentī, ae, a, *eight hundred.*

Octodūrus, ī, m., *Octodurus,* a city of the Veragri.

octōgintā, indecl., *eighty.*

oculus, ī, m., *eye.*

ōdī, ōdisse, *hate* (§ 198).

offerō, ferre, obtulī, oblātus, *offer;* sē offerre, *volunteer.*

officium, ī (iī), n., *duty.*

omnīnō, adv., *altogether;* with negatives, *at all.*

omnis, e, *all, every.*

onerārius, a, um, *burden-bearing;* nāvēs onerāriae, *transports.*

opera, ae, f., *assistance.*

opīniō, ōnis, f., *opinion, expectation.*

oportet, ēre, oportuit, *it behooves* (§ 202).

oppidum, ī, n., *town, walled town.*

opportūnus, a, um, *fit, opportune.*

opprimō, ere, pressī, pressus, *overwhelm.*

oppūgnō, I, *attack, assault.*

ops, opis, f. (nom. sing. is not used), *power, help;* in pl., *resources.*

optimē, sup. of bene (§ 79, I).

optimus, a, um, sup. of bonus (§ 73).

optiō, ōnis, f., *choice.*

optō, I, *desire.*

opus, indecl., n., *need;* opus est, *it is necessary.*

opus, eris, n., *work, fortification.*

ōra, ae, f., *coast.*

ōrātiō, ōnis, f., *speech.*

ōrātor, ōris, m., *orator; envoy.*

orbis, orbis, m., *circle;* orbis terrārum, *the world.*

ōrdinō, I, *institute.*

ōrdō, inis, m., *rank.*

orior, orīrī, ortus sum, *arise.*

ōrnō, I, *adorn.*

ōrō, I, *beseech.*

ortus, perf. participle of orior.

os, ossis, n., *bone.*

ostendō, ere, tendī, tentus, *show, explain.*

Ōstia, ae, f., *Ostia,* a Latin town at mouth of the Tiber.

ōstium, ī (iī), n., *mouth.*

ovis, ovis, f., *sheep.*

ōvum, ī, n., *egg.*

P., abbreviation of Pūblius.

pābulum, ī, n., *forage, food* (of animals).

paene, *almost, nearly.*

paenitet, ēre, paenituit, impers., *it causes regret* (§ 202).

palūs, lūdis, f., *marsh.*

Papīrius, ī (iī), m., *Papirius,* a man's name.

pār, gen. paris, *equal.*

parcō, ere, pepercī, parsūrus, *spare* (§ 220, II, *a*).

pariō, ere, peperī, partus, *bring forth; lay* (an egg).

parō, I, *prepare, get ready.*

pars, partis, f., *part; side.*

parvus, a, um, *small.*

pāscō, ere, pāvī, pāstus, *feed;* deponent, pāscor, pāscī, pāstus sum, *graze.*

passus, ūs, m., *pace* (five feet).

pāstor, ōris, m., *herdsman, shepherd.*

patefaciō, ere, fēcī, factus, *open.*

pateō, ēre, uī, *lie open.*

pater, patris, m., *father.*

paternus, a, um, *paternal; of one's father.*

patior, ī, passus sum, *suffer; allow.*

patria, ae, f., *country, fatherland.*

patrimōnium, ī (iī), n., *inheritance, property.*

paucī, ae, a, *few;* used only in pl.

paucitās, ātis, f., *fewness, small number.*

paulō, abl., *by a little.*

paulum, *a little.*

pāx, ācis, f., *peace.*

pecūnia, ae, f., *money.*

pedes, itis, m., *foot-soldier;* in pl., *infantry.*

peditātus, ūs, m., *infantry.*

pelliciō, ere, lexī, lectus, *allure, entice.*

pellō, ere, pepulī, pulsus, *drive; drive out, banish; rout, defeat.*

Peloponnēsus, ī, f., *Peloponnesus,* the southern part of Greece.

per, prep. w. acc., *through, by means of, through the instrumentality of; on account of; during.*

percutiō, ere, cussī, cussus, *strike.*

perdō, ere, didī, ditus, *lose.*

perdūcō, ere, dūxī, ductus, *conduct.*

pereō, īre, iī, itūrus, *perish* (§ 197).

perferō, ferre, tulī, lātus, *carry through, convey, endure* (§ 188).

perficiō, ere, fēcī, fectus, *accomplish.*

perfidia, ae, f., *treachery.*

perfuga, ae, m., *deserter.*

perfugiō, ere, fūgī, fugitūrus, *flee.*

pergō, ere, rēxī, rēctus, *proceed.*

perīculum, ī, n., *danger.*

permittō, ere, mīsī, missus, *permit, grant, cede* (§ 220, II, *a*).

permūtātiō, ōnis, f., *exchange.*

perpetuus, a, um, *perpetual.*

persequor, ī, secūtus sum, *follow up.*

persuādeō, ēre, suāsī, suāsum, *persuade.*

perterreō, ēre, uī, itus, *terrify.*

perturbō, 1, *agitate.*

perveniō, īre, vēnī, ventum, *come, arrive.*

pēs, pedis, m., *foot.*

petō, ere, īvī (iī), ītus, *seek, request; attack.*

Pīsō, ōnis, m., *Piso,* a man's name.

placeō, ēre, uī, itūrus, *please.*

plānitiēs, ēī, f., *plain.*

plēbs, plēbis, f., *common people.*

plēnus, a, um, *full.*

plērīque, aeque, aque, *most.*

plūrēs, a, *more; several;* plural of plūs (§ 68).

plūrimus, a, um, sup. of multus (§ 73).

plūs, comp. of multus (§§ 68, 73).

poena, ae, f., *penalty, punishment.*

Poenus, a, um, *Carthaginian.*

polliceor, ērī, itus sum, *promise.*

Pompējus, Pompēī, m., *Pompey,* a man's name.

Pompilius, ī (iī), m., *Pompilius,* a man's name.

pōnō, ere, posuī, positus, *put; place; establish;* castra pōnere, *pitch a camp.*

pōns, pontis, m., *bridge.*

Pontius, ī (iī), m., *Pontius,* a man's name.

populus, ī, m., *people.*

Porsena, ae, m., *Porsena,* a king of Etruria.

porta, ae, f., *gate.*

portus, ūs, m., *harbor.*

poscō, ere, poposcī, *demand.*

possessiō, ōnis, f., *possession.*

possideō, ēre, sēdī, sessus, *possess.*

possum, posse, potuī, *be able, can* (§ 183).

post, adv., *afterwards.*

post, prep. with acc., *after.*

posteā, *afterwards.*

posterus, a, um, *following* (§ 74, 2); posterī, ōrum, m., *descendants.*

postquam, conj., *after.*

postrīdiē, adv., *on the next day.*

postulō, 1, *demand.*

Postumius, ī (iī), m., *Postumius,* a man's name.

potēns, entis, pres. participle of possum, used as adj., *powerful.*

potestās, ātis, f., *power.*

potior, īrī, ītus sum, *gain possession of.*

praecipiō, ere, cēpī, ceptus, *enjoin.*

praecipitō, 1, *hurl down headlong.*

praeda, ae, f., *booty.*

praedō, ōnis, m., *robber.*

praeferō, ferre, tulī, lātus, *choose, prefer* (§ 188).

praeficiō, ere, fēcī, fectus, *put in charge, place in command* (§ 220, III).

praemium, ī (iī), n., *reward.*

Praeneste, is, n., *Praeneste,* a Latin town.

praesēns, praesentis, *present,* pres. participle of praesum, used as adj.

praesaepe, is, n., *manger.*

praesidium ī (iī), n., *garrison.*

praestantia, ae, f., *preëminence.*

praestāns, gen., stantis, *eminent, excellent.*

praestō, āre, itī, itus, *perform, show.*

praesum, esse, fuī, *be in charge of* (§ 182).

praeter, *except, besides.*

praetereā, *besides.*

praetereō, īre, iī, itūrus, *pass by* (§ 197).

praetor, ōris, m., *praetor.*

prātum, ī, n., *meadow.*

premō, ere, pressī, pressus, *press, crowd.*

pretium, ī (iī), n., *price.*

(prex, precis), f., *prayer* (nom. and gen. sing. not used).

prīmō, *first, firstly.*

prīmum, *first, for the first time.*

prīmus, a, um, *first;* superl. of comp. prior (§ 74).

prīnceps, ipis, m., *chief.*

prior, us, *former, before (another).*

Prīscus, ī, m., *Priscus,* a man's name.

prīstinus, a, um, *pristine.*

priusquam, *before.*

prīvātus, a, um, *private;* as noun, prīvātus, ī, m., *a private citizen.*

prō, prep. w. abl., *before, in front of; for, instead of.*

probō, 1, *approve.*

Procās, ae, m., *Procas,* a king of Alba.

prōcēdō, ere, cessī, cessūrus, *advance.*

procul, *far.*

prōcūrō, 1, *care for, have charge of.*

prōcurrō, ere, cucurrī, cursum, *run forward.*

prōditor, ōris, m., *traitor.*

proelium, ī (iī), n., *battle.*

proficīscor, ī, profectus sum, *set out.*

profugiō, ere, fūgī, fugitūrus, *flee, escape; flee for refuge.*

prōgredior, ī, gressus sum, *advance, go forward.*

prohibeō, ēre, uī, itus, *keep away, keep off.*

prōiciō, ere, jēcī, jectus, *throw forward; cast.*

prōmittō, ere, mīsī, missus, *promise.*

prōmuntūrium, ī (iī), n., *promontory.*

prōpāgō, 1, *propagate, continue.*

properō, 1, *hasten.*

prōpōnō, ere, posuī, positus, *propose.*

propter, prep. w. acc., *on account of.*

prōsum, prōdesse, prōfuī, prōfutūrus, *benefit* (§ 182).

prōtinus, *forthwith, straightway.*

prōvideō, ēre, vīdī, vīsus, *provide, take care.*

prōvincia, ae, f., *province.*

prōvocātiō, ōnis, f., *challenge.*

prōvocō, 1, *challenge.*

proximus, a, um, *nearest, next* (§ 74, 1).

prūdēns, *wise, sensible.*

Pūblicola, ae, m., *Publicola,* a man's name.

pūblicus, a, um, *public.*

Pūblius, ī (iī), m., *Publius,* a man's name.

puer, ī, m., *boy.*

puerīlis, e, *youthful.*

pueritia, ae, f., *boyhood.*

pūgna, ae, f., *battle.*

pūgnō, 1, *fight.*

pulcher, chra, chrum, *beautiful.*

pulsus, perf. pass. participle of pellō.

Pulvīllus, ī, m., *Pulvillus,* a man's name.

Pūnicus, a, um, *Punic.*

pūniō, īre, īvī, ītus, *punish.*

pūpillus, ī, m., *ward.*

pusillus, a, um, *weak.*

putō, 1, *think.*

Pyrrhus, ī, m., *Pyrrhus,* king of Epirus.

quā, adv., *where.*

quadrāgēsimus, a, um, *fortieth.*

quadrāgintā, indecl., *forty.*

quadringentēsimus, a, um, *four hundredth.*

quaerō, ere, quaesīvī, quaesītus, *inquire.*

quālis, e, rel., *as; such as;* interrog., *of what sort?*

1. quam, *how?*

2. quam, *than.*

quamquam, *although.*

quamvīs, *though, although.*

quandō, interrog., *when.*

quantum, *how much.*

quantus, a, um, *how great.*

quārē, rel. and interrog., *wherefore.*

quārtus, a, um, *fourth.*

quasi, *as if.*

quattuor, indecl., *four.*

quattuordecim, indecl., *fourteen.*

-que, enclitic conj., *and.*

queror, ī, questus sum, *complain.*

quī, quae, quod, rel. pron., *who, which.*

quīcumque, quaecumque, quodcumque, *whoever, whatever* (§ 102, 4).

quīdam, quaedam, quiddam or quoddam, *a certain* (§ 102).

quidem, *indeed, even; of course;* nē ... quidem, *not even.*

quīlibet, quaelibet, quidlibet or quodlibet, *any you please* (§ 102, 1).

Quīnctius, ī (iī), m., *Quinctius,* a man's name.

quīngentī, ae, a, *five hundred.*

quīnquāgintā, indecl., *fifty.*

quīnque, indecl., *five.*

quīntus, a, um, *fifth.*

Quīntus, ī, m., *Quintus,* a man's name.

quis, quid, interr. pron., *who, what?*

quis, qua (quae), quid, indef. pron., *any* (§ 102).

quisquam, quaequam, quidquam (quicquam), *any, any one* (§ 102).

quisque, quaeque, quidque (quicque), *each* (§ 102).

1. quō, rel. and interrog. adv., *whither.*
2. quō, conj., *in order that.*

quod, *because,* on the ground that.

quōminus, *from* (after verbs of *hindering*).

quondam, *formerly.*

quoniam, conj., *inasmuch as.*

quoque, *also,* always placed after the word it modifies.

rapiō, ere, uī, tus, *seize.*

raptor, ōris, m., *one who seizes.*

ratiō, ōnis, f., *reason.*

recēdō, ere, cessī, cessūrus, *retire.*

recēns, gen. recentis, *recent.*

recipiō, ere, cēpī, ceptus, *take back, receive;* with reflexive sē, *to retreat.*

recūsō, 1, *refuse.*

reddō, ere, reddidī, redditus, *return, give back; render, make.*

redeō, īre, iī, itūrus, *return, go back* (§ 197).

redigō, ere, ēgī, āctus, *reduce.*

redimō, ere, ēmī, ēmptus, *ransom.*

redūcō, ere, dūxī, ductus, *lead back.*

referō, ferre, rettulī, relātus, tr., *bring back, return* (§ 188).

reficiō, ere, fēcī, fectus, *rebuild.*

refluō, ere, *flow back.*

regiō, ōnis, f., *region.*

rēgius, a, um, *of the king; regal.*

rēgnō, 1, *reign.*

rēgnum, ī, n., *regal power, kingdom.*

regredior, ī, gressus sum, *march back, return.*

Rēgulus, ī, m., *Regulus,* a man's name.

rēiciō, ere, rejēcī, jectus, *hurl back.*

relātus, perf. pass. participle of referō.

relictus, perf. pass. participle of relinquō.

religiō, ōnis, f., *religion.*

relinquō, ere, līquī, lictus, *leave, leave behind.*

reliquus, qua, quum, *remaining.*

remaneō, ēre, mānsī, mānsūrus, *remain.*

rēmex, igis, m., *rower.*

removeō, ēre, mōvī, mōtus, *remove.*

Remus, ī, m., *Remus,* brother of Romulus.

renovō, 1, *renew.*

renūntiō, 1, *bring back word.*

repellō, ere, reppulī, repulsus, *drive back, repel.*

repente, *suddenly.*

repentīnus, a, um, *sudden.*

reperiō, īre, repperī, repertus, *discover, find.*

rēs, reī, f., *thing, affair, circumstance.*

rescindō, ere, rescidī, rescissus, *tear down.*

resistō, ere, restitī, *resist* (§ 220, II, *a*).

respondeō, ēre, respondī, respōnsus, *answer, reply.*

rēs pūblica, gen. reī pūblicae, f., *state, republic.*

respuō, ere, uī, *reject.*

restituō, ere, uī, ūtus, *restore.*

retineō, ere, uī, tentus, *retain.*

reverentia, ae, f., *reverence.*

revertor, ī, *return.*

rēx, rēgis, m., *king.*

Rhea Silvia, gen. Rheae Silviae, f., *Rhea Silvia,* mother of Romulus and Remus.

Rhēnus, ī, m., *Rhine.*

Rhodanus, ī, m., *Rhone.*

rīpa, ae, f., *bank.*

rīxor, ārī, ātus sum, *quarrel, wrangle.*

rōbur, oris, n., *strength.*

rogō, I, *ask.*

Rōma, ae, f., *Rome.*

Rōmānus, a, um, *Roman;* as noun, *a Roman.*

Rōmulus, ī, m., *Romulus.*

Rulliānus, ī, m., *Rullianus.*

rumpō, ere, rūpī, ruptus, *break, break down.*

ruō, ere, ruī, ruitūrus, *rush.*

rūrsus, *again.*

rūsticus, ī, m., *farmer.*

Sabīnus, a, um, *Sabine.*

Sabīnus, ī, m., *Sabinus,* a lieutenant of Caesar.

sacer, cra, crum, *sacred;* in pl., sacra, ōrum, n., *sacred rites.*

sacerdōs, ōtis, c., *priest, priestess.*

saepe, *often.*

salūs, lūtis, f., *safety.*

salūtō, I, *salute, hail.*

Samnīs, ītis, m., *a Samnite.*

Sardinia, ae, f., *Sardinia.*

satelles, itis, m., *a bodyguard.*

satis, adv., *enough.*

Sāturnia, ae, f., *Saturnia,* name of a citadel.

Sāturnus, ī, m., the god *Saturn.*

saxum, ī, n., *rock.*

Scaevola, ae, m., *Scaevola,* a man's name.

scelestus, a, um, *wicked.*

scelus, eris, n., *crime.*

sciō, īre, scīvī, scītus, *know.*

scrība, ae, m., *secretary.*

scrībō, ere, scrīpsī, scrīptus, *write;* of laws, *draw up.*

scūtum, ī, n., *shield.*

sē, reflexive, *he; himself, herself* (§ 86).

sēcēdō, ere, cessī, cessūrus, *secede, withdraw.*

secundus, a, um, *second.*

sed, *but.*

sedeō, ēre, sēdī, sessūrus, *sit.*

sēdēs, is, f., *seat.*

sēditiō, ōnis, f., *uprising, mutiny.*

semper, *always.*

senātor, tōris, m., *senator.*

senātus, ūs, m., *senate.*

senex, senis, m., *old man;* as adj., *old.*

Senonēs, um, m., the *Senones,* a Gallic tribe.

sententia, ae, f., *opinion, sentiment.*

sentiō, īre, sēnsī, sēnsus, *feel, perceive.*

septem, indecl., *seven.*

septimus, a, um, *seventh.*

septingentī, ae, a, *seven hundred.*

septuāgintā, indecl., *seventy.*

Sēquanī, ōrum, m. pl., *Sequani,* a Gallic tribe.

sequor, ī, secūtus sum, *follow; seek.*

sermō, ōnis, m., *conversation.*

Servius Tullius, Servī (iī) Tullī (iī), *Servius Tullius,* sixth king of Rome.

servō, 1, *save; preserve.*

servus, ī, m., *slave.*

sescentī, ae, a, *six hundred.*

sex, indecl., *six.*

sexāgintā, indecl., *sixty.*

sextus, a, um, *sixth;* sextus decimus, *sixteenth.*

sī, *if.*

sīc, *so* (of manner).

siccus, a, um, *dry.*

Sicilia, ae, f., *Sicily.*

sīgnificō, 1, *show; mean.*

sīgnum, ī, n., *standard.*

silentium, ī (iī), n., *silence.*

silva, ae, f., *forest.*

Silvius, ī (iī), m., *Silvius,* a man's name.

similis, e, *like.*

simul, *together, at the same time.*

simul ac (atque), *as soon as.*

sine, prep. w. abl., *without.*

singulāris, e, *single.*

singulī, ae, a, *one at a time, each.*

sinister, tra, trum, *left, left-hand.*

socer, erī, m., *father-in-law.*

societās, tātis, f., *partnership.*

socius, ī (iī), m., *ally, comrade.*

sōl, is, m., *sun.*

soleō, ēre, solitus sum, semi-dep., *be accustomed.*

sōlitūdō, dinis, f., *solitude.*

sōlum, *only;* nōn sōlum . . . sed etiam, *not only . . . but also.*

sōlus, a, um, *alone, only* (§ 61).

solvō, ere, solvī, solūtus, *loose;* of ships, *unmoor;* nāvēs solvere, *set sail.*

sonitus, ūs, m., *sound.*

sonus, ī, m., *sound.*

spatium, ī (iī), n., *space; time.*

spectō, 1, *look on.*

spērō, 1, *hope, hope for;* governs the acc.

spēs, speī, f., *hope.*

spoliō, 1, *despoil.*

Spurius, ī (iī), m., *Spurius,* a man's name.

statim, *at once, immediately.*

statuō, ere, uī, ūtus, *decide.*

stō, āre, stetī, stātūrus, *stand.*

strēnuus, a, um, *energetic.*

stultitia, ae, f., *folly.*

suādeō, ēre, suāsī, suāsūrus, *urge, advise.*

sub, prep. w. abl., *under.*

subdūcō, ere, dūxī, ductus, *withdraw, lead away; snatch away.*

subeō, īre, iī, itūrus, *approach* (§ 197).

subigō, ere, ēgī, āctus, *subdue.*

subitō, *suddenly.*

sublevō, 1, *relieve.*

sublīmis, e, *high, lofty;* in sublīme, *on high.*

submittō, ere, mīsī, missus, *send, dispatch.*

subrīdeō, ēre, rīsī, rīsum, *smile.*

subsidium, ī (iī), n., *assistance.*

succēdō, ere, cessī, cessūrus, *follow, succeed.*

suī, *self, oneself* (§ 86, 1).

sum, esse, fuī, futūrus, *be.*

summus, *highest, greatest, top of* (§ 283); sup. of superus (§ 74, 2).

sūmō, ere, sūmpsī, sūmptus, *take.*

super, prep. w. acc., *above.*

superbia, ae, f., *pride, haughtiness.*

superbus, a, um, *proud, haughty.*

superior, us, *higher, upper;* comp. of superus (§ 74, 2.)

superō, 1, *overcome, defeat, surpass; be superior.*

supersum, esse, fuī, *remain, be over; survive.*

superveniō, īre, vēnī, ventum, *come up, arrive.*

supplicium, ī (iī), n., *torture, punishment.*

suprā, prep. w. acc., *above.*

suprēmus, a, um, superl. of superus (§ 74, 2).

suscipiō, ere, cēpī, ceptus, *undertake, receive.*

suspīciō, ōnis, f., *suspicion.*

suspicor, ārī, ātus sum, *suspect.*

sustineō, ēre, uī, *withstand.*

sustulī, perf. ind. act. of tollō.

suus, a, um, *his; her; its; their.*

Syrācūsae, ārum, f., *Syracuse,* a city of Sicily.

T., abbreviation of Titus.

talentum, ī, n., *a talent* (about $1200).

tālis, e, *such.*

tam, *so* (of degree).

tamen, *nevertheless, yet.*

Tanaquil, ilis, f., *Tanaquil,* wife of Tarquinius Priscus.

tandem, *at length.*

tantum (n. of tantus), *so much.*

tantus, a, um, *so great.*

tardō, 1, *retard, check.*

Tarentīnus, a, um, *Tarentine.*

Tarentum, ī, n., *Tarentum,* a city.

Tarpēia, ae, f., *Tarpeia,* a woman's name.

Tarpēius, a, um, *Tarpeian.*

Tarquiniī, ōrum, m. pl., *Tarquinii,* a city.

Tarquinius, ī (iī), m., *Tarquin,* a Roman king.

tēctum, ī, n., *roof.*

Telesīnus, ī, m., *Telesinus,* a man's name.

tēlum, ī, n., *javelin.*

temere, *rashly.*

tempestās, tātis, f., *tempest.*

templum, ī, n., *temple.*

temptō, 1, *attempt, make trial of.*

tempus, oris, n., *time.*

teneō, ēre, uī, *hold.*

tergum, ī, n., *back;* ā tergō, *from behind.*

terra, ae, f., *land, a land.*

terreō, ēre, uī, itus, *frighten.*

territōrium, ī (iī), n, *territory.*

terror, ōris, m., *terror, fear.*

tertius, a, um, *third.*

testūdō, inis, f., *tortoise.*

Themistoclēs, is, m., *Themistocles,* an Athenian statesman.

Tiberis, is, m., *Tiber.*

timeō, ēre, uī, *fear.*

timidus, a, um, *timid.*

timor, ōris, m., *fear.*

tintinnābulum, ī, n., *bell.*

Titus, ī, m., *Titus,* a man's name.

tollō, ere, sustulī, sublātus, *raise; take, take away.*

tonitrus, ūs, m., *thunder.*

tonō, āre, tonuī, *thunder.*

Torquātus, ī, m., *Torquatus,* a man's name.

torquēs, is, m., *necklace.*

tot, indecl., *so many.*

tōtus, a, um, *whole, entire* (§ 61).

tractō, 1, *treat.*

trādō, ere, trādidī, trāditus, *hand over.*

trādūcō, ere, dūxī, ductus, *lead across.*

trāiciō, ere, jēcī, jectus (orig. transitive, *throw across, send across*), *cross over.*

trāns, prep. with acc., *across.*

trānseō, īre, iī, itus, *cross; cross over.*

trānsferō, ferre, tulī, lātus, *transfer.*

trānsigō, ere, ēgī, āctus, *pass, spend.*

trānsiliō, īre, uī, *leap over.*

trānsmarīnus, a, um, *across the sea, from across the sea.*

trānsnō, 1, *swim across.*

trānsportō, 1, *transport.*

trecentēsimus, a, um, *three hundredth.*

trecentī, ae, a, *three hundred.*

tredecim, indecl., *thirteen.*

trēs, tria, *three* (§ 80, 2).

Trēverī, ōrum, m. pl., *Treveri,* a tribe of Belgians.

tribūnus, ī, m., *tribune,* officer in a Roman legion; also a *tribune of* the plebs.

tribuō, ere, uī, ūtus, *assign, award; grant.*

tribūtum, ī, n., *tax.*

trīcēsimus, a, um, *thirtieth.*

trīduum, ī, n., *three days.*

trigeminī, ōrum, m. pl., *triplets.*

trīgintā, indecl., *thirty.*

triumphō, 1, *celebrate a triumph.*

Trōja, ae, f., *Troy.*

Trōjānus, a, um, *Trojan.*

trux, gen. trucis, *savage.*

tū, tuī, *thou, you* (§ 85).

tuba, ae, f., *trumpet.*

tubicen, inis, m., *trumpeter.*

tueor, ērī, *guard, watch.*

Tullia, ae, f., *Tullia,* a woman's name.

Tullus Hostīlius, Tullī Hostīlī(iī), m., *Tullus Hostilius,* third king of Rome.

tum, *then, at that time.*

tumultus, ūs, m., *uprising.*

turbō, 1, *disturb.*

turpis, e, *base.*

turris, is, f., *tower.*

Tusculum, ī, n., *Tusculum,* a town.

tūtor, ōris, m., *guardian.*

tūtus, a, um, *safe.*

tuus, a, um, *thy, your* (§ 87).

tyrannus, ī, m., *a tyrant.*

ūber, eris, n., *udder.*

ubi, rel. and interr. adv., *where; when.*

Ubiī, ōrum, m., *Ubii,* a Gallic tribe.

ubique, *everywhere.*

ulcīscor, ī, ultus sum, *avenge.*

ūllus, a, um, *any* (§ 61).

ulterior, us, *farther, more distant* (§ 74, 1).

ultrā, prep. w. acc., *beyond.*

ūnā, *together.*

unde, *whence.*

ūndēquīnquāgintā, indecl., *forty-nine.*

undique, *from all parts* or *sides.*

unguis, is, m., *talon.*

ungula, ae, f., *talon.*

ūnus, a, um, *one, alone* (§ 61).

urbs, urbis, f., *city.*

Usipetēs, um, m., *Usipetes,* a German tribe.

ūsque, *even.*

ūsus, ūs, m., *use, service.*

ut, *that, in order that;* with verbs of fearing, *that not.*

uterque, utraque, utrumque, gen. utrīusque (cf. § 61), *each* (of two); in pl., *both* (of two parties).

utinam, affirmative particle (§ 305).

ūtor, ī, ūsus sum, *use* (§ 258, 1).

utrum, *whether.*

uxor, ōris, f., *wife.*

vadum, ī, n., *ford, shallow water.*

vāgītus, ūs, m., *crying.*

valeō, ēre, uī, valitūrus, *avail, prevail.*

Valerius, ī (iī), m., *Valerius,* a man's name.

vallis, vallis, f., *valley.*

vāllum, ī, n., *intrenchment.*

vāstō, 1, *lay waste.*

Vējentānus, a, um, *Veientine.*

Vējentēs, ium, m., *Veientines* (inhabitants of Veii).

vēndō, ere, didī, ditus, *sell.*

venēnum, ī, n., *poison.*

Venetī, ōrum, m. pl., *Veneti*, a Gallic tribe.

veniō, īre, vēnī, ventum, *come*.

venter, tris, m., *stomach*.

ventus, ī, m., *wind*.

verber, eris, n., *blow*.

verberō, 1, *beat, strike*.

verbum, ī, n., *word*.

vereor, ērī, itus sum, *fear*.

vērō, *indeed, but*.

versor, ārī, ātus sum, *be engaged in*.

vertō, ere, vertī, versus, *turn;* terga vertere, *flee*.

vescor, ī, *feed upon*.

Vesta, ae, f., the goddess *Vesta*.

Vestālis, is, adj., *Vestal*.

vester, vestra, vestrum, *your*.

Veturia, ae, f., *Veturia*, a woman's name.

Veturius, ī (iī), m., *Veturius*, a man's name.

vetus, gen. veteris, *old, long-standing*.

vexō, 1, *harass, annoy; ravage*.

via, ae, f., *way, road*.

vīcēsimus, a, um, *twentieth*.

victor, ōris, m., *victor*.

victōria, ae, f., *victory*.

vīcus, ī, m., *village*.

videō, ēre, vīdī, vīsus, *see;* in pass., *be seen; seem, appear*.

vigilia, ae, f., *watch* (of the night).

vīgintī, indecl., *twenty*.

vinciō, īre, vinxī, vinctus, *bind, tie*.

vincō, ere, vīcī, victus, *conquer*.

vinculum, ī, n., *chain*.

vindex, icis, m., *champion*.

vindicō, 1, *claim*.

vir, ī, m., *man*.

vīrēs, pl. of vīs.

virga, ae, f., *rod, switch*.

Virginia, ae, f., *Virginia*, a woman's name.

Virginius, ī (iī), m., *Virginius*, a man's name.

virgō, inis, f., *virgin, maiden*.

virgula, ae, f., *rod*.

virtūs, tūtis, f., *valor, virtue*.

vīs, vis, f. (acc. vim), *violence; number;* vim facere, *do violence, violate;* pl. vīrēs, ium, *strength*.

vīsus, perf. pass. participle of videō.

vīta, ae, f., *life*.

vītō, 1, *avoid*.

vix, *scarcely, with difficulty*.

vocō, 1, *call, summon; name*.

volō, 1, *fly*.

volō, velle, voluī, *wish, be willing* (§ 192).

Volscī, ōrum, m. pl., *Volsci*, a Latin tribe.

volucer, cris, cre, *flying, capable of flight*.

Volumnia, ae, f., *Volumnia*, a woman's name.

vōx, vōcis, f., *voice, word, exclamation*.

vulnerō, 1, *wound*.

vulnus, eris, n., *wound*.

vultus, ūs, m., *countenance; look*.

Xanthippus, ī, m., *Xanthippus*, a man's name.

ENGLISH-LATIN VOCABULARY.

abandon

abandon, dēserō, ere, seruī, sertus.
(able), be able, possum, posse, potuī.
absent, be absent, absum, esse, āfuī,
 āfutūrus.
(account), on account of, propter,
 prep. w. acc.
accuse, accūsō, 1.
across, trāns, *prep. with acc.*
adjudge, jūdicō, 1.
advance, prōgredior, ī, gressus sum.
advice, cōnsilium, ī (iī), *n.*
after (*adv.*), post.
after (*conj.*), postquam.
after, post, *prep. w. acc.*
afterwards, posteā.
against, contrā, *prep. w. acc.*
all, omnis, e.
almost, paene.
already, jam.
although, though, quamquam;
 quamvīs; cum.
always, semper.
ancestors, mājōrēs, um, *m.*
and, et; -que (*enclitic*); atque.
announce, nūntiō, 1.
another, alius, a, ud.
answer, respondeō, ēre, spondī,
 spōnsum.
any, ūllus, a, um (§ 61).
anybody, anyone, anything, quisquam, quaequam, quidquam; quis,
 quid.
any you please, quīlibet, quaelibet,
 quidlibet *or* quodlibet (§ 102).
appoint, dīcō, ere, dīxī, dictus; *lit.,*
 say.

begin

approach, aditus, ūs, *m.*
approach, *v.*, appropinquō, 1; adeō,
 īre, iī, itus.
approve, probō, 1.
Ariovistus, Ariovistus, ī, *m.*
arm, armō, 1.
army, exercitus, ūs, *m.*
army on the march, agmen, minis, *n.*
as long as, dum.
as soon as, simul atque (ac).
ask, rogō, 1.
assemble (*intrans.*), conveniō, īre,
 vēnī, ventum.
assistance, subsidium, ī (iī), *n.*;
 auxilium, ī (iī), *n.*
(at hand), be at hand, adsum, esse,
 adfuī, adfutūrus.
at once, statim.
Athens, Athēnae, ārum, *f.*
attack, adorior, īrī, ortus sum.
attack, assault (*a town*), oppūgnō, 1.
avoid, vītō, 1.

bad, malus, a, um.
barbarian (*adj.*), barbarus, a, um;
 (*noun*), barbarus, ī, *m.*
battle, proelium, ī (iī), *n.*
be, sum, esse, fuī, futūrus.
be able, possum, posse, potuī (§ 183).
bear, ferō, ferre, tulī, lātus.
beast of burden, jūmentum, ī, *n.*
because, quod; quia; cum (§ 319).
become, fīō, fierī, factus sum.
before (*prep. and adv.*), ante.
before (*conj.*), antequam, priusquam.
begin, coepī, coepisse (§ 198).

behoove, it behooves, oportet, ēre,
oportuit (§ 202).
Belgians, Belgae, ārum, *m.*
believe, crēdō, ere, crēdidī, crēditus.
betake oneself, cōnferō, ferre, tulī,
collātus, *with the reflexive pron.*
better, melius.
between, inter, *prep. w. acc.*
blame, culpō, āre, āvī, ātus.
boat, nāvis, is, *f.*
booty, praeda, ae, *f.*
born, be born, nāscor, ī, nātus sum.
born, nātus, a, um.
both, each, uterque, utraque, utrumque.
boundary, fīnis, is, *m.*
boy, puer, erī, *m.*
brave, fortis, e.
bravely, fortiter ; *from the adj.,* fortis, e.
bridge, pōns, pontis, *m.*
brief, brevis, e.
bring, afferō, ferre, attulī, allātus.
bring about, efficiō, ere, fēcī, fectus.
bring against, īnferō, ferre, tulī
illātus, *with dat. of indirect obj.*
(§ 220, III).
bring back, referō, ferre, tulī, lātus.
Britain, Britannia, ae, *f.*
brother, frāter, tris, *m.*
by (*of personal agent*), ā, ab, *prep. w.*
abl.

Caesar, Caesar, is, *m.*
call (*name*), appellō, 1.
call (*summon*), vocō, 1.
call together, convocō, 1.
camp, castra, ōrum, *n.*
can (*be able*), possum, posse, potuī.
captive, captīvus, ī, *m.*
capture, capiō, ere, cēpī, captus.
cause, causa, ae, *f.*
cavalry, equitēs, um, *m. pl. of,* eques,
itis ; of cavalry, equestrian,
equester, tris, tre.

cease, dēsistō, ere, dēstitī.
certain, certain one, quīdam, quaedam, quiddam *or* quoddam (§ 102).
charge, be in charge, praesum, esse,
fuī, *construed with dat.* (§ 220,
II, *a*).
charge, put in charge, praeficiō,
ere, fēcī, fectus, *construed with dat.*
(§ 220, III).
children, līberī, ōrum, *m.*
choose, dēligō, ere, lēgī, lēctus.
circumstance, rēs, eī, *f.*
citizen, fellow citizen, cīvis, is, *m.*
city, urbs, urbis, *f.*
coast, ōra, ae, *f.*
cohort, cohors, rtis, *f.*
come, veniō, īre, vēnī, ventum.
command (*noun*), mandātum, ī, *n.*
command (*verb*), imperō, 1.
commander, imperātor, ōris, *m.*
common, commūnis, e.
compel, cōgō, ere, coēgī, coāctus.
concern, it concerns, interest, esse,
fuit.
concerning, dē, *prep. w. abl.*
confer, colloquor, ī, locūtus sum.
conference, colloquium, ī (iī), *n.*
consul, cōnsul, is, *m.*
consult (with), dēlīberō, 1.
contend, dīmicō, 1.
contented, contentus, a, um.
council, concilium, ī (iī), *n.*
country, native country, patria, ae,
f.
courageously, audācter, *from adj.*
audāx, ācis.
cowardly, ignāvus, a, um.
Crassus, Crassus, ī, *m.*
cross, trānseō, īre, iī, itūrus.

danger, perīculum, ī, *n.*
dare, audeō, ēre, ausus sum, *semi-*
dep.
daughter, fīlia, ae, *f.*
day, diēs, ēī, *m.*

decide, cōnstituō, ere, uī, ūtus.
decree, dēcernō, ere, crēvī, crētus.
deep, altus, a, um.
defend, dēfendō, ere, fendī, fēnsus.
deliberate, dēlīberō, āre, āvī, ātus.
delight, dēlectō, 1.
demand, flāgitō, 1.
depth, altitūdō, inis, f.
desire, wish, optō, 1.
difficult, difficilis, e.
dignity, dīgnitās, ātis,
discover, reperiō, īre, repperī, repertus.
dismiss, dīmittō, ere, mīsī, missus.
distant, be distant, absum, esse, āfuī, āfutūrus.
do, faciō, ere, fēcī, factus.
doubt, be in doubt, dubitō, 1.
drive back, repellō, ere, reppulī, repulsus.
drive out, expellō, ere, pulī, pulsus.
duty, officium, ī (iī), n.

each, quisque, quaeque, quidque.
each (of two), uterque, utraque, utrumque.
each other, suī, sibi, sē; *also* nōs, vōs *used reflexively* (§ 289).
eager, alacer, alacris, alacre.
easily, facile, *from adj.* facilis, e.
easy, facilis, e.
else, alius, a, ud.
embankment, rampart, agger, eris, m.
encourage, incitō, 1.
endeavor, cōnor, ārī, ātus sum, *dep.*
endure, perferō, ferre, tulī, lātus.
enemy (*in military sense*), hostis, is, c.; (*collectively*) hostēs, ium, m.
enemy (*personal*), inimīcus, ī, m.
enough, satis (§ 236).
entreat, implōrō, 1.
envoy, lēgātus, ī, m.
establish, cōnfīrmō, 1.
even, etiam.

not even, nē . . . quidem, *with the emphatic word or phrase between.*
ever, always, semper.
exhaust, wear out, cōnficiō, ere, fēcī, fectus.
expect, exspectō, 1.

family (stock), genus, eris, n.
farmer, agricola, ae, m.
father, pater, patris, m.
favor, beneficium, ī (iī), n.
fear (*noun*), timor, ōris, m.
fear (*verb*), timeō, ēre, uī.
fellow citizen, cīvis, is, m.
fertile, ferāx, ācis.
few, paucī, ae, a.
field, ager, agrī, m.
fiercely, ācriter; *from the adj.,* ācer, ācris, acre.
fifteen, quīndecim.
fight, pūgnō, 1.
fill up, compleō, ēre, ēvī, ētus.
find (*by searching*), reperiō, īre, repperī, repertus.
find (*come upon*), inveniō, īre, vēnī, ventus.
first, *adj.,* prīmus, a, um.
first, *adv.,* prīmum.
fit out, equip, īnstruō, ere, ūxī, ūctus.
five, quīnque.
flee, flee from, fugiō, ere, fūgī, fugitūrus.
fleet, classis, is, f.
(following), on the following day, postrīdiē.
fond, fond of, cupidus, a, um.
foot, pēs, pedis, m.
forage, pābulum, ī, n.
ford, vadum, ī, n.
forest, silva, ae, f.
forget, oblīvīscor, ī, oblītus sum.
fortify, mūniō, īre, īvī, ītus.
fortune, fortūna, ae, f.
fortune (*in sense of property*), fortūnae, ārum, f.

four, quattuor.
free (*adj.*), līber, a, um
free, set free, līberō, 1.
friend, amīcus, ī, *m.*
friendship, amīcitia, ae, *f.*
from, ā, ab.
from, out of, ē, ex.
from (= of), *with verbs of demand-ing, etc.*, ā, ab.
from, *after verbs of hindering, etc.*, quōminus, nē.
front (*adj.*), prīmus, a, um.

Galba, Galba, ae, *m.*
garrison, praesidium, ī (iī), *n.*
gate, porta, ae, *f.*
Gaul (*a Gaul*), Gallus, ī, *m.*
Gaul (*the country*), Gallia, ae, *f.*
Geneva, Genēva, ae, *f.*
German (*a German*), Germānus, ī, *m.*
Germany, Germānia, ae, *f.*
get ready (*trans.*), parō, 1.
give, dō, dare, dedī, datus.
glad, laetus, a, um.
go, eō, īre, īvī (iī), itum (§ 197).
go around, circumeō, īre, īvī (iī), itus (§ 197).
go away, abeō, īre, iī, itūrus.
good, bonus, a, um.
great, māgnus, a, um (§ 73).
greatest (*of qualities*), summus, a, um.
greatly, māgnopere.
(ground), on the ground that, quod.
guard, watch, tueor, ērī.

Haedui, Haeduī, ōrum, *m.*
happen, be done, fīō, fierī, factus sum.
happen, it happens, it befalls, *impersonal,* accidit, ere, accidit.
happy, beātus, a, um.
harass, vexō, āre, āvī, ātus.
harbor, portus, ūs, *m.*
harm, dētrīmentum, ī, *n.*

hate, ōdī, ōdisse (§ 198).
have, habeō, ēre, uī, itus.
he, is (ea, id) (§ 94).
hear, audiō, īre, īvī, ītus.
heart, courage, animus, ī, *m.*
help, auxilium, ī (iī), *n.*
Helvetii, Helvētiī, ōrum, *m.*
her, suus, a, um (§ 87, 1), *reflexive.*
here, hīc.
high, altus, a, um.
highest (*of qualities*), summus, a, um.
hill, collis, is, *m.*
himself, herself, *etc.*, suī, sibi, sē, *reflexive.*
hinder, impede, impediō, īre, īvī, ītus.
his, suus, a, um, *reflexive.*
(home), at home, domī (§ 277, 2).
home (to one's home), domum (§ 216, 1, *b*).
honor, honor, ōris, *m.*
hope, spēs, eī, *f.*
horseman, eques, itis, *m.*
hostage, obses, idis, *c.*
house, domus, ūs, *f.*
how much, *followed by gen. of the whole* (§ 236), quantum.
how many, quot, *indecl.*
hundred, centum.
hurry, contendō, ere, tendī, tentum.

I, ego, meī.
if, sī, *conj.*
in, in, *prep. w. abl.*
inasmuch as, quoniam (§ 319).
increase (*trans.*), augeō, ēre, auxī, auctus.
infantry, peditēs, um, *m.*
inform, certiōrem faciō, ere, fēcī, factus.
be informed, certior fīō, fierī, factus sum.
inhabitant, incola, ae, *m.*
injure, noceō, ere, uī, itūrus, *with the dat.* (§ 220, II, *a*).

into, in, *prep. w. acc.*
island, īnsula, ae, *f.*
Italy, Italia, ae, *f.*

javelin, tēlum, ī, *n.*
join (battle), committō, ere, mīsī, missus.

keep away, ward off, prohibeō, ēre, uī, itus.
kill, interficio, ere, fēcī, fectus.
king, rēx, rēgis, *m.*
know, sciō, īre, īvī, ītus.

lack, be lacking, dēsum, dēesse, dēfuī (§ 182).
land, ager, agrī, *m.*
land (*as opposed to the water*), terra, ae, *f.*
large, māgnus, a, um (§ 73).
last, last part of, *limiting a noun*, extrēmus, a, um (§ 283, 1).
law, statute, lēx, lēgis, *f.*
lead, dūcō, ere, dūxī, ductus.
lead, lead out, lead away, dēdūcō, ere, dūxī, ductus.
lead across, trādūco, ere, dūxī, ductus.
leader, dux, ducis, *c.*
leave, relinquō, ere, līquī, līctus.
legion, legiō, ōnis, *f.*
lend (*help*), ferō, ferre, tulī, lātus.
less, minus.
lest, nē.
letter (*an epistle*), litterae, ārum, *f.*
liberty, lībertās, ātis, *f.*
lieutenant, lēgātus, ī, *m.*
life, vīta, ae, *f.*
like, similis, e.
line of battle, aciēs, ēī, *f.*
little (*a little*), paulum.
long (*adj.*), longus, a, um.
long (*adv.*), diū.
love, amō, āre, āvī, ātus.
loyalty, fidēs, eī, *f.*

make, faciō, ere, fēcī, factus.
make (*somebody or something safe, bold, clear, etc.*), reddō, ere, reddidī, redditus.
man, homō, inis, *c., the general term ; man as opposed to woman, or as a complimentary designation,* vir, virī, *m.*
many, multī, ae, a ; very many, complūrēs, a ; *gen.,* complūrium.
march (*noun*), iter, itineris, *n.*
march (*verb*), iter facere, *lit., make a march.*
march forth, ēgredior, ī, gressus sum.
messenger, nūntius, ī (iī), *m.*
mile, mīlle passūs, *lit., thousand paces ; pl.,* mīlia passuum.
money, pecūnia, ae, *f.*
more (*adv.*), magis.
more (*substantive*), plūs, plūris, *n.*
most, plērīque, aeque, aque.
mountain, mōns, montis, *m.*
move, moveō, ēre, mōvī, mōtus.
much, multus, a, um.
my, meus, a, um.

name, nōmen, īnis, *n.*
narrow, angustus, a, um.
naval, nāvālis, e.
necessary, it is necessary, necesse est.
need, there is need, opus est (§ 258, 2).
neglect, neglegō, ere, lēxī, lēctus.
next, proximus, a, um (§ 73, 1 ; 228).
no, nūllus, a, um; *in answers, see* § 203, 3.
no one, nēmō, *dat.* nēminī, *acc.* nēminem; *gen. and abl., wanting.*
noble, nōbilis, e.
not, nōn, nē.
(not), is not? does not? *etc.,* nōnne (§ 203, 2).
not even, nē . . . quidem, *with the emphatic word between.*

not yet, nōndum.
nothing, nihil, *indecl.*
now (*at the present time*), nunc.
number, numerus, ī, *m.*

of, concerning, dē, *prep. w. abl.*
often, saepe.
on, in, *prep. w. abl.*
on all sides, undique, *adv.*
one, ūnus, a, um.
one . . . another, alius . . . alius;
the one . . . the other, alter . . .
alter.
onset, impetus, ūs, *m.*
opinion, sententia, ae, *f.*
opportunity, occāsiō, ōnis, *f.*
order, levy, imperō, 1.
order, command, jubeō, ēre, jussī,
jussus.
other, another, alius, a, ud.
other, the other, alter, a, um.
others, all the others, cēterī, ae, a.
ought, dēbeō, ēre, uī, itus; it behooves, oportet, ēre, oportuit.
our, our own, noster, tra, trum.
overcome, superō, āre, āvī, ātus.

pace (= *5 feet*), passus, ūs, *m.*
part, pars, partis, *f.*
peace, pāx, pācis, *f.*
people, populus, ī, *m.*
perish, intereō, īre, iī, itūrus (§ 197).
permit, permittō, ere, mīsī, missus.
persuade, persuādeō, ēre, suāsī, suāsum (§ 220, II, *a*).
pity, misericordia, ae, *f.*
pity, it excites pity, miseret, mise-
rēre, miseruit, *impersonal.*
place, locus, ī, *m.*
place in charge, in command over,
praeficiō, ere, fēcī, fectus, *with the
dat. of indirect obj.*
plan, cōnsilium, ī, *n.*
plunder, dīripiō, ere, ripuī, reptus.
Pompey, Pompējus, Pompēī, *m.*

power, potestās, ātis, *f.; denotes the
power that is vested in an official.*
praise, laudō, 1.
prefer, mālō, mālle, māluī (§ 192).
present, give, dōnō, 1.
present, be present, adsum, esse,
fuī, futūrus.
prevail, valeō, ēre, valuī.
put in charge, praeficiō, ere, fēcī,
fectus (§ 220, III).
put to flight, fugō, āre, āvī, ātus.

quickly, celeriter, *adv., from the adj.,*
celer, eris, ere.

rampart, agger, eris, *m.*
ravage, vexō, 1.
receive, accipiō, ere, cēpī, ceptus.
recollection, memoria, ae, *f.*
regret, it causes regret, paenitet,
ēre, uit, *impersonal* (§ 245).
remain, maneō, ēre, mānsī, mānsūrus.
remaining, reliquus, a, um.
remember, bear in mind, meminī,
isse (§ 242).
remind, admoneō, ēre, uī, itus.
reply, respondeō, ēre, respondī,
respōnsus.
report (*noun*), fāma, ae, *f.*
report (*verb*), nūntiō, 1.
reputation, fāma, ae, *f.*
request, seek, petō, ere, petīvī (iī),
ītus.
resist, resistō, ere, restitī, *with dat.*
rest, the rest, cēterī, ae, a.
retard, tardō, 1.
return (*intrans.*), revertor, ī; redeō,
īre, iī, itum.
reward, praemium, ī (iī), *n.*
Rhine, Rhēnus, ī, *m.*
river, flūmen, inis, *n.*
Roman, Rōmānus, a, um ; a Roman,
Rōmānus, ī, *m.*
Rome, Rōma, ae, *f.*

safety, salūs, ūtis, *f.*
sake, for the sake, causā, *with gen.;*
  the gen. always precedes.
same, īdem, eadem, idem (§ 95); **at**
  same time, simul.
save, servō, 1.
say, dīcō, ere, dīxī, dictus.
scarcely, vix.
sea, mare, is, *n.*
see, videō, ēre, vīdī, vīsus.
seem, videor, ērī, vīsus sum.
seize, occupō, 1.
self, oneself, suī, sibi, sē.
self, (*i.e. I myself, you yourself, etc.*),
  ipse *in apposition with the subject*
  or object.
sell, vēndō, ere, vēndidī, vēnditus.
Senate, senātus, ūs, *m.*
send, mittō, ere, mīsī, missus.
Sequani, Sēquanī, ōrum, *m.*
set out, proficīsor, ī, fectus sum.
she, ea, *f. of* is (§ 94).
ship, nāvis, is, *f.*
(sides) on all, undique.
since (*causal*), cum.
six, sex, *indecl.*
slave, servus, ī, *m.*
small, parvus, a, um (§ 73).
so (*of degree*), tam.
so, thus (*of manner*), ita, sīc.
so great, tantus, a, um.
so many, tot, *indecl.*
soldier, mīles, itis, *m.*
some, something, aliquis, aliqua,
  aliquid *or* aliquod.
some . . . others, aliī . . . aliī.
son, fīlius, ī, *m.*
Spain, Hispānia, ae, *f.*
spare, parcō, ere, pepercī, parsūrus
  (§ 220, II, *a*).
speak, loquor, ī, locūtus sum; dīcō,
  ere, dīxī, dictus.
standard, sīgnum, ī, *n.*
state, cīvitās, ātis, *f.*
station, collocō, 1.

stone, lapis, idis, *m.*
such, tālis, e.
suddenly, subitō.
suffer, patior, ī, passus sum.
suitable, idōneus, a, um.
summer, aestās, ātis, *f.*
summon, vocō, 1.
(superior), be superior to, superō, 1.
surpass, superō, 1.
surrender (oneself), dēdō, ere, dēdidī, dēditus.
surround, circumveniō, īre, vēnī,
  ventus.
suspicion, suspīciō, ōnis, *f.*
sword, gladius, ī (iī), *m.*

take, seize, capiō, ere, cēpī, captus.
take by storm, expūgnō, 1.
talent, talentum, ī, *n.*
tarry, moror, ārī, ātus sum.
teach, doceō, ēre, uī, doctus.
tell, say, dīcō, ere, dīxī, dictus.
ten, decem, *indecl.*
terrify, perterreō, ēre, uī, territus.
than, quam, *conj.; see also* § 254.
that, is, ea, id; ille, illa, illud.
that of yours, iste, ista, istud.
that, *rel. pron.*, quī, quae, quod.
that, in order that, ut; quī, quae,
  quod *with the subj.; with comp.*,
  quō.
that, lest, *with verbs of fearing,* nē.
that not, in order that not, nē.
that not, *with verbs of fearing,* ut.
that (*of result*), ut.
that not, ut nōn.
that, on the ground that, quod.
their, their own, suus, a, um.
they, *see he, she, etc.*
thing, rēs, reī, *f.*
this, hīc, haec, hōc.
those, *as antecedent of rel.*, eī, eae, ea.
thou, tū, tuī.
though, quamquam, quamvīs, etsī,
  cum.

thousand, mīlle; *pl.*, mīlia, ium, *n.*
three, trēs, tria.
three hundred, trecentī, ae, *a.*
till, dum, dōnec, *conj.*
time, tempus, oris, *n.*
to, ad, *prep. w. acc.*
(top) top of, *with a noun*, summus, a, um (§ 283).
torture, supplicium, ī (iī), *n.*
touch, moveō, ēre, mōvī, mōtus.
tower, turris, is, *f.*
town, oppidum, ī, *n.*
tree, arbor, oris, *f.*
trench, fossa, ae, *f.*
tribe, gēns, gentis, *f.*
tribune, tribūnus, ī, *m.*
troops, cōpiae, ārum, *f.*
trust, cōnfīdō, ere, fīsus sum, *semidep.* (§ 220, II, *a*).
try, make trial, temptō, āre, āvī, ātus.
twenty, vīgintī.
two, duo, duae, duo.

under, sub, *prep. w. acc.*
unharmed, incolumis, e.
until, dum, dōnec, quoad.
unwilling, invītus, a, um ; be unwilling, nōlō, nōlle, nōluī.
us, nōs, nostrum, nostrī, *pl. of* ego. *Cf.* § 287, 2.
use, ūtor, ī, ūsus sum.

valor, virtūs, ūtis, *f.*
Veneti, Venetī, ōrum, *m.*
very many, complūrēs, a; *gen.*, complūrium.
victory, victōria, ae, *f.*
village, vīcus, ī, *m.*
virtue, virtūs, ūtis, *f.*
voice, vōx, vōcis, *f.*

wage, gerō, ere, gessī, gestus.
wait, exspectō, I.
war, bellum, ī, *n.*
watch, vigilia, ae, *f.*
welcome, grātus, a, um.
what ? quis (quī), quae, quid (quod).
whatever, quisquis, quidquid.
when ? quandō.
when, *rel.*, ubi, ut, cum.
where ? ubi.
where, *rel.*, ubi.
whether, num, -ne.
whither, quō.
while, *conj.*, dum (§ 331).
who ? quis.
who, which, *rel. pron.*, quī, quae, quod.
whole, tōtus, a, um (§ 61).
winter quarters, hīberna, ōrum, *n.*
wish, volō, velle, voluī.
with, cum, *prep. w. abl.*
withdraw, discēdō, ere, cessī, cessūrus.
without, sine, *prep. w. abl.*
withstand, sustineō, ēre, uī, tentus.
word, verbum, ī, *n.*
work (*a work*), opus, eris, *n.*
worthy, dīgnus, a, um.
wound (*noun*), vulnus, eris, *n.*
wound (*verb*), vulnerō, āre, āvī, ātus.
write, scrībō, ere, scrīpsī, scrīptus.

year, annus, ī, *m.*
yes, *see* § 203, 3.
yet, not yet, nōndum.
you, tū, tuī.
young man, adulēscēns, entis, *m.*
your, your own, tuus, a, um; vester, tra, trum.

A Latin Grammar.

By Professor CHARLES E. BENNETT, Cornell University. 12mo, cloth, 265 pages. Price, 80 cents.

IN this book the essential facts of Latin Grammar are presented within the smallest compass consistent with high scholarly standards. It covers not only the work of the preparatory school, but also that of the required courses in college and university. By omitting rare forms and syntactical usages found only in ante-classical and post-classical Latin, and by relegating to an Appendix theoretical and historical questions, it has been found possible to treat the subject with entire adequacy in the compass of 250 pages exclusive of Indexes. In the German schools, books of this scope fully meet the exacting demands of the entire gymnasial course, and those who have tried Bennett's Grammar find that they are materially helped by being relieved of the mass of useless and irrelevant matter which forms the bulk of the older grammars.

Professor William A. Houghton, *Bowdoin College, Brunswick, Maine :* The Grammar proper is admirably adapted to its purpose in its clearness of arrangement and classification, and in its simplicity and precision of statement, giving definitely just what the pupil must know, and not crowding the page with a mass of matter that too often disheartens the young student instead of helping him. I trust it will come into general use, for I think for the reasons just given, and because of its moderate compass and attractive appearance, students are likely to get more practical grammatical knowledge out of it than they generally do from the larger grammars.

Professor Alfred M. Wilson, *Lewis Institute, Chicago, Illinois :* I have examined it very carefully, and I can say, truly and with pleasure, that my first impressions have become positive convictions as to the very great value and utility of the book. I am daily using it with increasing delight and satisfaction. It is clear, concise, and independent.

The Critic, *Feb.* 29, 1896. The book is a marvel of condensed, yet clear and forcible, statement. Just enough examples are given to illustrate each principle without discouraging the pupil by their number and variety. The ground covered in the treatment of forms and syntax is adequate for ordinary school work and for the use of freshmen and sophomores in college.

CPSIA information can be obtained at www.ICGtesting.com
Printed in the USA
BVOW06s1024081015

421591BV00021B/338/P